GARDENING with NATURE in TEXAS

Karen M. Breneman

Republic of Texas Press
Plano, Texas

Library of Congress Cataloging-in-Publication Data

Breneman, Karen M.
    Gardening with nature in Texas / Karen M. Breneman.
        p. cm.
    Includes index
    ISBN 1-55622-891-0
    1. Gardening--Texas. I. Title.
    SB453.2.T4 B74 2002
    635.9'09764--dc21   2002000460

Republic of Texas Press is an imprint of Wordware Publishing, Inc.
No part of this book may be reproduced in any form or by
any means without permission in writing from
Wordware Publishing, Inc.

Printed in the United States of America

ISBN 1-55622-891-0
10 9 8 7 6 5 4 3 2 1
0201

All inquiries for volume purchases of this book should be addressed to
Wordware Publishing, Inc., at 2320 Los Rios Boulevard, Plano, Texas 75074.
Telephone inquiries may be made by calling:

(972) 423-0090

Dedication

This book is dedicated to all nature's creatures including man and to the ability to live together benefiting all.

CONTENTS

INTRODUCTION

Nature is defined by Webster's dictionary as "the material world, esp. as surrounding humankind and existing independently of human activities; the natural world as it exists without human beings or civilization; the elements of the natural world, as mountains, trees, animals, or rivers; natural scenery; the sum total of the forces at work throughout the universe; a primitive, wild condition; an uncultivated state."

Nature is all these and more. In the above definition Webster states, "existing independently of human activities." Nature can exist without humans, but humans cannot exist without nature. Nature is all around us, part of every breath we take, yet many never acknowledge her presence. The food we eat; the clothes we wear, even the power to generate cars, computers, phones, and other essentials of modern life all began with nature. Have you ever tasted Texas wildflower honey? A special treat from nature.

Texas is a diverse state that can be divided into ten ecoregions or zones based on geologic features, soil types, and climate with plant and animal life adapted to the unique conditions in each region. Starting with the forces of nature that created these differences and continue to work today, the gardener can begin to understand nature and how to work with the differences—the first step to successfully working with nature. Simple adjustments to current gardening practices can solve problems with gardening in the shade, turf grasses, use of ground covers, and growing vegetables.

Wildlife, an added attraction to all landscapes, is an important indicator of environmental health. Selection of plant material and easy changes in landscape design can provide wildlife friendly habitat, less maintenance, and allow time to observe the attracted wildlife.

Texas is facing serious water and energy shortages. Air pollution is a major issue, and not only in metropolitan areas. Streams, lakes, and rivers are polluted. Overuse and misuse by the homeowner of fertilizers and pesticides is considered one of the greatest sources of this pollution.

Beginning after World War II with the introduction of DDT, pesticide use has been promoted, even strongly encouraged. The dangers made public with the publication in 1962 of Rachel Carson's *Silent Spring* started organic gardening movements. These movements viewed in the beginning as radical are still around and many try to practice the concept. Truly organic gardening is difficult and if not understood can be as hazardous to humans as the non-organic methods. Organic pesticides do not have the same long-term environmental effects as the non-organic but still need to be used with caution and only when truly needed. By using a simple system called Integrated Pest Management, the best of both organic and non-organic methods, contamination of soil, water, and death of wildlife can be greatly reduced.

Native plants are key to wise use of natural resources, requiring less water, fertilizer, and pesticides. The use of native plants is encouraged throughout the book and after reading this book hopefully will be the first plants you consider in any landscape project. To many true gardeners plants are not only green growing entities to please the senses, but extensions of friends and family. Reserve a special corner or favorite view for these friends whether native or exotic. Utilize the properties of the natives to enhance and at times protect that special green growing friend.

Understanding the terminology—definitions of native, nonnative, and exotic vegetation—aids in proper planting and maximum conservation of resources. We all need to preserve nature and use our natural resources wisely. The place to start to remedy and rehabilitate is with the home gardener. By working with our natural resources, we can improve our health, environment, and pleasure.

The principles of sustainability described throughout the book work not only in the home landscape but in the commercial/public sector. The Roy Lee Walker Elementary school in McKinney ISD near Dallas continues to prove the feasibility of working with nature including a few unexpected benefits.

You as a gardener can make a difference and improve the environment, your health, and your quality of life. Simple, easy changes in gardening practices to work with the elements of nature rather than fighting against them can and do make a significant impact. Plants adapted to a site need less water, fertilizer, and pesticides than exotic species. Native plant species provide food sources for wildlife. Without bees and other pollinators, the wonderful honey will not be the only casualty.

"Gardener" is defined here as anyone who plants a plant. Even a single flower on a balcony can provide nectar to a passing bee, butterfly, or hummingbird. Ideas and suggestions in this book are intended to help nature and in the process increase the enjoyment and lessen the drudgery of gardening. Nature can be a wonderful partner in gardening, not an enemy. The time saved will enhance all aspects of life.

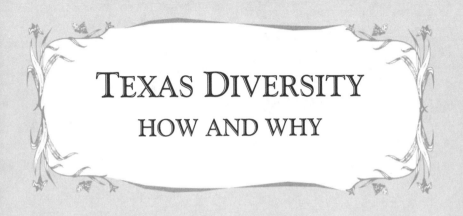

TEXAS DIVERSITY
HOW AND WHY

Texas! A large wonderful state. A gardener's paradise and a gardener's nightmare. The diverse climate and soil conditions create challenges encountered nowhere else in the United States. The extremes of annual rainfall from less than eight inches in the western portions to near sixty inches in the eastern piney woods; winter temperatures from below zero in the northern plains to rarely freezing at the southern subtropical tip make the state unique and difficult for gardeners. By working with instead of against these forces of nature, both the gardener and nature can benefit.

To understand, appreciate, and work with these differences requires a basic knowledge of the ecological zones or ecoregions and how they formed. Ecoregions are areas that exhibit unique characteristics and relationships among soil, water, plants, animals, and their environments. Ten different ecoregions evolved in Texas: Piney Woods, Gulf Coast Prairies and Marshes, Post Oak Savannah, Blackland Prairies, Cross Timbers and Prairies, South Texas Plains, Edward's Plateau, Rolling Plains, High Plains, and Trans Pecos. Several different region designations exist with slight variations and combinations depending on source. For the purposes of this book, the ten listed above are described.

A summary of the geological history that shaped the regions

follows. The accompanying geologic map of Texas (Figure 1) combines each major era into single groups for simplicity: the Precambrian 1200 to 2000 million years, Paleozoic 570 to 245 million, Mesozoic 245 to 66 million years, and Cenozoic 58 to 2 million years.

Geological History

The recorded history visible in rock strata across the state documents a changing geography that began several billion years ago in the Precambrian Era. Mountains, seas, rivers, volcanoes, and earthquakes are all part of the story with oil, coal, metals, ground water, salt, limestone, ceramic

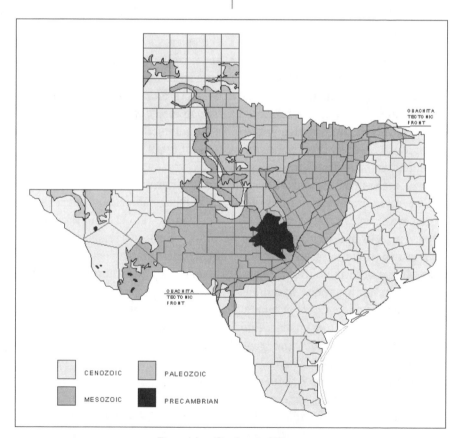

| CENOZOIC | PALEOZOIC |
| MESOZOIC | PRECAMBRIAN |

Figure 1—Geology of Texas

clays, and soils the result of the changes. Precambrian rocks more than 600 million years old are exposed in the Llano uplift and a few small areas in Trans Pecos.

During the early Paleozoic, broad inland seas covered West Texas, depositing limestones and shales. Paleozoic rocks are exposed around the Llano uplift and the mountains of Trans Pecos. A deep marine basin extended from Arkansas and Oklahoma to Mexico. Sediments accumulated in the Ouachita trough until late in the Paleozoic Era when the European and African continental plates collided with the North American plate. This collision produced mountainous uplifts (Ouachita Mountains) and small basins filled by shallow inland seas that made up the West Texas basin.

Broad limestone shelves and barrier reefs surrounded the deeper parts of the saltwater basins. Rivers flowed to the landward edges of the basins, forming deltas; coastlines shifted continually as sediments were deposited and then eroded away. Inland seas retreated southwest, and West Texas became the site of broad basins where salt, gypsum, and red muds existed in a hot, arid climate. The layers originally deposited in the Permian basin

are exposed in the Rolling Plains of West and Northwest Texas and Trans Pecos.

The Mesozoic Era began 245 million years ago when the European and African plates began to break away from the North American plate, producing a belt of elongated basins from Mexico to Nova Scotia. Streams deposited sediment in these basins. As the plates drifted farther away, the basins were buried beneath saltwater as the East Texas and Gulf Coast basins were created. During the remainder of the Mesozoic Era, coastal plains and deposits periodically buried broad limestone shelves as the Texas continental margin gradually shifted southeastward into the Gulf of Mexico. In the East Texas basin, deeply buried salt deposits moved upward forming salt ridges and domes, providing a variety of folded structures and traps for oil and gas.

In West Texas, during the early Mesozoic Era, a large shallow lake occupied the abandoned site of the Permian basin. Eventually waters from the Gulf of Mexico reached and flooded West Texas beneath a shallow sea where dinosaurs roamed the land and shallow waters. Marine reptiles dominated the Mesozoic seas until waters withdrew from West

Texas near the end of the era. Mesozoic layers are exposed along the western and northern edges of the Gulf Coast and East Texas basins and prominently across West Texas.

With the Cenozoic Era about 66 million years ago, the East Texas basin filled with lignite-bearing deposits of river and delta origin. The early Cenozoic Mississippi River flowed across East Texas. A large delta covered the area north of Houston with smaller deltas and barrier islands extending southwestward into Mexico, much like the present Texas coast. Delta and river sands were carried southeastward into the deeper waters of the Gulf of Mexico. In the Gulf Coast basin, deeper buried lower Mesozoic salt moved upward to form domes. Today, Cenozoic layers are exposed throughout East Texas and in a broad belt in the coastal plain that become younger toward the Gulf of Mexico.

In Trans Pecos, numerous Cenozoic volcanoes erupted resulting in thick lava flows that covered older Mesozoic and Paleozoic layers forming basins. Cenozoic volcanic rocks are now exposed in this arid region.

In northwestern Texas, late Cenozoic streams deposited gravel and sand carried from the Rocky Mountains of southern Colorado and northern New Mexico. Beginning about two million years ago during the Pleistocene Epoch (the Ice Age), the Pecos River eroded northward into eastern New Mexico and isolated the deposits of the Texas High Plains from their Rocky Mountain source. Several Texas rivers eroded the isolated High Plains during and since the Ice Age, causing the eastern caprock to retreat westward to its present location.

While the northern part of the continent was covered by thick Pleistocene ice caps, streams meandered southeastward across a cool, humid Texas, carrying great volumes of water to the Gulf of Mexico. The Colorado, Brazos, Red, and Canadian Rivers slowly deepened their meanders as gradual uplift occurred across the state during the last one million years. Sea level changes during the Ice Age alternately exposed and flooded the continental shelf. River, delta, and coast sediments deposited during high sea level stages are exposed along the outer 80 kilometers of the coastal plain. Since sea level reached its approximate present position about 3,000 years ago, thin coastal-barrier, lagoon, and delta sediments have been deposited along the Gulf Coast.

The differing geological features stabilized, soil formed followed by plant and animal life, and the ecological regions as defined today developed. Highly erratic rainfall with droughts either temporary or prolonged a common occurrence force vegetation to adapt. Cold fronts sweep down from the north often dropping temperatures 20 to 40 degrees in a short time with severe freezes usually a result of these "blue northers." The northern High Plains has the distinction of holding the state record for most total miles of wind with the average at Amarillo of 7.1 miles per hour year round.

Climatic zones have been characterized variously as arid or semi-arid to humid to sub-humid, even though the state lies within temperate latitudes. All these features help to define the ten

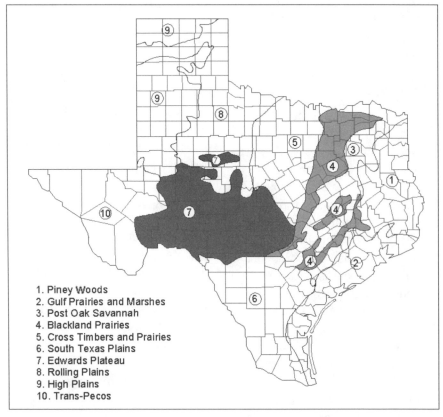

1. Piney Woods
2. Gulf Prairies and Marshes
3. Post Oak Savannah
4. Blackland Prairies
5. Cross Timbers and Prairies
6. South Texas Plains
7. Edwards Plateau
8. Rolling Plains
9. High Plains
10. Trans-Pecos

Figure 2—Ecoregions of Texas

ecoregions. The boundaries are not all clearly defined, gradually merging one into the next. Compare the map of the ecoregions (Figure 2) with the geologic map (Figure 1).

Ecoregions

A brief description of each ecoregion follows with the basic characteristics of each summarized in Table 1 and characteristic native plant life identified by region in Table 2 at the end of this chapter.

Region 1

Region 1 is the **Piney Woods**, part of a much larger area of pine-hardwood forest that extends into Louisiana, Arkansas, and Oklahoma. The amounts of moisture and soil differences limit the forest on the west with the area comparatively free from persistent winds. The dominant vegetation type is a mixed hardwood-pine forest on the uplands and a mixed hardwood forest on the lowlands. The Longleaf Pine Forest, one of two divisions, once dominated the southeastern part of the Piney Woods of Texas. Only a few pockets remain today after extensive logging in the late nineteenth and early twentieth centuries.

The Mixed Pine-Oak Forest occurs to the west and north of the longleaf pine area. Swamps are common and are largest in the southern part of the Pine-Oak Forest. Caddo Lake, the only true lake in Texas, is located in this region. All other lakes in the state are the result of manmade dams.

Region 2

The **Gulf Prairies and Marshes** region (region 2) is divided into two major divisions, the Coastal Prairie and Gulf Coast Marshlands. The Prairies division is a slowly drained plain dissected by streams and rivers flowing into the Gulf of Mexico. The original vegetation types were tall grass prairie and post oak savannah. Oak mottes or islands are a curious feature of this division. Also referred to as maritime woodlands, oak mottes appear as clusters of oak trees in the midst of prairies. Actually the individual trees in an oak motte began as root sprouts from one or a few trees that took hold on the sandy prairie soils.

The coast marsh is limited to narrow belts of low wet marsh immediately adjacent to the coast and includes the barrier islands lining the coast, which protect the shoreline from the constant buffeting of ocean waves, and the highly productive estuaries and marshes. The areas provide excellent natural wildlife habitat and contain most of our National Seashore parks.

Region 3

The **Post Oak Savannah** (region 3) borders the Piney Woods on the east and mixes with the Blackland Prairie area in the south. In addition to this area, both the East and West Cross

Table 1. Summary of Characteristics of the Ten Ecoregions of Texas

Region	Size Million Acres	Annual Precipitation in Inches	Frost Free Days	Topography
1. Piney Woods	15.80	40-56	235-265	Nearly level to gently undulating
2. Gulf Prairies & Marshes	10.0	26-56	245-320	Nearly level
3. Post Oak Savannah	6.85	30-45	235-280	Nearly level to gently rolling
4. Blackland Prairies	12.6	30-45	230-280	Nearly level to rolling
5. Cross Timbers & Prairies	15.3	25-35	230-280	Gently rolling
6. South Texas Plains	20.9	18-30	260-340	Nearly level to rolling
7. Edwards Plateau	25.45	12-32	220-260	Deeply dissected hilly, stony plain
8. Rolling Plains	24.0	18-28	185-235	Nearly level to rolling
9. High Plains	19.4	14-21	180-220	Nearly level high plateau
10. Trans Pecos	17.95	8-18	220-245	Mountain ranges rough, rocky land, flat basins and plateaus

Table 1. Continued

Region	Elevation in Feet	Major Soil Types	Month of Peak Precipitation (secondary peak)
1. Piney Woods	200-700	Acid sandy loams, sand	Even distribution
2. Gulf Prairies & Marshes	0-250	Prairie: Acid clay loams, clay Marsh: Alkaline sandy loam, clay	September (May)
3. Post Oak Savannah	300-800	Acid sand & clay	May (September)
4. Blackland Prairies	250-700	Slightly acid clay	May (September)
5. Cross Timbers & Prairies	500-1500	Acid loam & clay	May (September)
6. South Texas Plains	0-1000	All types	September (May)
7. Edwards Plateau	1200-3000	Shallow soils all types	May (September)
8. Rolling Plains	1000-3000	Neutral to alkaline sandy & clay loams, clay	May (September)
9. High Plains	3000-4500	Neutral to alkaline clay, clay loams, sand caliche	May (September)
10. Trans Pecos	2500-8751	All types including gypsum & saline	July, August, September (November)

Timbers are classed as Post Oak Savannah. Some authorities consider this plant association as a part of the oak-hickory or deciduous forest formation. Others prefer to classify the area as a part of the true prairie association of the grassland formation. This latter view is because the understory vegetation is typically tall grass. There also is evidence that the brush and tree densities have increased tremendously from the virgin condition, suggesting more original prairie than forest.

Region 4

The name **Blackland Prairie** is derived from the fairly uniform dark-colored alkaline clays, referred to as "black gumbo." This rolling, well-dissected prairie is divided into the San Antonio and Fayette Prairies and represents the southern extension of the true prairie that occurs from Texas to Canada. Research on the native vegetation confirms the true prairie designation with little bluestem as a dominant species.

Livingston State Park owned by the state is an example of this community. Isolates of the Blackland Prairies occurring in the Post Oak Savannah region are easily identified by the characteristically dark clay soils.

Region 5

The **Cross Timbers and Prairies** area (region 5) in North Central Texas represents the southern extension of the Central Lowlands and the western extreme of the coastal plains. The wide variances in geologic formations bring about sharp contrasts in topography, soils, and vegetation, although the predominate grasses are uniform through the region.

Region 6

The **South Texas Plains** (region 6) lie south of a line from San Antonio to Del Rio and are the western extension of the Gulf Coastal Plains merging with the Mexico Plains on the west. Periodic droughts occur in the area with an all-time low annual record of 2.82 inches at Cotulla in 1917. The original vegetation was an open grassland or savannah type along the coastal areas and brushy chaparral grassland in the uplands. Originally oaks and mesquite and other brushy species formed dense thickets only on the ridges, and oak, pecan, and ash were common along streams. Continued grazing and cessation of fires altered the vegetation to such a degree that the region is now commonly called the Texas Brush Country.

Region 6 has a greater diversity of animal life than any other in Texas, home for many near tropical species which abound in Mexico, many grassland species that range northward, and some desert species commonly found in the Trans Pecos. The southern tip of Texas, a highly modified subregion because of certain climatic factors such as high rainfall, contains remnants of original vegetation. Many of these areas where subtropical species such as ebony and anaqua dominate the relict plant communities are now in public ownership. Santa Anna State Park is one example.

Region 7

The **Edwards Plateau** (region 7) is an area of west Central Texas known as the "Hill Country." On the east and south the Balcones Escarpment forms a distinct boundary, while on the north it blends into the Cross Timbers and Prairies and Plains regions. The Pecos River and eastern edge of the Stockton Plateau define the western extent of the Edwards Plateau.

The Balcones Canyonlands subregion has the most rugged topography in the Edwards Plateau with steep grades and exposed geological strata. Springs abound amid the woodlands of oaks and mesquite. Many plants are native to the area.

The Llano Uplift part of the northern border is a 5,000-square-mile area contained within the Edwards Plateau region. This area is also known as the central mineral region and has elevations ranging from 825 feet to 2,250 feet above sea level. Geologically this region is a large dome with rolling to hilly topography. Bare granite domes, the largest known as Enchanted Rock, are common. In contrast to the clays and clay loams of the Edwards Plateau, sandy soils predominate on the Llano Uplift. Over thousands of years, weathering of granite deposits has produced these coarse soils.

Region 8

The **Rolling Plains** (region 8) together with the High Plains (region 9) is the southern end of the Great Plains of the central United States. The eastern portion is sometimes known as the Reddish Prairies. This region is bordered on the west by the Caprock Escarpment, on the south by the Edwards Plateau, and on the east by the Cross Timbers and Lampasas Cut Plain. A summer dry period with high temperatures and high evaporation rates is typical.

The original prairie vegetation included tall and midgrassses such as bluestems and gramas. The Mesquite Plains subregion typifies the Rolling Plains region, a gently rolling plain of mesquite, short-grass savanna. Escarpment breaks are steep slopes, cliffs, and canyons occurring just below the edge of the High Plains Caprock.

Region 9

The **High Plains** (region 9) is separated from the Rolling Plains by the Caprock Escarpment. The southern edge adjoins the Edwards Plateau and the Trans Pecos regions. A transition from productive grazing land to sand hills marks the boundary between the High Plains and the Trans Pecos. The Canadian River breaks divide this region into southern and northern sections. Notable canyons include Tule and Palo Duro along the Caprock. This relatively level plateau contains many shallow siltation depressions, or "playa lakes," which sometimes cover as much as forty acres and contain several feet of water after heavy rains. These depressions support unique patterns of vegetation. Extended droughts have occurred here several times during the twentieth century with the worst in 1917-18, 1930s, and 1951-56. Caliche generally underlies these surface soils at depths of two to five feet.

The vegetation on the High Plains is variously classified as mixed-prairie, short-grass prairie, and in some locations tall-grass prairie. Distinctly different plant communities exist on the hardlands, mixed lands, sandy lands, and draws. The region characteristically is free from brush, but mesquite and yucca have invaded parts of the area.

Region 10

The last region, the **Trans Pecos** in far West Texas, the most complex of all the regions, is traversed by the chain of the Rocky Mountains and is typical of the southwestern United States. It occupies the extreme western part of the state eastward to the Pecos River and includes the Stockton Plateau and the Sand Hills near the southeast corner of New Mexico. It is a region of diverse habitats and vegetation varying from desert valleys and plateaus to wooded mountain slopes. Even the mountain masses vary in the environments offered for plant and animal life. Some are characterized by volcanic rocks, others by limestone. The soils have developed from outwash materials from the mountains and are varied in surface texture and profile characteristics.

Due to the diversity of soils and elevations, many vegetation types exist in the region. Treatment of this region as a single vegetation area is justified only in view of its extreme variability and the impracticability of recognizing more vegetation units. The grass vegetation, especially on the higher mountain slopes, includes many southwestern and Rocky Mountain species not present elsewhere in Texas. Poisonous plants present considerable problems in this harsh environment.

The ten ecoregions describe the major soil types, altitude, and average rainfall across the state. The plant material native to each region has adapted to the conditions of that region and grows best when grown in native conditions. Many plants will grow successfully in other areas. Soil and water conditions can be duplicated; however, temperature requirements are not as easy. Plants grow only within a set temperature range.

The USDA Plant Hardiness Zone Map (Figure 3) determined by the U.S. National Arboretum is used as a guide for minimum temperature ranges. Texas is divided into four different zones, which are each subdivided into two zones. Planting guides and catalogs use the zones in plant descriptions. Determine your hardiness zone. If the plant has a number smaller than your zone, it should survive the winter; if larger, treat as an annual or

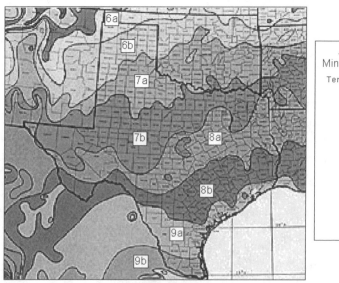

Average Annual Minimum Temperature	
Temperature (F)	Zone
-5 to -10	6a
0 to -5	6b
5 to 0	7a
10 to 5	7b
15 to 10	8a
20 to 15	8b
25 to 20	9a
30 to 25	9b

Figure 3—Plant hardiness zone map

provide additional protection.

The Minimum Temperature Range map does not take into consideration the summer heat in the southern part of the state. The warm to hot nights can be as deadly for some plant material as the cold nights in the winter. To avoid losing plants in the summer, check the heat-tolerance zone map compiled by the American Horticulture Society. The map is based on number of days above 86 degrees. The map compiled in the late 1990s is gradually being used in the nursery industry as the minimum temperature map is used. More and more plant descriptions will include these zone designations.

Working with nature and acknowledging the variations will make a difference. Think about where you live, what region. What are the general characteristics of your area? What zones do you fall into? Nature encourages diversity, resulting in pockets of different soils and plants within regions. Consider this: Sometimes trying something not recommended for your region will work, but do you really want to spend the time, money, and effort to try?

In the following chapters, ideas and suggestions are presented on ways to accept and work with the variety of growing conditions found in Texas. Understanding and accepting this great diversity will enhance quality of life for you, the gardener, and improve the environment for all Texans.

Table 2. Representative Native Plants

COMMON NAME/GENUS SPECIES	Ecoregions found
Trees	
Acacia *Acacia*	2P, 6
American beech *Fagus grandifolia*	1
Ashes *Fraxinus*	1
Bald cypress *Taxodium distichum*	1
Black gum *Nyssa sylvatica*	1
Brazil *Zizyphus obvata*	6
Cottonwoods *Populus*	1, 4
Elms *Ulmus*	1, 3, 4, 5
Hackberry *Celtis*	3, 6
Hickories *Carya*	1, 3
Honey mesquite *Prosopis glandulosa*	2P, 6, 7
Junipers *Juniperus*	3, 7
Lime prickly ash *Zanthoxylum fagara*	6
Lotebush *Zizyphus obtusifolia*	6
Magnolias *Magnolia*	1
Maples *Acer*	1
Native pecan *Carya*	4, 5, 6
Oaks *Quercus*	1, 2, 3, 4, 5, 6, 7
Pines *Pinus*	1, 10
Shrubby blue sage *Salvia ballotiflora*	6
Sweeetgum *Liquidambar styraciflua*	1
Texas persimmon *Diospyros texana*	6
Walnuts *Juglans*	1
Water tupelo *Nyssa aquatica*	1

COMMON NAME/GENUS SPECIES	Ecoregions found
Understory Shrubs-Small Trees	
American beautyberry *Callicarpa americana*	1, 3
Blackhaws *Viburnum*	1
Bumelia *Bumelia lanuginosa*	5
Bushy sea ox-eye *Borrichia frutescens*	2P, 2M
Coralberry *Symphoricarpos orbiculatus*	3
Creosote bush *Larrea tridentata*	10
Dogwoods *Cornus*	1
Redbud *Cerces canadensis*	1
Skunkbush *Rhus aromatica*	5
Southern wax myrtle *Myrica cerifera*	1
Tarbush *Flourensia cernua*	10
Yaupon *Ilex vomitoria*	3
Vines	
Blueberries *Vaccinium*	1
Dewberry *Rubus*	1
Grapes *Vitis*	1, 3
Greenbriars *Smilax*	1, 3, 5
Hawthorns *Crataegus*	1
Morning glories *Ipomoea*	2M
Poison ivy *Rhus toxicodendron*	1, 5
Rattan-vine *Berchemia scandens*	1
Trumpet honeysuckle *Lonicera sempervirens*	1
Yellow jessamine *Gelsemium sempervirens*	1

COMMON NAME/GENUS SPECIES	Ecoregions found
Annuals and Perennials	
Asters *Aster*	2P, 4, 5
Bluebonnets *Lupinus*	2P
Broadleaf milkweed *Asclepias latifolia*	7, 8
Bush sunflowers *Simsia*	6, 7
Clovers *Trifolium*	I
Crotons *Croton*	3, 6, 9
Engelmann daisy *Engelmannia pinnatifida*	7
Evening primroses *Oenothera*	2P
Fimbries *Fimbristylis*	2M
Gayfeathers *Liatris*	5
Glassworts *Salicornia*	2M
Goldenrods *Solidago*	I
Greenthread *Thelesperma nuecense*	6
Indian paintbrush *Castilleja indivisa*	2P
False indigo *Amorpha fruticosa*	3
Lambert crazyweed *Oxytropis lambertii*	8
Late coneflower *Rudbeckia serotina*	4
Lazy daisies *Aphanostephyus*	6
Lespedezas *Lespedeza*	3, 5
Maritime saltwort *Batis maritima*	2M
Milkpeas *Galactia*	I
Orange zexmania *Zexmania hispida*	6, 7
Phloxes *Phlox*	2P
Plains beebalm *Monarda pextinata*	9
Poppy mallows *Callirhoe*	2P
Prairie bluet *Hedyotis nigricans*	4
Prairie clovers *Petalostemon*	3, 4
Sageworts *Artemisia*	5

COMMON NAME/GENUS SPECIES	Ecoregions found
Sea-rockets *Cakile*	2M
Sennas *Cassia*	1, 3
Shrubby oxalis *Oxalis berlandieri*	6
Slimleaf scurfpea *Psoralea tenuiflora*	8, 9
Sneezeweeds *Helenium*	3, 7
Snoutbeans *Rhynchosia*	4, 6
Spikesedges *Eleocharis*	2M
Tallowweeds *Plantago*	6, 9
Tephrosias *Tephrosia*	5
Tickclovers *Desmodium*	1, 3
Velvet bundleflower *Desmanthus velutinus*	6
Vetches *vicia*	1, 4
Western ragweed	4, 5, 6, 7, 8
Western yarrow *Achillea millefolium*	8
Wild indigos *Baptisia*	1, 3
Wooly loco *Astragalus mollissimus*	9
Grasses	
Beakrushes *Rhynchospora*	1
Big bluestem *Andropogon gerardii*	2P, 4,5, 7, 8
Big sandbur *Cenchrus myosuroides*	6
Bristlegrasses *Setaris*	6
Buffalograss *Buchloe dactyloides*	4, 5, 7, 9
Bulrushes *Scirpus*	2M
Burrograss *Scleropogon brevifolius*	7
Cane bluestem *Bothriochloa barbinodis*	7
Chino grama *Bouteloua breviseta*	10
Common reed *Phragmites australis*	2M
Eastern gamagrass *Tripsacum dactyloides*	2P

COMMON NAME/GENUS SPECIES	Ecoregions found
Grasses (cont.)	
Fall witchgrass *Leptoloma cognatum*	7
Galleta *Hilaria jamesii*	9
Gulf cordgrass *Spartina spartinae*	2P, 6
Gulf muhly *Muhlenbergia capillaris*	2P
Indian grass *Sorghastrum nutans*	2P, 3, 4, 5, 6, 7, 8,9
Knotweed bristlegrass *Setaria geniculata*	2M
Little bluestem *Schizachyrium scoparius*	2P, 3, 4, 5, 6, 7, 8, 9, 10
Longtom *Paspalum lividum*	2M
Lovegrasses *Eragrostis*	3
Maidencane *Panicum hemitomon*	2M
Marshmillet *Zizaniopsis miliacea*	2M
Narrow leaf wood-oats *Chasmanthium sessiliforum*	3
Panicum spp.	2P
Paspalum spp.	2P, 3, 6
Rushes *Juncus*	2M
Seacoast bluestem *Schizachyrium scoparium*	6
Seashore dropseed *Sporobolus virginicus*	2M
Seashore saltgrass *Distichlis spicata*	2M, 6
Sedges *Carex* and *Cyperus*	1, 2P, 2M, 5
Cordgrasses *Spartina*	2M
Sideoats grama *Bouteloua curtipendula*	4, 5, 7, 8, 9, 10
Silver bluestem *Bothriochloa saccharoides*	3, 6
Silveus dropseed *Sporobolus silveanus*	4
Switchgrass *Panicum virgatum*	3, 5, 6, 7, 8, 9
Tall dropseed *Sporobolus asper*	4
Tanglehead *Heteropogon contortus*	2P
Texas wintergrass *Stipa leucotricha*	3, 4, 5
Windmillgrasses *Chlois*	6, 8

COMMON NAME/GENUS SPECIES	Ecoregions found
Water plants	
Bushy seedbox (evening primrose) *Ludwigia alternifolia*	2M
Docks *Rumex*	2M
Duckweeds *Lemna*	2M
Green parrotfeather *Myriophyllum pinnatun*	2M
Narrowleaf cattail *Typha domingensis*	2M
Pennyworts *Hydrocotyle*	2M
Pepperweeds *Lepidium*	2M
Smartweeds *Polygonum*	2M, 9
Spiderworts *Tradescantia*	2M
Water lilies *Nymphaea*	2M
Miscellaneous	
Candelilla *Euphorbia antisyphilitica*	10
Lechuguilla *Agave lecheguilla*	10
Ocotillo *Fouquieria splendens*	10
Orchids *Orchidaceae*	1
Prickly-pear *Opuntia*	2P, 6, 9
Sotols *Dasylirion*	10

NATIVE, NATURALIZED, HEIRLOOM, AND DEGENERATES

All gardeners plant plants and hope they grow, but often despite our best efforts the plants die. A professor from Louisiana recently stated at a conference I attended: "If you are not killing plants you are not gardening." This made the attendees feel better, but we all want plants to survive. Many dollars and much time and energy are spent and wasted trying. Nature has worked for years to provide the proper requirements to support life. We as gardeners can be more successful with less wasted effort by paying attention.

Using native and adapted plants is a good place to start, but what is a native plant? What are adapted or naturalized plants? Where do heirloom plants fit into

the mix? All these plants have a place in our landscapes. To answer the previous questions, we need to define the terms used in this book.

What is a native plant? Answers vary depending on whom you ask. The strictest definition is a plant growing on a site before arrival of European settlers in 1492, genetics unaltered by intervention from humans, and ability to survive on a site without care from humans. Vegetation types have moved around the country for centuries without intervention by man. Buffalo herds roaming the plains moved grasses and wildflowers during their migrations by eating seeds in one area and depositing them in their droppings in a distant location. The nutrients in the droppings acted as fertilizer to aid the seeds' germination and growth.

The same movement of plant populations continues today with bird migrations. Wind helps to carry seeds. Rivers and streams, especially during floods, carry seeds and sometimes entire plants downstream. When a seed or plant lands in an acceptable environment, growth occurs. The transported seeds and plants grow and over time adapt to their new homes.

This is where the native controversy lies. Did the new "subtropical vegetation" found at a site arrive by bird from the south and grow because of a more favorable climate, or is the plant the result of escape from a home garden? Research is required to know for sure, and with some plants, the answer may never be determined.

A plant that is not a native but grows as a native without intervention by man is called a naturalized or adapted plant.

A good example of a naturalized plant is the crepe myrtle. This native of China has adapted extremely well and is called the "lilac of the South." Old specimens can be found thriving on abandoned home sites throughout the state.

Plant Nomenclature

Plants are identified by name, often common name. Many plants can have the same common name. A single plant can have multiple common names. What do you think of when you hear "bachelor button"? In the southern part of the state the flower is *Gomphrena globosa* or globe amaranth, while in the north the "bachelor button" is *Centaurea cyanus* or cornflower. Two distinctly different genus with differing growth requirements. The cornflower will not survive the heat and humidity in the southern part of the state and if grown must be planted in the fall and enjoyed as a cool season annual. The globe amaranth is an ideal summer annual throughout most of the state, able to withstand the heat and varied moisture conditions, although they do prefer well-drained soil.

The confusion over common names extends into the nursery trade. Last spring I purchased *Gomphrena* with a label and picture for *Centaurea* in each pot. The four-inch pots had arrived at the garden center with the labels. No one caught the error, and they were sold mislabeled. To try and avoid possible confusion, the genus and species names will be used as much as possible in plant descriptions with common names listed to aid in identifying favorite plants.

Scientific names are based on the binomial system, which was devised by the Swedish botanist Linnaeus, the father of modern taxonomic botany, in 1753. Before his time an accepted or uniform method of naming plants or any other living group did not exist. He started using Latin names, which has continued by Latinizing non-Latin words. Some scientific names are also the common name such as rhododendron, magnolia, and viburnum.

International Congresses determine the scientific names or classifications for all plants from the smallest algae to the largest oak. The names are used worldwide and continue to be based on Latin terminology, often incorpo-

rating the name of the discoverer. As with all science, more advanced technology leads to a greater understanding of plant components and changes in and within families occur. This is an important point to remember when using older source material for identification.

Botanists divide the plant kingdom into Division, Class, Order, Family, Genus, and Species. For the scope of this book we will start the classification with families. A plant family is a large group of plants that share general characteristics usually based on fruit and flower similarities. Leaf and root characteristics are noted but are not as important in identifying a family. Often the members of a family appear as a diverse group. Sunflowers and lettuce belong to the same family of Asteraceae (formerly Compositaceae). Roses and apples belong to the family Rosaceae. Family names end in -aceae.

Members of each family are divided into groups based on more closely related characteristics. Each of these groups is called a genus. Plural form, more than one genus, is genera. In the examples used above, the difference between roses and apples is noted in the specific genera names of *Rosa* for roses and

Malus for apples. Sunflowers are *Helianthus* and lettuce is *Lactuca*. Most families contain many genera, although a few consist of only one genus. The family Ginkgoaceae has only one genus *Ginkgo*. The genus is generally in italics and the first letter capitalized. The genus once stated is often denoted with the capitalized first letter followed by a period then the species name.

The first part of the scientific name is the genus. The second part of the name is the species. The species is also in italics, but the first letter is not capitalized. Species are plants that are genetically distinct one from another and reproduce with little genetic variation. The species name is often the name of the person who discovered the plant. In Texas many native plants have the species name of "lindheimerii" for the early German botanist Ferdinand Lindheimer, who was first to identify and categorize the state's plant life. He is the Father of Texas Botany, born in May 1801; he traveled extensively through Texas in the early and middle nineteenth century. The Lindheimer senna found in the Trans Pecos is *Cassia lindheimeriana*. Other species names are derived from the location of the first identified plant. The Texas bluebonnet is *Lupinus texensis*.

Species Selection

Different genera may have the same species name. This does not mean they are related, but that the same individual identified them, they were found in the same area, or they share a single characteristic such as flower color. The prairie iris (pinewoods lily) *Eustylis purpurea*, a member of the lily family found in the piney woods of East and Southeast Texas, has purple flowers. The unrelated gerardia *Agalinis purpurea*, a member of the Scrophulariaceae family (figwort, snapdragon, or foxglove family), is a vine-like plant native to the Gulf Coast and Big Thicket. The only thing these two plants have in common is their flower color.

Species may be divided further into variety, either botanical or horticultural. The botanical variety denotes a natural geographic or other variant of a given species. The name is in italics as a third word following the species or denoted by the abbreviation *var.* The redbud (*Cercis canadensis*) has three varieties. The Eastern redbud *var. canadensis*, the Texas redbud *var. texensis*, and the Mexican redbud *var. mexicana*. All three varieties are native in Texas and interbreed where ranges cross, resulting in the possibility of more than three varieties.

The varieties become smaller and more drought tolerant farther west. The redbuds found in the Piney Woods, Post Oak Savannah, and Blackland Prairies are Eastern redbud. The ones on limestone escarpment in the center of the state are the Texas variety. Their leaves are rounder, heavier, and very glossy. Mexican redbud is found in Trans Pecos. This variety has small, glossy, wavy leaves, making it the most drought tolerant. All varieties have similar blooms in the early spring and exhibit fall color. A few of the varieties also come in white. All varieties are winter hardy even in the Panhandle and although not native to the Valley, will naturalize. Many other genus and species exhibit this same type of variation.

The horticultural variety is a plant of garden origin that results from hybridization or selection. Also called a selection or cultivar, the name is in Roman type and set off by single quotation marks. Examples are found in the crepe myrtles. The crepe myrtles belong to the Lythraceae family.

All of the more than twenty-five different varieties are selections of *Lagerstroemia indica* or hybrids of *L. indica* with *L. fauriei*. My favorite crepe myrtle is *L. indica* 'Natchez.' This variety is a small tree to 30 feet with cinnamon brown peeling bark and a high resistance to mildew and requires no maintenance. All I do is enjoy its many faces through the seasons. Covered with ice after an early spring storm, it was magnificent and received no damage.

Read labels carefully on all crepe myrtles. The size varies from low ground cover to small tree, and mildew resistance varies widely. The proper variety in the proper location is the key. Even though nature was not directly involved in many of the varieties, she is important in maintenance. Chapter 15 covers proper pruning; most crepe myrtles are "murdered" rather than pruned.

In 1834 near Gonzales another early botanists, Thomas Drummond, this time from England, gathered seeds of the plant he named Drummond phlox (*Phlox drummondii*). He took the seeds to England, and for the next 100 years they were hybridized to grow in English gardens. With growing interest in cottage gardens, the Drummond phlox returned to the United States. Roy Bedichek wrote in *Adventures with a Texas Naturalist* in the 1940s the following about the Drummond phlox: "...after its 100 year cruise around the world, tamed and subdued, an expatriate, nurseryman's pet, hothouse darling—in short, a degenerate." Most of the Drummond phlox found in the nursery trade today are descendants of the "degenerates" Bedichek describes. They are still classified as *P. drummondii*, but are not our true natives and do not perform nearly as well as the true native. Is any part of Texas similar in climate to England?

This native phlox, one of many species of phlox found in Texas, can still be found where Drummond originally discovered it. The species are difficult to tell apart with colors varying from brilliant rose-red to red to pink, violet, or white with purple or darker red eyes (centers).

When purchasing phlox or any native for your garden, question where the seeds were obtained. One of the wildflower seed suppliers in Texas should have true natives and not degenerates. Collecting plants or seeds from the wild is not recommended. More details in Chapter 4, Wildflowers.

Degenerates exist in other genera besides the phlox. Hybridizing to single out certain "desirable characteristics" usually reduces other characteristics. Hybrid roses are a good example. Hardiness and resistance to disease have been selected out to obtain longer stems and larger blooms.

Heritage Plants

Heirloom or heritage plants are often described in literature. These are plants that may or may not be native but have naturalized to an area. When one thinks of grandmother's garden, certain plants come to mind. These are the heirloom plants. The German red carnations (*Dianthus caryophyllus*) are found in areas of Texas settled by the Germans. This double dark red ever-blooming member of the Caryophyllaceae family does well in the Hill Country and other parts of Texas. Requiring good drainage and full sun, even in ideal conditions it may only survive a few years. Most other members of this genera are cool season annuals in the southern half of the state. In the northern half, most *Dianthus* spp. are perennials.

The white cemetery iris (*Iris*

albicans), named because it is found in old cemeteries and abandoned home sites, is one of the few bearded irises to do well in the Gulf Coast area and other humid, hot regions of the state. Originally from Yemen, the species has naturalized so extensively to be considered by many a native. A purple iris also found on old home sites and cemeteries is a different color form of *I. albicans*. This is a nice little once-blooming iris well adapted to most of the state. Most bearded iris cannot handle the hot, humid regions, requiring moist, not wet, soil and cool temperatures. Many of the estimated 10,000 to 20,000 varieties of iris do well in the northern and drier regions.

Several hibiscus, members of the Malvacea (mallow) family, are heritage plants. The Texas star hibiscus or rose mallow, *Hibiscus coccineus*, is not a native of Texas but of the coastal swamps of Florida and Georgia and is found more frequently in Texas gardens than in its native states. The plant is perennial only through zone 9, the southern half of the state. With good drainage and full sun it can be grown as an annual in the rest of the state. The plant can reach five to six feet with dark green leaves and bright red

flowers up to three inches across. It makes a striking drought tolerant accent plant.

H. coccineus has caused trouble for gardeners and embarrassment for police officers. The leaves closely resemble leaves of the illegal member of the family—marijuana—resulting in destruction of many plants by overzealous officials.

The giant rose mallow, common rose mallow, and perennial hibiscus are all *H. moscheutos*. This hibiscus is perennial throughout the state, although it will die back to the ground in many areas. This species has the largest flowers in the genera, reaching up to twelve inches across on a six- to eight-foot-tall plant. This relative of the native hibiscus has several different named varieties varying in color and size of flower and plant.

The third member of this family to be considered a heritage plant is the Confederate rose, *H. mutablis*. This mallow is often found growing as a small tree to large shrub around old home sites in zones 8b through 9. Farther north it is more of a perennial.

The hibiscus species most commonly found in nurseries are tender tropical descendants of the Chinese hibiscus *H. rosa-sinensis*. Many of the multitude of varieties available fall into Bedichek's classification of degenerates and do not work well with nature.

Most regions of the state do have native hibiscus varieties that will work in landscapes. The flowers may not be as showy as the degenerates, but they do not attract whitefly and other pests and do not need to be moved into the garage in the winter. *H. militaris*, the halberd-leaf hibiscus, is one found in all regions including the Panhandle. The four-inch blooms are white and sometimes pink with maroon or purple centers on three- to eight-foot stalks, grows in most soils, even poorly drained ones, and the plant is easily propagated from seed.

Most regions of the state do have native hibiscus varieties that will work in landscapes.

Annuals and Perennials

In the previous plant descriptions I have used the terms annual and perennial. Most gardeners do know the meaning of the terms, but I realize some readers may be beginning gardeners and not familiar with the terms. I apologize in advance to experienced gardeners. You may skip the next few paragraphs.

A perennial is a plant that returns from the same root every year. Some perennials are evergreen, others are deciduous. Evergreen refers to any plant or tree that does not lose its leaves or needles in the winter, such as pine trees, live oaks, and citrus trees. The vegetable pepper is an evergreen perennial in warmer climates. Deciduous perennials die back to the roots each year. In the spring after danger of frost the dead stems and branches should be removed without disturbing the dormant root system. New stems and leaves grow from the root each season.

Annuals are plants that complete their entire life cycle in one growing season. A reseeding annual is one that produces viable, easily germinated seeds. Once you plant one of these, you tend to always have this annual. Many of the wildflowers are good examples of reseeding annuals.

Biennials are plants that require two years to complete their life cycles. The first year they produce only leaves, the second year they complete their lives by flowering and producing seeds before they die. Parsley and digitalis are examples of common biennials.

Soil Requirements

Soil is the term used to describe the substance that covers the ground and where plants grow. "Dirt" will not be used in this book. The word does not exist in any other language as a synonym for soil. Soil when ground into the knees of your gardening slacks then becomes dirt.

All plants have specific soil requirements for optimum growth. Soil types listed in the regions in the first chapter are important when determining proper conditions for the native you are planting. The basic soil types are sand, loam, clay, caliche, and limestone. The soil type often determines the pH of the soil.

pH is a scientific measurement of hydrogen ion concentration and is based on a scale of 0 to 14 with 7 being neutral. A pH below 7 is acidic. Black coffee is a mild acid with a pH of 5. Hydrochloric acid (HCl) is a strong acid with a pH of 0. Rainwater has a pH of 6.5. The smaller the number the more corrosive the acid.

A pH above 7 is alkaline. The higher the number the more corrosive the substance. Lye, sodium hydroxide (NaOH), is alkaline with a pH of 14. When an acid and an alkaline substance are mixed together, salt and water are the result. Mixing sodium hydroxide and hydrochloric acid results in NaCl, table salt, and water. Houston city water is alkaline with a pH between 8 and 8.5. Alkaline tap water results in salt build-up in potted plants. Try to water with collected rainwater to avoid problems.

Sand is the loosest (more air spaces between particles) of the soil types. The pH tends to be neutral or slightly acidic because most calcium and other salts are washed through. Sandy soils do not hold water, making them optimum for plants requiring good drainage.

Clay soils are dense, heavy soils with the consistency of heavy glue when wet and adobe when dry. In many areas clay soils are referred to as "gumbo." Clay retains water and can be either alkaline or acid depending on the amount of rainfall. Native prairie plants require the heavy clay soils. Organic matter, gypsum, and other amendments need to be added to heavy clay soils for most plants to grow successfully in home landscapes.

Loam is a combination of sand and clay with organic matter.

Sandy loam is predominately sand, while clay loam is predominately clay. Loam generally drains well and with the organic matter has a neutral to slightly acidic pH. This soil is the closest to perfect type for most plants.

Caliche is found in areas with little rainfall where the calcium and other salts do not wash through the soil. A hard layer of lime (calcium carbonate) forms sometimes on the surface but can be from one to three feet below the surface. These soils are alkaline.

Limestone is calcium carbonate that was deposited in the form of shells during the time of the shallow seas across Texas. The exposed limestone outcroppings are soft in terms of rocks and are easily worn away by erosion, producing lime, alkaline soils.

Regional Conditions

Over five thousand native plant species are found in the state of Texas with very few native to the entire state. Each region has a unique set of native species that have learned to deal with the challenges of that region. To utilize this ability to survive, the native region of a specific plant must be determined and the conditions of the region duplicated in the landscape. A Trans Pecos native Texas mountain laurel (*Sophora secundiflora*) will only grow in the Piney Woods if planted in a high, well-drained alkaline soil in a sunny location. Maidenhair ferns are native over most of the state around seeps and springs where they have continual moisture. Don't try to grow them in the wet, heavy clay soils and sun of the Gulf Coast without providing good drainage and shade.

Attracting Wildlife

To grow beautiful, healthy plants is the goal of all gardeners. Native and adapted species will thrive when given proper conditions. An added benefit of growing native species is the wildlife. Hummingbirds, butterflies, song birds are all attracted to plants for food, nesting, and with butterflies, reproduction. Exotic plants, those not native to an area, are unknown to the local wildlife and will be largely ignored.

The red passionflower, native to Brazil, will adapt to a large area of Texas and is a beautiful flower, but if you grow only this passionflower, you will not have Gulf fritillary butterflies *Agraulis vanillae*. The spectacular bright red-orange butterfly requires passionvine to reproduce. The seven native *Passiflora* spp. all act as host plants for the caterpillars. This relationship is important to mention because the host plant will be completely denuded—no leaves by the time the butterfly completes the caterpillar stage of development. The chrysalis stage lasts about two weeks with emergence of the butterflies. By the time the butterflies are flying, new leaves are opening on the vine. With rapid growth the leaves are soon ready. The cycle is complete.

Host and butterfly relationships occur between many native species. The monarch butterfly and the milkweed *Asclepias* spp. are another example. The adapted nonnative Mexican milkweed is acceptable to the monarch, because Mexico is part of its natural migration route. All of the many native milkweed species are host plants and will be stripped of leaves during the caterpillar stage. Place the host plant to the rear of a planting to conceal the bare branches, if desired. The short time of bare stalks is more than rewarded by the profusion of beauty with the flights of color.

Pest insects are attracted to all plants. With over 30,000 different species of hungry aphids, every plant is susceptible. Native plants also attract predators—good guys. Nonnative plant species are not familiar to all predators and can be ignored. The *Asclepias* spp. discussed above also attract aphids, but this is good. The aphids in turn attract predators to your garden. The lady beetle or ladybug, lacewings, and assassin bugs all "know" the milkweeds have aphids. The predators, especially the larval forms, are voracious eaters and when finished with the milkweed move on to other plants in your garden. Most aphids are species specific, meaning they will suck the life out of only one specific species of plant. The aphids attacking the milkweed are not able to feed on the roses, but the predators are not concerned about the host plant and will move on to a new crop of aphids. This natural predator/prey relationship eliminates the need for pesticides. Chapter 11 covers this in more detail.

Specific native and adapted plants are discussed in following chapters. Many good reference books exist detailing native plants and requirements for growth. A few of my favorites are listed in Appendix A.

WATERWISE GARDENING

Water, an essential element of life, is all around us but not always accessible. If all Earth's water fit in a gallon jug, available freshwater would equal just over a tablespoon—less than half of one percent of the total. About 97 percent of the planet's water is seawater, another 2 percent is locked in icecaps and glaciers. Vast reserves of freshwater underlie Earth's surface, but much is too deep to economically tap.

Except for floods and drought, we ignore water, accepting it as always there. On a typical day, the average person in the United States uses about 83 gallons of water: 24 for flushing; 32 for bathing, laundry, and dishwashing; and 25 for swimming pools and watering the lawn. A mere two gallons is used for drinking and cooking—the only water required for survival.

Water in Texas is no exception. Thirteen river basins provide water; all have been altered by man with dams, levees, or engineered channels and wastewater treatment plants. Not one exists in its natural state along its entire length. Five of the basins originate outside Texas: the Rio Grande and Canadian in Colorado; the Red River, Brazos, and Colorado in New Mexico. The remaining: Guadalupe, Lavaca, Neches, Nueces, Sabine, San Antonio, San Jacinto, and Trinity originate within Texas. The Canadian and the Red Rivers have outlets outside Texas. The rest empty into the Gulf of Mexico.

Aquifers supply nearly 60 percent of the total freshwater demand of the state and are the sole source of water in numerous areas of Texas. Aquifers are underground water recharge areas; most consist of sand and gravel through which water moves slowly. The Edwards Aquifer in the San Antonio River basin is different. Here the water flows through highly permeable limestone, sometimes large caverns. This aquifer is like a huge tilted Swiss cheese that fills from its northwestern side and spills water out the springs to the southeast. Because water moves through it so easily, how much is pumped depends mainly on the size of the pump.

The Edward's Aquifer is increasingly threatened with more water pumped out than flows in. In the early 1990s a local farmer posted the following sign on his wall. "Yes, you can have my water. Just like you can have my gun . . . When you pry it out of my dead hands." This sentiment is strong in the area and has led to fights and lawsuits.

The state of Texas controls surface water with laws based on prior appropriation and permits based on principles outlined by an Ohio judge who wrote in 1861 that groundwater movement was "secret" and "occult" and could not be administered. Texas law, with few restrictions, lets a landowner take as much groundwater from private land as desired.

If groundwater were really occult and came from the places people used to think it did, like the mysterious bottom of Crater Lake, nobody would mind how much was used. However, the hydrology of the Edwards Aquifer is well known. An average of 640,000 acre-feet a year goes in, and at present about the same amount leaves the aquifer from wells and springs. San Antonio wants to ensure its future supplies, and the Endangered Species Act requires flowing springs; neither may be possible if users have the right to pump water at will.

In 1992 following several court battles over uses of water from the aquifer, the Texas Water Commission announced that the Edwards was not occult groundwater at all. It was a river that happened to flow underground and was thus subject to state regulation. The idea was quickly thrown out by a state district court. In 1993 with lawsuits involving the Endangered Species Act and the Texas legislature, a management plan was passed into law. Controversy still exists over use of the water from the Edwards Aquifer.

As a result of the severe droughts in 1996, in 1997 the 75th Texas State Legislature passed Senate Bill 1, sweeping water reform legislation championed by the late Lt. Gov. Bob Bullock. For the first time drought and conservation planning at the local, regional, and statewide levels was required. The bill also tightens rules for moving water from one river basin to another. Before SB1, Texas was one of only three western states without an approved drought management plan. The deadline for statewide water plans set at September 2000 continues to be rolled back, although communities across the state are making progress towards full compliance.

Texans have pumped so much water from the ground beneath Houston that the city and surrounding areas have subsided several feet and homes have been invaded by seawater from Galveston Bay. The subdivision of Brownwood in Baytown, southeast of Houston, once an upscale thriving development called the River Oaks of Baytown, succumbed to subsidence. In August of 1983, due to the subsidence of as much as a foot a year at one point or a total of nine feet between 1900 and 1980, the Baytown city council passed an ordinance which stated that Brownwood was unfit for human occupation and in effect barred anyone from ever rebuilding or living there again.

Brownwood prompted the formation of the Galveston-Harris County Coastal Subsidence District in 1975 to regulate ground water removal and was the first place in the state to become eligible for national flood insurance. The word "subsidence" became part of conversations along the Gulf Coast.

The 450-acre site with the support of the community, city of Baytown, and industrial neighbors is being restored as a saltwater marsh and is currently listed in the Texas Parks and Wildlife Departments "Coastal Birding Trail."

Brownwood is an amazing area and an example of how working against nature to build a community results in nature winning. If the original developers had thought more about the former uses of the land—grazing cattle on salt grass during the winter —and less of manipulating nature, much money, heartache, and time would have been saved.

Flooded Brownwood subdivision, December 2000

Visit this area when traveling along the Gulf Coast. It is hard to imagine people living here. Abandoned houses, palm trees, and roads remain as stark reminders.

In landscaping, water may be the single most important and valuable element. Recent droughts and increased demand for usable water have resulted in more legal battles over water rights in parts of the state. Even in the heavy rainfall areas such as the coastal plain and the piney woods, water usage has become an important issue. Legislation has been proposed to limit use of ground water to prevent more Brownwoods. As is true with many things in Texas, there is either too much or not enough, nothing in between. As gardeners we must learn to manage the water resources available. Waterwise gardening is the first step.

Water conservation movements began in 1978 in Denver, Colorado, with "Xeriscape" and were originally promoted in parts of the United States where the native plant material consists of cactus and other succulents. The pictures and other literature implied gardeners had to transform their landscapes into deserts. Partly because of this connotation the movement met with resistance.

Because of increasing demands for water conservation and current legislation, forty states have initiated water conservation projects. The new more accurate term is "waterwise," although the terms "sustainable landscape," "resource efficient landscape," and "low input landscape" are all found in current literature. Whatever the term the message is simple. We all, not only gardeners, have to conserve our water usage.

Data obtained by Texas A&M in 1999 indicates that in urban areas of Texas between 40 and 60 percent of the water supply is used for landscape and garden watering. This is higher than the national usage of 30 percent. A world without gardens and the creatures that inhabit them, to me, is absolutely unthinkable! Following simple rules reflecting nature, we can ensure future generations will enjoy what we enjoy.

Principles of Efficient Landscape Design

Waterwise landscapes do not have to be cactus and rock gardens. They can be green, cool landscapes full of beautiful, healthy plants maintained with water efficient practices. The waterwise landscape is truly sustainable, reducing inputs of water, pesticides, fertilizers, energy, and labor.

Seven principles are the standard for conserving water in the landscape. These principles are **good design**, **soil analysis**, **appropriate plant selection**, **practical turf areas**, **efficient irrigation**, **use of mulch**, and **appropriate maintenance**.

The first principle, good design, is not an option we all have. Most gardeners are not working with a new landscape but with an established yard. Chapter 16 suggests ways to update landscapes to incorporate ideas presented in this and other chapters.

If you are able to start from scratch to develop a new landscape, all aspects of the location should be considered. Begin with a sketch of existing structures, trees, shrubs, and grass areas. Consider budget, appearance, function, maintenance, and water requirements. Local experts, landscape architects, designers, nurserymen, and county extension agents can help with this process. In addition to water conservation, consider energy conservation with regard to placement of plantings to maximize sun and decrease wind exposure in winter and decrease summer sun intensity, etc. A good plan in the beginning, even if it takes several years to implement, will save time, money, and energy in the future.

recommended four inches of material is not economically feasible or necessary.

Proper plant selection is extremely important. Water is a critical component of photosynthesis, the process used by plants to manufacture food from carbon

Waterwise landscapes do not have to be cactus and rock gardens. They can be green, cool landscapes full of beautiful, healthy plants maintained with water efficient practices.

Before planting, determine what type of soil and pH exists on your site. Texas A&M offers soil analysis. Kits describing how to collect the sample and applicable fees are available at your local county cooperative extension office. Many nurseries and garden centers also offer this service. Addition of organic matter to shrub and flowerbed areas will increase plant health and conserve water no matter what the soil type and pH by increasing the soil's ability to absorb and store water in a form available to the plant. More details regarding organic material are covered in Chapters 13 and 14. For tree and grass areas, incorporating the

dioxide and water in the presence of light. Water is one of several factors that can limit plant growth. Other factors are nutrients, temperature, and light. Plants take in carbon dioxide through their stomata, microscopic openings on the undersides of leaves. Water is also lost through the stomata in the process called transpiration. The plant is breathing. Transpiration, combined with evaporation from the soil surface, accounts for the moisture lost from the soil.

When there is a lack of water in the plant tissue, the stomata close to try to limit water loss. Wilting occurs when the tissues lose too much water. Plants adapted to dry conditions have developed numerous mechanisms for reducing water loss, including narrow leaves, hairy leaves, and thick fleshy stems and leaves. Pines, hemlocks, and junipers are also well adapted to survive extended periods of dry conditions encountered each winter when frozen soil prevents the uptake of water. Cacti with leaves reduced to spines and thickened stems are the best example of plants well adapted to extremely dry environments. Not all adapted plants are cacti.

Native plants are adapted to the conditions of a region. Most have lower water demands, fewer pest problems, and less fertilizer needs than many nonadapted, exotic plants introduced into landscapes. The example of different species of redbud used in the last chapter describes the most drought tolerant species, the Mexican redbud, native to the drier regions, as having thick, shiny leaves. This is an adaptation within species to survive low water stress.

Native plants are becoming more available in nurseries and garden centers. If your local center does not carry them, make a request. Oftentimes the only way the nursery knows what you as a gardener wants is if you ask.

Many small, independent nurseries specialize in natives and often grow their own stock. These are the best places to find true natives to your area. Suggestions of natives to fill specific needs are listed throughout this book with references in the appendix. Check with your local chapter of the Native Plant Society of Texas for recommended plants and where to find them. See Appendix B for contact information.

Practical turf areas refers to lawns. Turf grasses require more water and maintenance than most other landscape plants. Across the United States, 20 million acres of land, an area roughly the size of Maine, are covered by lawn. It takes, on average, 27,000 gallons of water per week to maintain one acre of lawn, which translates into 540 billion gallons used to water all 20 million acres. Buffalograss is the only turf grass native to Texas. All other grasses used for lawns are imported. St. Augustine, the most popular grass in the eastern two-thirds of the state, was imported into Texas for use as cattle feed in the 1850s. I have yet to see cattle grazing in the home landscape.

Early Texas homes did not have lawns. Areas around most farmhouses were swept dirt to reduce dangers from fire and concealment of snakes and other critters. The current "need" to have large turf areas is a result of the English settlers duplicating their home traditions. In England large green lawns were a sign of wealth and upper class. Only the rich could afford the land and the upkeep. The English settlers wishing to show pride in their new homes planted turf. The tradition has continued today. As asked previously—Are Texas and England climates similar? With the current droughts and water availability, large turf areas are once again approaching the extravagance and ostentation of the English wealthy.

Some turf areas are needed in home landscapes for play areas and pets, but the amount can be reduced and managed more efficiently. Planting the lowest water use turf grass adapted to the region is an effective way to reduce water usage. (See Table 3. Recommended Grasses from Texas A&M.)

Consider using patios, decks, shrub beds, and ground covers in place of turf. Make paths using mulch, stones, or gravel to replace grass walkways or hard-to-water narrow strips. Blocky, square areas of grass are more efficient to maintain. Chapter 6 suggests alternatives to turf.

Irrigation

Landscape watering is the largest use of water by the homeowner. Of the tremendous amounts of water applied to lawns and gardens, the plants never absorb much of it. Some is lost to runoff by being applied too rapidly, some evaporates from exposed, unmulched soil. The greatest waste of water is applying too much, too often.

Runoff caused by overwatering carries polluting fertilizer and pesticides to bayous, creeks, rivers, and lakes. In aquifer regions, the overwatering can leach fertilizer and pesticides into the aquifers. This misuse by the homeowner creates more pollution than runoff from agriculture. By using proper watering techniques, this needless contamination can be avoided and precious water resources conserved.

Most lawns receive twice as much water as required to remain healthy. The key to watering lawns is to apply the water infrequently, yet thoroughly. This creates a deep, well-rooted lawn that efficiently uses water stored in the soil and is better able to withstand drought stress. Water only when needed—let the grass tell you when. Wilting of the

Table 3. Texas A&M Recommended Turf Grasses

Common name	Scientific name	Ecoregion	Notes
Bermuda grass	*Cynodon dactylon*	All	Good drought tolerance; produces dense turf; poor shade tolerance; seed or sod
Buffalograss	*Buchloe dactyloides*	3, 4, 5, 7, 8, 9, 10	Excellent drought tolerance; produces thin turf; moderate shade tolerance (variety dependent); seed; Texas native
Carpet grass	*Axonopus affinis*	1	Adapted to moist sites; tolerates partial shade; many seed heads; thin turf; seed
Centipede grass	*Eremochloa ophiuroides*	1	Low maintenance; tolerates partial shade; drought tolerant; seed or sod
St. Augustine grass	*Stenotaphrum secundatum*	1, 2, 3, 4, 5, 6, 7,	Produces dense turf; good shade tolerance; poor drainage tolerance; sod
Tall fescue	*Festuca arundinacea*	5, 8, 9	Under irrigation, remains green year round; good shade tolerance; poor drought tolerance; seed
Zoysiagrass	*Zoysia* spp.	All	Produces dense turf; good shade tolerance; good drought tolerance; sod; varieties: Meyer and Emerald

blades and change of color to a blue-green from a yellow-green indicate water stress. Serious injury will not occur to the grass if watered within 24 to 48 hours. Apply one inch of water. If runoff occurs before the one inch is reached, turn the water off for approximately 30 minutes then continue watering until one inch is reached. Use a coffee can or a rain gauge set in the range of the sprinkler to determine when one inch is achieved. Repeat the procedure the next time the lawn "talks to you." Lawns are healthier with fewer weeds and pest problems and more able to handle nature's changes when watered correctly.

All trees and shrubs need more frequent watering when first planted. Once the plant is established, one to two years after planting, reduce watering. In the absence of rain, most trees and shrubs need a thorough watering once a month. Normal lawn watering is not a substitute for tree and shrub watering.

The feeding root system of a tree or shrub is located within the top twelve inches of the soil at the drip line of the plant. The drip line is the area directly below the outermost reaches of the branches. Apply water and fertilizer just inside and a little beyond the drip line, not at the trunk. The best way to water is to lay a slowly running hose on the ground and move it around the drip line as each area becomes saturated to a depth of 8 to 10 inches. A soaker hose laid along the drip line works well and doesn't have to be moved. Use a sharp stick or pole to measure how deep the water has reached. For large trees, this technique may take several hours, but remember you are only doing it once a month.

Drought stress on large trees is usually not evident until several years after the stress. Trees are an important part of the landscape. Proper watering reduces stress that can result in pest and disease problems that can be very difficult to treat. Often the only solution to severe problems such as pine bark beetle is removal of the tree before the problem spreads to other trees. Prevention by avoiding stress is the most effective way to treat tree problems.

Irrigation systems are an important part of proper watering. Sprinkler irrigation is the most commonly used method of watering. The two most common are the hose-end sprinkler and permanent underground system. Both systems require little maintenance and apply large volumes of water in a short time. These are also the two most abused and often the most wasteful systems. Large sprinklers spraying water into the air allow for evaporation of as much as half of the water depending on time of day and temperature. To avoid the evaporation, water only in the early morning or late evening and use sprinklers that have flat, low to the ground spray heads. Avoid the high, arching, moving back and forth heads.

Water droplets hitting the soil splash soil and possibly fungal spores back onto the lower leaves of the plants. This is a real problem in the areas of the state where red-tipped photinia

Photinia fraseri (a native of China) grows. This shrub is highly susceptible to fungal leaf spot. The spores are present on the leaf litter under the shrubs. When sprayed with water the spores reinfect lower new leaves, making this disease almost impossible to treat without heavy use of fungicides, which add to pollution. Even then the only real treatment may be to remove the infected plant and replace it with another shrub (a Texas native such as wax myrtle) resistant to leaf spot.

With permanent underground systems, frequently check sprinkler heads to avoid watering sidewalks, driveways, fences, and walls. When using a timer, install a device that will shut off the timer if measurable rain falls. This device will cost a little more but in the long run will save money in water bills and overwatering stress on plants. Work with your system to determine how long it should run to deliver the proper amount of water, then set the timer to deliver the amount. A few minutes every morning is not an efficient use of your system.

Trickle or drip irrigation systems eliminate many of the problems of the sprinkler system by increasing efficiency. Drip irrigation slowly applies water to the soil. The water flows under low pressure through emitters, bubblers, or spray heads placed at each plant. Water applied by drip irrigation has little chance of waste through evaporation or runoff.

The simplest system is a soaker hose laid around the plants and connected to an outdoor spigot. No installation is required, and the hose can be moved as needed to water the entire garden. A slightly more sophisticated system is a slotted pipe. This is a more permanent system that is laid on the ground in rows with a connection at one end for attachment of the garden hose. This is a good system for vegetable or other gardens with straight rows.

Many different types of drip or trickle systems exist. All basically consist of tubing, heads, and emitters. Sizes of each of the three components vary by system, each meeting specific requirements. These systems need more planning but are neither difficult nor expensive. Drip systems require periodic maintenance to check emitters to make sure they are not clogged. Information on different systems is available through irrigation suppliers, home centers, and some nurseries.

Turf areas, shrubs and trees, and annual and perennial beds all have differing water requirements. Zoning the system to deliver water to different areas at different intervals is the most efficient way of watering. Different zones or areas are designated and timed to meet the needs of that area. A combination of different drip systems may be most effective. Take the time to determine the needs of your landscape. An improperly placed and/or timed system can create many more problems than it solves as well as wasting precious water and money.

Mulch conserves moisture, reduces weed populations, soil compaction, and soil-borne diseases, and moderates soil temperatures. Mulch is a layer of nonliving material covering the soil surface around plants. Organic material such as pine bark, compost, wood chips, and inorganic materials such as rocks or permeable plastic all make good mulches. Mulches are covered in more detail in Chapters 13 and 14.

> Proper landscape maintenance is essential to a water-wise garden. A well-designed landscape can decrease maintenance by as much as fifty percent through reduced mowing, proper mulching, elimination of weak, unadapted plants, and efficient watering techniques.

Turf grass is the biggest maintenance item in a landscape. Mowing consumes energy, human and petroleum, produces pollutants from engines, and generates yard wastes. Reducing the size of turf areas immediately reduces energy consumption and pollution. Proper mowing and not collecting clippings in combination with the "Don't Bag It" programs discussed in Chapter 14 ensure lawn clippings do not take up valuable landfill space.

Fertilizing the lawn at the proper time and in the proper amount can save time, effort, and money through reduced mowing and watering. Fertilizers can be and are a major source of pollution of streams and groundwater when excessive amounts are applied.

St. Augustine grass is healthy when it is yellow-green in color. It is not a blue grass like the

Kentucky bluegrass grown in northern climates. Excess nitrogen promotes blade growth, produces the dark green color, stresses the grass making it more susceptible to fungal and other pest problems, and increases frequency of mowing. Established St. Augustine lawns do not need frequent fertilizing. They are healthy when fertilized only every three or four years, then with a slow release turf fertilizer applied after the grass is actively growing, generally after the second mowing in the spring.

Weed and feed fertilizers are not effective on St. Augustine. To work, the weed and feed should be applied to actively growing weeds and turf. Weeds found in St. Augustine are most active when the grass is still dormant. Mowing weeds closely in the early spring will do more good than a weed and feed. When the grass begins to grow, a good, healthy turf will suppress weeds. Herbicides will not be needed.

If you do use an herbicide on lawn weeds, be very careful to not place it near the drip line of trees and shrubs or near flower beds. Herbicides will kill or damage all broad leaf plants—weeds, trees, shrubs, perennials. They are not discriminatory. Before purchasing an herbicide, determine if you really have the need for one. Cheaper and more environmentally friendly alternatives may be available.

Managing pest problems in the landscape improves plant health and conserves water. **Studies show that the amount of chemical pesticides used per square foot in urban areas for landscape maintenance exceeds that used on agricultural land.** Homeowners must learn to better manage the pests. Integrated Pest Management (IPM) is an effective way to control pests with a minimum use of pesticides. The object of an IPM program is not to totally eliminate pests, but to keep pest populations below the level at which they cause unacceptable damage. The system is covered in detail in Chapter 11.

Water conservation is important. You can make a difference by applying simple changes to your landscape. Work with your neighbors, community associations, and cities to implement some if not all of the seven principals of waterwise gardening. Only you can stop the water filled with pesticides and fertilizer running down the gutter into the storm drain, creeks, rivers, and bayous!

TEXAS WILDFLOWERS

What are wildflowers? Some field guides define them as plants that have a mainly aboveground growth and die at the end of one growing season and generally lack a woody stem. Another definition is any flower, native or nonnative, that grows without the aid of humans. Many wildflowers are annuals as in the first definition; however, many of the flowers listed as wildflowers in seed catalogs and enjoyed along the roadways are perennials with a few biennials.

Wildflowers in Texas are synonymous with Lady Bird Johnson. Her interests and efforts for roadside beautification as first lady brought Texas and its wonderful wildflowers to national attention. "For me, wildflowers have been part of the joy of living," she wrote in the foreword to *Texas Wildflowers* by Campbell and Lynn Loughmiller. Many of us share this sentiment.

Lady Bird Johnson played a part in Texas Department of Transportation (TxDOT) planting of wildflowers along the roads across the state. Yes, man plants most of the wildflowers enjoyed by visitors every spring! TxDOT cares for the more than 800,000 acres of unpaved highway right-of-way. Landscape architects and maintenance personnel design and maintain the roadsides, sowing, fertilizing, mowing, and planting shrubs and trees. Over 47,000 pounds of seeds, including bluebonnet, buttercup, and Indian paintbrush are planted each fall.

TxDOT has learned from sixty years of beautification experience that plantings of single species do not do well. The most effective roadside horticulture mimics nature. Roadsides are most stable when natural combinations of grasses, legumes (bluebonnets), and wildflowers are planted. The varieties complement each other, form better ground cover, and are healthier, hardier, and more drought tolerant. A drive along the roadways reveals the success of this philosophy. Once again working with nature had to be learned by man.

Wildflower Viewing

Wildflower viewing is big business throughout the state. Spring brings an influx of visitors from all over the world to view the more than 79,000 miles of Texas highways with March, April, and May the prime blooming months. Many of the large national tour companies have special tours for events related to wildflowers.

The bluebonnet, *Lupinus texensis*, became the state flower in 1901, beating out the prickly pear cactus and the open cotton boll. In 1971 legislation was amended to include all *L. texensis* and "any other variety of bluebonnet not heretofore recorded." Six species are currently recognized as the Texas state flower. Bonnet flower, buffalo clover, Texas lupine, Quaker's bonnets, wolf flower, and *el conejo* are all common names for the Texas bluebonnet. In the wild the *L. texensis* is found only in Texas.

Lupinus texensis

The first bluebonnet plantings along highways were done for erosion control. The plants have deep root systems and as members of the legume family add atmospheric nitrogen to the soil by fixating the nitrogen through root nodules. Nature at work through beauty.

Bluebonnets reach their peak in April. One of the oldest Bluebonnet Trails is at Ennis with more than 40 miles of well-marked trails. A popular trail charted in Washington County runs from Brenham to Chappell Hill. La Grange marks Bluebonnet Trails in Fayette County. The Highland Lakes Bluebonnet Trail loops through the Hill Country usually on the first two weekends in April. Many other activities such as antique shows, herb fairs,

and quilt shows run in combination with the various trails on weekends.

Dogwood festivals celebrate the season in Tyler, Woodville, and Palestine usually the last weekend in March and the first weekend in April. In northeast Texas, a signed wildflower route on a three-day weekend at the end of April highlights dozens of beautiful wild species between the towns of Avinger, Hughes Springs, and Linden. Around Gilmore, the annual Cherokee Rose Festival explores wild roses in rural countrysides in mid-May.

Spring may create the most activity, but it is not the only time to view wildflowers. Indian blankets fill fields and roadsides with bright red and yellow blooms during May and June. Many members of the family Asteraceae (Compositacea), sunflowers and relatives, thrive during summer's hottest months. Elegant Queen Ann's lace blooms in September followed by fall blooms of goldenrod and purple gayfeather.

Fall color displays rival spring wildflowers with the autumn trails held the last weekend in October in Canadian and the four weekends of October in Winnsboro. In West Texas, colorful blossoms of cacti, succulents, and other desert species may erupt following any rain.

To obtain current information on wildflower viewing in the state, refer to Appendix B.

Lady Bird Johnson Wildflower Center

To promote and educate about Texas wildflowers and other North America native plants, Lady Bird Johnson and Helen Hays established the Lady Bird Johnson Wildflower Center in 1982. The center's mission is to educate people about the environmental necessity, economic value, and natural beauty of native plants. The center located at 4801 La Crosse Avenue in Austin serves all of North America, but the headquarters reflects the nature and culture of the Central Texas Hill Country, part of the Edwards Plateau. The southeastern edge of the plateau contains the Edward's Aquifer and the Wildflower Center. The Edwards Plateau is also the intersection of the Midwestern Prairies, the Chihuahuan Desert, the Tamaulipan Thorn Scrub, and the Southeastern Woodlands. This diversity is ideally suited to the study of wildflowers and other native plants.

The Wildflower Center is designed to fit into the local

environment. Plants native to the area are used in landscaping around the buildings. Rooftop water harvesting systems, passive solar heating, breezeways, and the use of recycled materials all demonstrate the feasibility and practical applications of alternative sources used to protect the delicate Hill Country ecosystems —an excellent example of a waterwise landscape. The conservation systems also allow the center to concentrate funds where most needed in research and promotion of working with our natural resources.

The grounds of the center are surrounded by savanna, a mix of grasses interspersed with oaks and junipers. One hundred and seventy years ago, Austin was a vast savanna. The land managers at the Wildflower Center are working to restore the area to its pre-European settlement beauty. Nature trails wind through the meadow and forest, allowing visitors an up-close look at mature native plants. Demonstration areas are maintained around the center to highlight different native plants and visibly show the difference between a native and a nonnative urban landscape. Native landscapes can be formal areas. Visit the center. See for yourself. See Appendix B for complete information.

Growing Wildflowers

Enjoyment of wildflowers does not have to be limited to viewing from a moving vehicle or walking through a restored meadow and woodlands or demonstration area. A wide variety of seeds are available by mail or at your local nursery. For best results look for seeds harvested in Texas, preferably in your area. Sources are listed in Appendix A.

Wildflowers fit easily into home landscapes, are easy to grow, and provide the first glimpses of spring. No matter which part of the state, the majority of the wildflowers require well-drained soil and plenty of sun. Observe where your favorite flowers grow in the wild and try to duplicate the conditions. Do not remove the plants growing in the wild! More about that later.

The optimum planting time for seeds for the majority of the spring blooming wildflowers is September to December. Plants can be planted in the spring as early as the soil can be worked. Seeds and plants for summer and fall blooming wildflowers can be planted anytime in the spring.

Site selection is the first step

to a successful wildflower garden. A sunny area along a fence where perennials or annuals grow in the summer but is bare or sparsely planted in the fall and winter, turf areas, spots under deciduous trees, open fields, and ditch banks are all good possibilities. No matter what site you select, make sure it does not have standing water and receives at least eight hours of direct sun. A few wildflowers will grow in less sun, but not less than five hours per day. The purple coneflower *Echinacea purpurea* will grow in partial to dappled shade, but the blooms will not be as large or prolific. An indication of not enough sun is a spindly or leggy plant that leans toward the sun and does not bloom.

Once selected, the site needs to be prepared. The soil needs to be cleared of weeds and loosened to no deeper than an inch. Thousands of dormant seeds lie beneath the soil waiting to germinate when exposed to light. Extensive tilling of the soil greater than one inch releases the dormant seeds, allowing them to outcompete the wildflower seeds. In turf areas, mow the turf as low as possible, rake the selected site to loosen the soil around the leaf blades, and remove any accumulated leaf debris. The seeds must be able to make contact with the soil's surface.

After the site is selected and prepared, you are ready to plant. Since most wildflower seeds are small, to achieve better seed distribution it is helpful to mix them with a carrier, an inert material such as masonry sand, perlite, or potting soil. Four parts of inert material to one part seed is recommended. Mix desired seeds and carrier; using a mechanical hand spreader or by hand, broadcast one half of the seeds as uniformly as possible over the area. Sow the remaining seed in a direction perpendicular to the initial sowing. This process allows for more even coverage and can be applied to any size site.

The seeds then need to be pressed into contact with the soil. This can be accomplished by walking over the area, rolling with a mechanical roller, or pressing by hand on smaller sites. It is important that the seeds are not covered any deeper than 1/16 of an inch. Some of the seeds will remain visible. That's okay. The seeds need light to germinate.

Sprinkle the seeds lightly with water. Do not add fertilizer. Fertilizer will increase weed growth and promote lush foliage and few blooms on your wildflowers. The only exception is if the soil is severely depleted of nutrients, then work in a conservative amount of fertilizer at planting time. For best results use a low nitrogen fertilizer with an approximate ratio of 1-3-2 (one part nitrogen-three parts phosphorus-two parts potassium). If nature does not provide moisture, it is necessary to lightly sprinkle the area until the seeds germinate. After germination, do not allow the site to completely dry out but avoid overwatering. The seedlings are susceptible to root rot with too much water. After seedlings are one to two inches high, gradually reduce watering and apply only when plants show signs of stress. Once native plants are established, supplemental watering is not required, though a little water during drought conditions will be appreciated.

Weed control is necessary as the wildflowers germinate and grow. But what is a "weed"? Once again there is no clear-cut definition. The most accepted definitions are a plant in the wrong place; a plant that does not belong in the particular plant community and can overgrow other plants in the community; an introduced exotic that thrives in disturbed places crowding out desirable species. A weed is subjective. One person's weed may be another's prize plant. To paraphrase Ralph Waldo Emerson: "A weed is a plant whose virtue has yet to be determined."

Whatever you determine to be a weed, the chore of removal should be minimal if the area was properly prepared. Weeds do grow faster than newly planted seedlings. They shade seedlings and compete for soil moisture. One way to control weeds is to water correctly. Watering too

"A weed is a plant whose virtue has yet to be determined."

early or too late in the season or overwatering encourages weeds to grow.

To help differentiate a weed from a seed you planted, many of the seed catalogs and packets include a picture or drawing of the seedling stage of the flowers. Planting a few of the seeds left from the garden in a clay pot and keeping the pot in the house will aid you in identification of seedlings. If in doubt I recommend you do not pull. Wait until positive identification can be made. You may find you are pulling the wrong plant. I recently debated about pulling an unidentified plant that later turned out to be a pink gaura—a prized Texas native perennial wildflower. Where did it come from? I have no idea. I consider it a gift from nature. Be careful! You too may have many of these gifts from nature.

Wildflower Seeds

An often asked question is will the wildflowers come back next year? Some may and some may not. If you used a commercial wildflower mix, some or many of the flowers may be nonnative species or native species not adapted to your area. If you want only native species, be sure to carefully check your seed source. One of the Texas seed companies provides seeds designated as "Domesticated." These are seeds that are not native or have been altered from the original—degenerates. The company clearly labels these seeds and states they will not reappear next season under most situations. They provide lovely displays and are popular. Read your seed packets carefully to be sure you are planting seeds for the plants you want to grow.

Patience is required to allow wildflowers to reseed. The majority of the seeds in mixes are annuals and must be allowed to set mature seeds. Once the seeds are dry, either collect them or shake or mow them, allowing the seeds to cover the soil in the area you want them to reseed. For best results remove the plant or mow larger areas only after the seeds have been removed. Allow the area to remain relatively undisturbed to ensure the germination of the seeds in spring. Many find this leaves an unsightly area and find it easier to simply replant each fall. Working the annual wildflowers around perennials fills in an area during non-wildflower-blooming times.

Perennial wildflowers can be trimmed after blooming; however, cutting the foliage below three inches may permanently damage the plant. Many perennials also reseed if allowed to complete the seed cycle before dead heading or trimming, a good way to increase your perennial bed or to share with friends.

Collecting wildflowers in the wild is discouraged. It is not illegal to pick many wildflowers, but it is illegal to trespass and damage or destroy right-of-way or government property. It is also illegal to trespass on private property at any time without permission. Flowers picked along the road or plants dug up are not allowed to complete the cycle to seed formation. These plants will not reseed for next year's blooms. Be considerate of the land and the flowers. Allow for enjoyment in years to come.

Never collect seeds or plants in public areas of any kind: public parks, wildlife refuges, or preserves. Areas marked for development or destruction in the near future are excellent sites for seed and plant collection; however, permission still needs to be obtained. Once permission is obtained from a private landowner for collection of seeds, certain steps should be followed to ensure proper preservation of the seeds and/or plants. Timing is the most important. Desired plants are seen when blooming, but this is not the time to collect. Mark desired plants with a flag or stake, since dried plants are hard to find and almost impossible to identify. Be sure to make a detailed map of the locations of your markers. You will not be returning for several weeks.

Never collect seeds from rare or endangered species. Notify the local chapter of the Native Plant Society if you find rare or endangered species on a site soon to be destroyed. This organization has the authority and knowledge to handle rare and endangered species. Chances are they are already aware of the plants, but take the time to notify them.

Proper harvesting requires an understanding of seed ripening, dispersal mechanisms, and the influences of weather on the timing of seed maturation. First, you must be familiar with the approximate flowering and fruiting dates of the desired plants and be able to recognize mature fruit or seeds. Experience is often the best teacher. The production of mature seeds is very weather dependent with flowering and fruiting dates varying from year to year. An early spring and dry summer, for example, may cause early seed set. Seed quality also varies from year to year and from location to location.

After determining the general time period in which the fruit or seeds ripen, the next step is to carefully observe the plants. Begin collecting only when fruit and seeds mature. A delay of only a few days may be the difference between success or failure in collecting a good crop, especially for those species with seeds that disperse quickly or are attractive to birds and other animals.

Mature seeds are generally dark in color, firm, and dry. Seeds that are green and moist are immature and generally will not germinate or will produce unhealthy seedlings. Many pods or capsules dehisce (come open and expel seeds) when ripe and mature at staggered intervals, making collection difficult. Once maturation begins, those plants may need to be checked every few days to collect any newly matured seeds. Place a paper sack over the blooms and tie it off with string if unable to visit regularly. Enough light and air will reach the bloom to allow it to continue growing, and the sack will hold the seeds as they mature and drop, so that you only have to collect seeds once, at the end of seed set.

The flesh of pulpy fruits often becomes soft and changes from green or yellowish to reddish or blue-purple when ripe. Seeds are often mature a week or more before the fleshy fruits turn color and fall from the plant. You can determine seed maturity by cutting open the fruit and examining seeds for firmness, fullness, and dark color.

Collect seeds only from plants you find growing abundantly in a given area to ensure you do not eradicate an isolated population. Take no more than one-third of the seeds, leaving enough to reseed and increase the resident population. Gather fruits from the ground only if they have recently dropped. Avoid all fruits or seeds that have lain on moist ground. The chances are good they have begun to decay or are infested with insects. The potential to ruin the rest of the seed harvest if combined with other seeds is great. Do not collect seeds that have signs of insect or mold damage. Collect seeds in pods as soon as they are dry to prevent insect-infested seeds.

Equipment needed depends on the size of the harvest. Basic equipment includes gloves, boots, drop cloths, pruning shears, boxes, baskets, paper bags, and/or canvas bags (no plastic bags!). Many plants can be stripped by hand or the seed can be beaten onto drop cloths. Screens with large openings can be used to sift the seeds or fruits and reduce the amount of material to dry before threshing.

Once seeds are collected, specific procedures should be followed to insure viability of the seeds. Bluebonnets and other legumes should be collected just before or as the pod turns brown and dries and before the pod opens. The pods should be dried in single layers spread thinly on canvas cloths, screens, or trays elevated from the ground. Air-drying takes one to three days, depending on the humidity. After the seeds have dried, remove them from the pods by beating or threshing. A mature pod will often twist and split open to drop the seeds. Be sure the seeds are thoroughly dried before storing in a breathable container in a cool, dry place.

Not all seeds need to be cleaned before storage; however, those with pulpy fruit should be cleaned to prevent mold. Remove the pulp of large fruits by rubbing on a screen or mashing with a wooden block, rolling pin, or fruit press. With care to prevent damage to the seeds, smaller fruits can be cleaned in a blender. Using a ratio of two part fruits to one part water, blend with brief, intermittent agitations at low speed then strain the mixture to separate the seeds from the pulp.

Threshing seeds (separating seeds from the rest of the collected plant material) is optional, but it does have at least two advantages: It reduces the volume of seeds to be stored, which saves on storage space; and more seed-predators such as insect eggs, mold spores, and other seed disease vectors may be removed with the discarded chaff. The easiest way to thresh seeds is to rub the collected material against a coarse screen with a gloved hand. A more sophisticated method is to rub the plant material on the screen with one or more paddles covered with rubber matting.

The two most critical factors for storing seeds are constant temperatures and low humidity. A temperature of 50 degrees Fahrenheit or less and 50 percent humidity or lower is ideal. In general, fluctuating temperature and humidity harms seeds more than slightly higher constant values of each. The key to storing seeds is finding a cool dry place that will remain cool and dry throughout the storage period. Store the seeds in paper sacks to allow good air circulation and prevent molding. Do not store seeds in plastic bags or other non-breathable containers unless they are air dried thoroughly first. Glass or plastic jars with added desiccants (those things found in over-the-counter pill bottles) are ideal for the dried seeds.

Store seeds in the refrigerator, not the freezer, until ready to plant. Low temperatures, humidity, and light levels protect seed longevity. If it is not practical to store seeds in your refrigerator, store them in any place that is cool, dark, and dry, protecting them from insects as much as possible.

Fleshy fruits should be kept

moist to maintain viability. If allowed to dry out, they will either germinate prematurely or not at all. This type of seed should be planted immediately or mixed in a one-to-one ratio of moist sand, sphagnum moss, or a peat and perlite mixture, and stored in a cool place. If the root emerges from the seeds during storage, the seedling should be removed and planted immediately. Seed storage longevity varies from species to species. Some seeds may be viable after ten years of storage, while others may not germinate after two years in storage. Ideally, seeds should be planted within one year of collection.

When collecting plants in the wild, the same consideration of the land and landowner is essential. Collect plants only after receiving permission. One exception is ditch banks along roadways that are routinely cleaned to improve drainage. Plants from these areas may be "rescued" at any time. The time for collection is as important with plants as it is with seeds. Plants should only be dug at the beginning of their growth for the season or while dormant. Once again it is necessary to tag the desired plants, carefully mark location on a map, and come back at the proper time.

Digging large trees and shrubs is not recommended because of extensive damage that may occur during digging. Destruction of the plant and the area around it is not worth taking the chance. An exception is in plant rescues where the area and vegetation will be destroyed. For larger specimens, check your local nurseries.

Whether collecting seeds or plants, always pay careful attention to where the plant is growing. Check shade, soil, drainage, mulch cover—all are very important. For success with the seedling or transplant, the conditions of the site where collected must be duplicated.

An extension agent a few years ago collected sunflower seeds along a roadside, a nice low-growing plant covered with bright yellow flowers. He then planted the seeds in the test gardens at the extension, where they were fertilized, watered, and pampered. The sunflower turned out to be a *Bidens*, grew 6-8 feet tall, and tried to take over the garden. A few plants are still popping up in unexpected places several years later. With better conditions than the roadside, the small sunflower turned into a garden "thug." Beware of what you collect!

Wildflowers are a wonderful way to welcome spring to your garden. The butterflies and hummingbirds attracted to your yard by the flowers are an added benefit. Find a place, large or small, for seeds this fall. Apply the knowledge learned by TxDOT, increase the diversity in your landscape, and enjoy the rewards.

May all your weeds be wildflowers!

TEXAS WILDSCAPES
HABITAT GARDENING

Texas Parks and Wildlife created the Nongame and Urban Program division (now the Wildlife Diversity Program) in 1992-1993 with the Texas Wildscapes Backyard Habitat Program the first project. Looking for something to appeal to people interested in wildlife but not in hunting or fishing, TPWD staff realized the popularity of gardening and used it as a theme, implementing concepts learned from similar successful projects in other states. As people create wildlife habitat in their backyards, TPWD feels they learn to appreciate the importance of habitat conservation on a larger scale.

Certificates and signs are offered to participants as rewards for their efforts and to allow the opportunity to show off to neighbors and communities. The program is self-funding, allowing for printing and staff—a unique approach for a state agency. Workshops are given routinely around the state to provide the public with information and tools to help preserve and restore wildlife habitat. Call your local TPWD office or check their web site (Appendix B) to find locations and times.

In 1999 Texas Parks and Wildlife Press published *Texas Wildscapes Gardening for Wildlife* by Noreen Darmude and Kelly Bender, both among the originators of the project. This book, containing lists of plants recommended for birds and other wildlife, is an excellent gardening reference.

The Wildscapes program emphasizes habitat gardening. Habitat is defined by Webster as "the natural environment of an organism; place that is natural for the life and growth of an organism." A habitat garden must provide three basic elements—**food**, **water**, and **shelter**. The size of the garden area is not important. What is provided is. The principles of the Wildscape program can be applied to a balcony, a patio garden, a multi-acre site, and everything in-between. The only difference is the amount and form of wildlife attracted.

A habitat garden must provide three basic elements—food, water, and shelter.

Before starting a habitat garden of any size, consider your current gardening practices. Do you frequently use pesticides, herbicides, and fungicides in your garden? Why? Are they necessary? Chapter 11 offers safe and easy alternatives. To successfully attract wildlife to your garden, you first must stop killing what is there. Systemic pesticides kill all creatures drinking the nectar of the flowers (bees, butterflies, hummingbirds) as well as the insects sucking the leaves. Many birds are killed by direct contact with pesticides from eating the poison or being sprayed or indirect contact from eating poisoned prey. Think next time before picking up that spray bottle. Will you kill more than you intend?

Recent statistics reveal over 30 percent of Texans watch wildlife as a hobby with nearly 17 percent traveling away from home. Bird watching or "birding" is an increasingly popular form of wildlife observation with many organized activities and birding trails across the state. Interest in watching hummingbirds, butterflies, dragonflies, and even amphibians is increasing. Save gas, time, and money and watch from your porch swing, favorite chair by the window, or corner of the patio. Provide the basic habitat, and nature will do the rest. Imagine sharing your first cup of morning coffee with a bright red male cardinal gathering insects to feed his growing brood or your evening glass of wine with an owl silently gliding across the yard.

The habitat you provide depends on what you want to attract and the size of your garden. As TxDOT determined, diversity provides the healthiest wildflowers. Diversity also provides the best habitat for wildlife. Ideally, a landscape should offer a mix of different ecosystems: woodlands, prairies, and wetlands. The scale of each ecosystem does not have to be large.

Habitat Layers

The best habitats are multi-layered, providing a top, middle, and low or ground level. The top layer is in the trees. Again use of natives cannot be overstressed. Oaks attract thirty-seven bird species. Wax myrtle *Morella cerifera* seeds feed over forty species of birds. Maples, pecan, hackberry, sweetgum, southern magnolia, and conifers such as the Ashe's juniper and red cedar (twenty-two species of birds) all have important functions for wildlife.

The type of wildlife attracted depends on the form or type of the essentials of food, water, and shelter provided. Trees, not limited to the ones listed above, provide food, shelter, and nesting sites. Seeds, fruit, new green leaves, and the insects attracted to them all provide food sources. The branches provide shelter and

nesting sites. Trunks of large trees offer home sites for woodpeckers, flickers, owls, and others.

Trees do not have to be alive to function in a habitat. Leaving a dead tree or snag allows additional nesting areas. Woodpeckers work on holes in trees for years to shape into proper nests; when abandoned, the hole is used as a nest site for many other bird species including owls. Planting a dead tree with holes already in place will attract an interesting variety of birds. When leaving a dead tree in place or "planting" a snag, be sure to consider safety. Make sure the snag is well placed and secured to avoid falling on buildings or people.

The second layer consists of mid-story trees and shrubs. In smaller or immature landscapes these may function as the top story. This layer also provides food and shelter with nesting sites for predominately song birds. A mix of evergreen and deciduous plantings is best. Small native trees and shrubs such as the American beautyberry *Callicarpa americana* (twelve bird species), canyon senna, roughleaf dogwood, hawthorns *Crataegus* spp. (nineteen bird species), coralbean, Virginia sweetspire, and cenozia are a few good examples.

The third or bottom layer is the ground. Many birds are ground feeders on seeds and insects. American robins scratch for worms and other insects. Doves eat seeds and rest on the ground. To provide proper habitat, the open area should be close enough to trees and shrubs to allow cover from predators and large enough to allow escape from predators hiding in the shrubs.

Food, Water, and Shelter

Food sources are best if natural but can be supplemented. Migrating birds and residents both appreciate seeds in feeders. Providing food does not prevent birds from normal migration; on the contrary the additional food often allows for healthier birds during migration. Birds will seek out natural food when available, but often with the fragmentation of habitat the natural food is not available. During the winter tremendous amounts of energy are required to keep warm. A few additional seeds from a feeder can make the difference between life and death. A sudden cold spell in the spring that sends insects into hiding can be serious. Again a few seeds can provide the necessary protein to continue.

Observing birds is easier at a feeder than in the trees. The type of seeds and feeder will determine what birds. Most birds like the small oil sunflower seeds. Sunflowers are American natives thus most seed eaters are familiar with them with over forty-six different bird species known to eat the seeds. Many finches like thistle, and various kinds of thistle feeders are available. Whatever feeder and feed you use, make sure you keep the feeder clean of debris and droppings and the seed fresh. Moldy, mildewed seed and dirty feeders can promote diseases.

The last and maybe the most important component to a habitat is water. Wildlife needs water for drinking, bathing, and reproduction. The water source can be any size and once again size depends on what will be attracted. The small ornamental bird baths are the least effective. For a bird bath to attract birds, it must have gently sloping sides to allow small birds easy access in and out and a rough surface to provide safe footing. Ideally a bird bath should also have a deep end about three inches for a large bird to soak and bathe without splashing out all the water. A bowl with a twelve-inch diameter meets the minimum requirement.

Place the bath near trees or shrubs where birds can fly to dry and preen in safety. Locating it in the middle of an open space may make a focal point of the bath but allows for easier predation, especially from birds of prey. Cleaning frequently and filling with fresh water is essential, since diseases can be transmitted through dirty water. Keep water in the bath all year round. The birds need water in the winter as much as in the summer. Birdbath heaters are available for use in areas of the state with freezing winters and do work.

When more space is available, in-ground and above-ground water features are a good way to provide water for birds. Leave areas around the edges with shallow levels to accommodate the smaller birds. An added benefit of larger bodies of water is increased wildlife. Dragonflies will breed in small ponds if proper conditions are provided. Frogs and toads appear whenever water is provided. Large ponds attract wading birds. More about water gardens in Chapter 9.

Attracting Humming-birds and Butterflies

Habitat gardening suggestions so far have been primarily for birds. Many landscapes are limited in size for attracting large numbers of birds. Smaller landscapes, patio gardens, and balconies can easily attract hummingbirds and butterflies. The same principles apply as for attracting birds: food, shelter, and water. Often the same plants attract hummingbirds and butterflies.

In Texas seventeen different species of hummingbird have been identified. Ten are regularly occurring, the remaining seven are visitors or vagrants from Mexico. In East Texas the ruby-throated hummingbird is the most common. In central, western, and more southerly areas, a good field guide is necessary to identify the different species. No matter what species, all require the same type of habitat.

Hummingbirds are the smallest warm-blooded vertebrates with the greatest relative energy output of any warm-blooded animal. They are often referred to as nature's jewels because of their iridescent feathers. The iridescence is due to barbules, tiny elliptical structures of varying sizes containing air bubbles. The thickness of the structure determines the color seen with greens, reds, and purples predominant.

Among nectar feeding birds, hummingbirds are the most specialized. Their bills are not used to sip the nectar but to probe the flower deeply as a protective covering over the grooved tongue. Nectar and insects, up to 25 percent of the diet, are ingested together with lapping motions of the tongue, which can protrude inches beyond the bill's tip. Any nectar-producing flower can provide food; however, hummingbirds prefer certain flower types: thick-walled, tubular flowers with little or no fragrance arranged in well-spaced clusters along tall upright stems. Since hummingbirds feed in flight, no perching spots are necessary, only open space.

Hummingbirds are very visual, attracted to red and orange. They will feed on other flower colors when it is determined the nectar contains proper sugar concentrations. The attraction to red extends to non-floral red objects, including clothing and other inert objects. People in red hats are often "checked out."

The tremendous amounts of energy exerted by the little birds require large quantities of nectar. The specific flowers adapted to meet these needs also make use of the visits by depositing pollen on the visitor's head that is then carried to another flower for pollination. The hummingbirds help in assuring a continuing source of nectar. Nature at work.

An appropriate habitat should be layered as in the general description. In small gardens vines can serve as mid layers. The crossvine *Bignonia capreolata* blooms during the times of hummingbird migration. This easily grown vine is native to the Piney Woods and Gulf Coast Prairies and Marshes regions but has been seen growing across the state. Another vine is the native coral honeysuckle *Lonicera sempervirens*. Nineteen other bird species feed on the fruit, and giant swallowtail butterflies feed on the nectar. Avoid the yellow and white Japanese honeysuckles *L. japonica* that have escaped and naturalized across the state. Remember native wildlife knows native plants.

Several small trees also provide nectar. Native to the Trans Pecos region are the yellow trumpets *Tecoma stans* and the desert willow *Chilopsis linearis*. Both can be grown across the state if provided good drainage and little water—very drought tolerant plants. Another drought tolerant plant attractive to the little birds is the red yucca *Hesperaloe parviflora*. Many other plants also attract hummingbirds to small or large areas; many of the salvias, wildflowers, cactus, mints, mallows, and lantana all provide nectar.

However, for a balcony with only one or two plants, supplemental feeding with a feeder may be necessary. Feeders are fun to provide no matter what other nectar sources are available. Many styles are available and any will work; however, red ones will attract visitors faster. Make sure the feeder comes apart easily for cleaning. To prevent disease the feeder must be kept clean and the sugar water changed regularly. Nectar mixes are available commercially but can be prepared easily by mixing four parts water to one part sugar. Add the sugar to boiled water, but do not boil the mixture. A higher concentration of sugar is not recommended because of the possibility of liver damage. Red coloring does not need to be added to the solution. A red area on the feeder is enough to attract the hummingbirds. Cleaning the feeders and adding fresh solution is recommended every three days to reduce the chance of fermentation of the sugar.

Placement of the feeder is important. Try to hang in the shade out of the wind and to attract the birds faster, close to native wildflowers. Hanging the feeder after establishing a habitat garden is most effective. Additional feeders increase visitors to the garden and increase squabbles over the nectar. Don't be concerned about these aggressive displays. They are normal and fun to watch as a "pecking order" is established. Often the smallest species is the most aggressive.

> Feeders will attract hummingbirds, but flower nectar is preferred. Providing both in your garden will keep the little birds around for your enjoyment.

Availability of feeders will not prevent migration. When the time comes the birds will leave. In the southern half of the state hummers can be seen almost year round. If you choose to leave your feeder out past migration to feed the stragglers, remember to maintain the cleaning and refilling. A stressed bird is more susceptible to disease.

A few species of hummingbird do nest in Texas. The preferred sites are deciduous trees or shrubs with dense foliage. The tiny nests, built in the fork of a very small limb, are made from and camouflaged with spider webs, hair, bits of lichens, and other materials. To optimize your chances of attracting a pair to nest, provide favorite flowers, feeders, and a shallow water source for bathing. Nest boxes are not used.

To provide habitat for butterflies, a basic understanding of the life cycle is important. Butterflies are insects that exhibit complete metamorphosis. Metamorphosis comes from the Greek word meaning change. Most creatures develop from an egg and gradually change into adults with all stages gradual progressions of the same form. Insects exhibiting complete metamorphosis go through stages completely different from one another. With the butterflies and all members of the order Lepidoptera, the four stages are egg, larva or caterpillar, chrysalis or pupae, and adult or reproductive stage. To successfully attract butterflies, a habitat must be provided for all four stages.

Butterflies are host specific, meaning each species requires a certain plant species for reproduction. Gulf fritillaries need passionvine, but not all *Passiflora* species will do. Once again only native species are suitable. The lovely red Brazilian *Passiflora* will be ignored. A caterpillar would rather die than eat a bite. Monarchs require members of the milkweed family Asclepiadaceae. Most North American species are used for both food and reproduction, since the monarch migrates between the U.S. and Mexico.

If eaten plants bother you, place host plants to the back of an area where they can be obscured by other foliage. The plants will be denuded by the caterpillars but not killed. The host/plant relationship, developed over centuries, allows the plants to replace leaves during the time of the third or chrysalis stage. The host will have a fresh crop of leaves by the time the reproductive stage of the butterfly is ready to lay more eggs.

Place nectar plants to provide optimum attraction for the butterflies, other visitors, and you. For nectar, butterflies prefer tubular flowers of the proper length depending on the length of the proboscis, with individual flowers arranged either in clusters or around a central flower head. Butterflies land to feed and need a platform. Purple, red, pink, orange, yellow, and white are preferred colors. Butterflies unlike hummingbirds use their proboscis as a straw and suck up nectar. Butterflies detect scent with their antennae and their feet. Females use their feet to determine if plants are suitable for egg-laying and proper development of the caterpillar.

Butterflies know the plants to look for and remain in your habitat only if you provide the proper plants. Addition of sunny rocks, small pools of water, and small open muddy areas for gathering to collect minerals and salts found in the soil provide added incentives to remain.

Again diversity and native plants are important. Texas has more than 450 species of butterflies, more than any other state in the U.S. Butterflies pollinate more than 65 percent of the world's flowering plants, second only to bees. Habitat destruction is the main cause of decline in numbers and species. With careful planning you can provide important habitat and share in the variety. Make your garden an inviting place and the butterflies will reward you with color, movement, and texture.

The Alamo Area Master Naturalists in San Antonio in 1998 established a Riverwalk Wildscape Demonstration site. The site located just north of the intersection of W. Durango and Aubrey adjacent to the Riverwalk Inn has received several awards including the Keep San Antonio Beautiful Environmental Leadership Award. The site is also the location for the annual TPWD Wildscapes workshop. The next time you're in San Antonio check it out.

Wildscapes Backyard Habitat Program

Plan your habitat, include all three elements, start planting, and apply to TPWD Texas Wildscapes Backyard Habitat Program for certification. Let your neighbors know what you have done and how they can help to maintain precious habitat. TPWD currently requires a minimum of 50 percent natives to qualify and recommends a minimum of turf. The 50 percent minimum is soon to be increased, but an exact number has not been determined. In your planning, try for a higher number.

The application asks for a plant list, a basic drawing of your landscape with all major features included, specific food sources, natural and supplemental, water sources, shelter, and nesting sites. One step above the certified habitat is demonstration garden designation. This requires a visit and approval by TPWD personnel.

My home landscape in a subdivision on the west side of Houston is a Texas Wildscapes Backyard Wildlife Habitat and a Certified Texas Wildscape Demonstration Site. In January 1999 my husband and I purchased the property next to us where a house had burnt in 1984. We have worked to combine the two lots into habitat gardens. The plan sent to TPWD and the plant list are in Appendix C.

Four ecosystems, woodland, desert, wetland with pond, and prairie are represented as closely as possible in the heat and humidity of the Gulf Coast. Many of the native plants were difficult to find,

but the search has been worth it. Drought tolerant plants from Trans Pecos have survived without water and bloomed! The landscape is still a work in progress with continued search for natives.

The diversity of wildlife is amazing! One morning in June 2001 on the short trip from the back door to the compost pile, I saw six different species of butterflies! During the winter of 2000-2001 we had a resident armadillo living under the front deck. He aerated the turf in the front yard and helped me weed several beds in the backyard as he removed the insects. The section of turf he worked is the healthiest in the yard. In the spring he

TPWD Habitat sign

Wildscape demonstration site sign

moved on. A pair of raccoons and an opossum moved into his old quarters. Slugs, snails, and tree roaches soon disappeared. The small amount of damage created by these creatures is more than offset by the good they do. More about these and other wanted and unwanted critters in Chapter 17.

The ponds attract frogs, toads, dragonflies, damsel flies, and myriad water inhabitants. I watched a male indigo bunting bathe on the edge of the large pond. He stayed for a few days then continued on his migration. Several different species of birds winter in the yard including Eastern Phoebes. Mosquitoes don't stand a chance with all the natural predators. More on the ponds and inhabitants in Chapter 9.

To obtain applications and more information, contact Texas Parks and Wildlife Department, Wildlife Diversity Program, Texas Wildscapes, 4200 Smith School Road, Austin, Texas 78744. For acreages between 10 and 200 acres use the same address as above, but request the Texas Wildacres Program. Information is also available on the web site listed in Appendix B.

Habitats are fun and necessary to maintain wildlife. To paraphrase, Provide the essentials and THEY will come!

ALTERNATIVES TO TURF
GROUND COVERS

Ground covers are used to stabilize soil, prevent erosion on slopes, moderate soil temperatures, hide "ugly" features such as utility boxes, fill in odd shaped trouble spots, cover soil surface tree roots, add color with flowers, foliage, or berries, and reduce weed growth. An often overlooked but important function is to increase available wildlife habitat at the ground level.

A ground cover is any material, plant or non-plant, used to cover the surface of the soil, rocks, or sand, etc. The most frequently used ground cover in the urban landscape is turf grass, the thirstiest part of the landscape. With media propaganda and encouragement to have "the greenest, insect free lawn," urban landscapes (turf) create more water pollution from overuse and misuse of fertilizers and pesticides than commercial agriculture. Turf grasses have limited habitat value, especially when sprayed with pesticides. Yet turf areas remain essential to all landscape plans. Why? The most frequently encountered answer is that turf areas are needed for pets and playgrounds, but even in these situations more habitat friendly alternatives are available.

Non-plant material is recommended for use for paths in high traffic areas, to cover problem drainage, or in any area where living plants are not practical, such as in too much shade (see Chapter 7). Frequently used non-plant

material is chipped and shredded yard wastes and leaves (Chapter 14), mulch, gravel, lava rocks, stones, newspapers, and wooden walks and decking.

I recently saw a school playground area covered with a thick mat made from recycled tires—softer and cleaner than turf and a good use for tires to keep them out of the landfills, also requires no maintenance. Alternatives are available.

Plant material is the most frequently used ground cover even excluding turf. The most desirable share the characteristic of spreading by suckers, rhizomes, or stolons. Suckers are shoots rising from the underground stem or root of the parent plant. Taller ground covers such as short varieties of plum produce thickets through suckers. Tomatoes and crepe myrtles also produce suckers.

Stolons are prostrate stems, at or just below the surface of the ground, that produce new plants from buds at tips or nodes. Frogfruit *Phyla incisa*, one of my favorite ground covers, grows this way.

Rhizomes are root-like underground stems, usually horizontal in position, that produce roots below and send up new plant shoots along the upper surface of the rhizome. Most ferns produce clumps through rhizomes.

The usual plants sold in the nursery trade are Asian jasmine, liriope, mondo or monkey grass, periwinkle (*Vinca major* and *minor*), non-native cinquefoils, Boston and fig ivy, and Japanese ardesia. All these do require less water, fertilizer, and pesticide than turf but provide only marginally better habitat. Native ground cover plants are harder to find but worth the effort. Table 4 lists native ground covers, growth requirements, and their wildlife significance.

Soil Preparation

No matter which ground cover is selected, proper soil preparation is essential before planting or placing any plant or non-plant material. Once in place, weed removal becomes difficult without disturbing the cover. The basic preparation principles apply to all ground covers, with exceptions noted for specific plants. After determining the area to be covered, remove all unwanted existing plant material, especially weeds.

A good safe method is solarization if time permits. This method works best in sunny locations. Remove existing plant material as much as possible; dig a trench a few inches deep around the site. Water the area thoroughly, then spread a piece of clear plastic 1-4 mil thick over the area and bury the edges. The idea is to "cook" the soil under the plastic. Weeds and weed seeds along with insects, such as nematodes will be destroyed. The hotter the temperature the quicker the process, but it will also work in cooler areas. Deep shade areas do not do well with this method and may damage tree and other roots near the surface. Leave the plastic in place for three to four weeks, longer in cooler, cloudy weather.

Solarization only treats the top three to five inches of soil; try to avoid cultivating the soil below this depth when planting. Remember weed seeds remaining below this depth only need a little light to germinate. This process may also kill beneficial soil microbes that can be added back by including compost with or around the new plants at planting time. After planting, place a thick layer of mulch around each new plant. This moderates soil temperature and will reduce weed growth from new seeds making contact with the soils surface.

If solarization is not a viable option, such as when the area is too shady or other desirable plant material exists, remove as much of the unwanted plants as possible, place a thick layer of newspapers, cardboard, or other permeable material (no plastic) around the plants, and cover with mulch or dried leaves. Leave this in place as long as possible. When it's time to plant, cut holes through the layers, remove only an area large enough for each individual plant, and set the plant in the hole. Water and re-cover the area with the removed material, leaving only the new plantings above the mulch. This process is good for covers that multiply with suckers or stolons; the permeable material layer will prohibit rhizome growth.

I do not recommend herbicides. The stronger products sterilize the soil and can prevent growth for up to a year, sometimes longer. The potential to kill or damage surrounding vegetation is always a possibility. A few years ago at the Harris County Cooperative Extension office, the tomato leaves started to curl on all the plants in the vegetable garden. The first thought was virus, and several plants were destroyed, but the curling continued on virus resistant varieties. Testing discovered no virus,

Table 4: Native Ground Covers

GROUND COVER	CHARACTERISTICS *Height/growth/spacing*	REQUIREMENTS *Soil/exposure*
Artemisia *Artemisia udoviciana*	Evergreen 1-3 feet, can be mowed, rhizomes. Space - 1 foot	Sand, loam, clay caliche, limestone, well drained. Part shade to full sun
Carolina jasmine *Gelsemium sempervirens*	Evergreen vine, screen and cover. Space - 6 to 8 feet	Sand, loam, clay, poor drainage okay. Part shade to full sun
Coralberry *Symphoricarpos orbiculatus*	Evergreen except in hard freeze, 1½ to 6 feet, stolons form thickets. Space - 1 foot	Sand, loam, clay, well drained. Shade
Fern acacia *Acacia angustissima,* *A. hirta, A. texensis*	Deciduous, 1-3 feet, small shrub, rhizomes. Space - 1½ feet	Sand, loam, clay, caliche, good drainage. Shade to full sun
Ferns: Maidenhair *Adiantum cappillus-veneris* Christmas *Polystichum acrostichoides* Wood *Thelypteris kunthii*	Maidenhair: dormant when dry. Space - 1 foot. Christmas: evergreen. Space - 1½ feet. Wood: dormant in winter, rhizomes. Space - 2 feet	Maidenhair: sand, loam, limestone, well drained. Christmas: sand, loam, acid to neutral, well drained. Wood: sand, loam, clay moist, poor drainage okay. Shade
Frogfruit *Phyla incisa*	Evergreen unless hard freeze, will return from roots, stolons. Space - 1 foot	Most soil types, including saline, well drained or seasonal poor drainage. Sun to shade
Horseherb *Calyptocarpus vialis*	Evergreen, dormant during freezing temps. 8-10 inches, mowed 2-4, stolons. Space - 1 foot	Sand, loam, caliches, clay, well drained. Shade to part shade
Lindheimer's globe berry *Ibervillea lindheimeri*	Vine, annual, good erosion control. Space - 1 foot	Well drained, loam, salt tolerant. Sun to part shade
Partridgeberry *Mitchella repens*	Evergreen, 2 inches, stolons. Space - 9 inches	Sand, loam, acid, well drained. Shade
Passionflower *Passiflora incarnata,* *P. lutea, P. foetida*	Deciduous vine screen and cover. Space - 2 to 3 feet	Well drained sand, loam, clay. Part shade to sun

REGION	WILDLIFE *Host/nectar*	NOTES
All except Coastal Plains and southern Brush Country	Cover, nectar, fragrant foliage	All year color in sunny locations, tolerates foot traffic if mowed
All, Rolling and High Plains may freeze back	Evergreen cover, nectar butterflies and hummingbirds	Flowers are toxic to humans
All if conditions favorable	Small red to purple berries eaten by birds	Provides good erosion control
All	Nectar and cover	Fine, ferny texture of leaves
All depending on soil conditions for specific fern	Cover	Texture in shade areas Wood will tolerate the most sun and is easiest to grow.
All	Nectar for butterflies-checkers and skippers	Tolerates light foot traffic and trimming
All except Trans Pecos, High and Rolling Plains	Cover	Outcompetes turf in shade, tolerates foot traffic and mowing
All except High and Rolling Plains rarely in Trans Pecos	Fruit food for birds, nectar	Also called balsam apple, balsam gourd
All	Food for birds, nectar for butterflies	Fussy to grow, but worth the effort
All depending on species	Host and nectar for Gulf fritillary & zebra long-wing, fruit for birds, cover	Avoid tropical red passiflora Also called maypop

Table 4 Continued

GROUND COVER	CHARACTERISTICS Height/growth/spacing	REQUIREMENTS Soil/exposure
Pigeonberry *Rivina humilis*	Evergreen except during hard freeze, 1½ feet, spreads by seeds. Space - 1 foot	Sand loam, clay, alkaline preferred, moist but well drained. Shade
Pink evening primrose *Oenothera speciosa*	Evergreen, except some areas in summer, rhizomes and seeds. Space - 1 foot	Sand, loam, clay, well-drained. Part shade to sun
Pipevine *Aristolochia tomentosa, A. reticulata*	Deciduous short vines to ground hugging vines. Space - 1 to 3 feet	Moist, but well drained. Sun to part shade
Plum *Prunus gracilis, P. angutifolia, P. rivularis*	Deciduous, 1½ to 6 feet, suckers form thickets. Space - 1½ to 3 feet	Sand, limestone well drained. Shade to full sun
Ponyfoot *Dichondra argentea, D. brachypoda*	Evergreen (*D. argentea* only in southern half of state), 2-4 inches, stolons. Space - 1 foot	*D. argentea*: sand, loam, limestone, well drained. Part shade to full sun *D. brachypoda*: cool, moist. Shade
Ruellia "Katie's Compact" *Ruellia brittoniana*	Dormant in winter, 6 inches, seeds. Space - 1 foot	Clay, loam, sand, well drained, seasonal poor drainage okay. Sun to part shade
Spiderwort *Tradescantia* spp.	Evergreen, 2-6 inches, stolons. Space - 1 foot	Sand, loam, clay, well drained. Shade
Verbena *Glandularia canadensis*	Evergreen annual in High and Rolling Plains 5-10 inches, stolons. Space - 1 foot	Sand, loam, acid, moist, well drained. Shade
Violets *Viola walteri, V. pedta, V. missouriensis*	Evergreen, dormant in some areas during summer, rhizomes and seeds. Space - 9 to 12 inches	Sand, loam, clay, limestone, well drained. Full to partial shade

REGION	WILDLIFE *Host/nectar*	NOTES
All, but rare in Piney Woods	Fruit for birds, nectar for butterflies	Blooms and produces fruit all season, deer don't like it
All regions, rare in High and Rolling Plains	Hummingbird and butterfly nectar	Wildflower reseeds readily
All, depending on variety	Host and nectar for Pipevine swallowtail	Avoid tropical varieties
All regions depending on variety	Fruits provide bird food Nectar for butterflies	Striking spring flowers
All *D. brachypoda* Southern half of state for *D. argentea*	Cover	Competes well with short grasses except Bermuda, forms mats *D. argentea*-gray foliage *D. brachypoda*-green foliage
All but High and Rolling Plains	Cover, nectar	Good performer in heat and humidity. May be aggressive
All depending on species	Cover, nectar	Grasslike foliage good in informal woodland setting, not aggressive
All	Nectar for butterflies and hummingbirds	Not aggressive
All depending on variety	Nectar for butterflies	*V. lanceloata* and *V. primulifolia* tolerate poor drainage

bacteria, or pests of any kind. The only thing all the plants had in common was the straw mulch around the base of each plant. Contact with the supplier revealed he had used an herbicide during growth of the crop, and with light rains before harvest the product had not been completely removed from the system of the plants. The herbicide was washing from the straw into the soil around the tomatoes and being absorbed by the plants. The straw was removed and most of the tomato plants recovered, although the crop was diminished.

If you do choose to use an herbicide, follow labeled directions very carefully and avoid root systems of desirable vegetation. In the long term a little elbow grease and other more nature friendly methods are much more effective and less costly to all. Think before you pick up that bottle!

Plant Spacing

What goes where? The ground is prepared, now how do you cover it? Most plants are offered in nurseries in small containers, two- to four-inch pots. These are the most economical but do require a larger number

depending on how fast they grow and how soon coverage is desired. Larger containers cost more (although generally fewer are required), need larger holes, but faster coverage is attained. Occasionally bare root stock is available. Determine size and rate and type of growth from literature with the material or a reliable reference. This information is important along with the usual soil, water, and sun requirements. A complete understanding of the plant material before planting makes the difference between success and failure.

Measure the area and determine square feet. For a rectangular or square plot multiply length by width. For a circular area multiple the radius (half of the distance across the circle) by itself then multiply by *pi* (3.1416). In the case of an oval, use an average radius in the above formula. Triangular areas, multiply one-half the height by the base. (Now you know why you should have paid more attention in math class.) Divide the number of square feet by the spacing in feet listed for desired plant. This is the number of plants recommended. Buying a few additional is a good idea; they can always be worked in. For example, a strip along a driveway or walkway 10 feet long by 3 feet wide has 30 square feet of space. Using frogfruit *Phyla incisa* for this strip with recommended spacing of 12 inches would require 30 plants. This sounds like a lot of plants, but for faster coverage it is the recommended number. Frogfruit will spread, although for me it did take a year to become established before it took off and then it covered rapidly.

A circle 3 feet across has a radius of 1.5 feet. 1.5 multiplied by 1.5 equals 2.25. Multiply 2.25 times 3.1416 equals 7.07 square feet. Using the frogfruit from the example above with one foot spacing, seven plants are recommended. Don't worry if you can't figure out an exact number. These are only recommendations and guidelines.

Groundwork

The number of plants are determined, now how to place them? In small areas setting the pot in the desired location before planting gives an indication of placement. For larger areas you may want to run a string with knots marking location of each plant, or set stakes. No set pattern is best for planting; straight rows, checkerboard, staggered, etc., all will work. As the plants grow, the various individual specimens will not be distinguishable; all the stems, branches, and leaves will intermingle. Use the pattern easiest for you.

Ready to plant, remove the plant from the pot and check the roots. If the plants are root bound (roots form a tight ball around the soil), gently loosen the ends of the roots with fingers or clippers to encourage new root development. Place the plants in the ground at the same depth as in the pot, firm the soil around each, and water in when finished. Replace any mulch material moved while planting and add additional mulch to the area if needed. Water the root systems as needed to prevent wilting. Once established—usually only a few weeks for the faster growing ground covers—water less frequently, only when needed.

Maintenance of ground cover is minimal when native plants are planted properly. Weeds or unwanted plants should be nominal if the area was properly prepared and mulched. Weeds that do occur should be removed by hand. Any herbicide use at this time will damage or may even kill plantings. Once active growth begins, the ground cover will outcompete most weeds. For deciduous ground covers, weeding in the early spring may be required for maximum health of the ground cover.

Most ground covers are low growing and spreading so they do not require pruning or trimming. Branching can be encouraged in new plantings by trimming ends of long runners. Deciduous covers will benefit by removal of dead material once all danger of frost has passed in the spring. Leaving dead material in place during the winter provides protection from harsh conditions, and for many, removal of dead branches and stems can stimulate new growth. Evergreen covers can be pruned in early spring if desired, although for most it is best to trim only when overgrowing an area, to maintain edges, or to remove damaged areas.

Ground Cover Choices

For some areas a combination of plant and non-plant covers works best. A berm (elevated area or slope) often requires mixing stones or other hard surfaces with the plant material to stabilize the soil. Placing rocks and broken halves of clay pots into the slope with ground covers at the top are attractive ways to highlight trailing, flowering covers. Broken garden tools, old rakes, handles, shovels, etc., also help to prevent erosion while plants grow and provide interesting peeks among the vegetation. Much more interesting than turf and easier to maintain.

Cacti are perfect stabilizers for slopes and mix well with rocks and broken pots. Many drought tolerant plants work in companion plantings. Trans Pecos natives such as Texas mountain laurel *Sophora secundiflora* and Texas sage *Leucophyllum frutescens* thrive under similar conditions. Other succulents also add variety and dimension to slopes, berms, and hard to water areas.

Texas has many native cacti adapted to all regions of the state. Some varieties are more cold hardy than others; all can handle the heat but do require good drainage. Try in the Piney Woods only in full sun and high ground. These are true "waterwise" plants. Do not collect in the wild unless given specific permission. Many of the desert species are endangered due to loss of habitat and illegal harvesting. Several nurseries across the state specialize in cacti. Contact your local native plant society for sources.

Instead of trying to hide unsightly areas—utility boxes,

poles, maintenance areas—with tall vegetation, cover them. Vines hide the "unsightly" and trail over the ground to tie into other areas of the landscape. Deciduous vines such as *Passiflora* or annual vines such as cypress vine *Ipomoea quamoclit* are less woody and if access is needed can easily be pruned or replanted.

Irregular shaped areas can add color with flowers, berries, and butterflies using the proper cover. Frogfruit produces a small white flower all summer long that attracts checkered and skipper butterflies. Pigeonberry and partridgeberry both produce flowers and berries attractive to birds and butterflies.

Traffic areas can be easily managed with a ground cover. Frogfruit and horseherb both survive traffic. In areas with higher traffic, stepping stones or walkways can be added over and through many ground covers.

Native Turf Grasses

Proper placement of ground covers affords maximum benefit and minimum maintenance. If you still feel you have to have turf, buffalograss *Buchloe dactyloides* is a native with less maintenance than the non-native turf grasses.

Buffalograss, a rugged, short prairie grass that once provided rich grazing for the buffalo herds across the American prairies, is ideal for residential and commercial turf, golf greens, and erosion control. A uniform, attractive turf varying in height from four to six inches and color from spring green to blue-green has narrow leaves that curl downward to produce a shorter-looking turf even without mowing. For a prairie look it can be left unmowed or cut to two to three inches for a tighter, neater turf.

When supplemental water is limited, buffalograss outcompetes weeds including Johnson grass, dallisgrass, and Bermuda grass. This native turf requires only moderate sun; four to six hours per day is sufficient for dense growth. It is very hardy and will survive drought conditions, periods of flooding, compacted soil, and temperatures ranging from above 120 to minus 30 degrees Fahrenheit. Commercial varieties are vegetatively propagated female strains, so no pollen or seed heads are produced.

For healthy growth of buffalo turf, fertilizers and pesticides are not needed, and with the lower, slower growth rate, less watering is necessary. Data from the Texas Water Commission indicates that buffalograss flourishes over most of Texas with only natural rainfall and thrives in central, south, west, and north Texas. The sandy, acidic soils of East Texas and the very wet conditions of the coastal region do not promote thick, lush growth. Texas Water Commission suggests the following watering schedule (when no rainfall): Buffalograss—every 21-45 days; Zoysia—every 7-10 days; Bermuda—every 5-10 days; and St. Augustine—every 5 days.

Buffalograss is the obvious choice for turf areas. Four varieties are available. Texoka, an early cultivation that produces a thinner turf with a spring green color, is ideal for planting in wildflower areas where the thin turf provides background to wildflowers. Prairie, developed at Texas A&M, performs best in soils with high clay content and neutral to alkaline soils. The turf is apple green in color, of medium density, and low growing with a slow rate of growth. 609, developed at the University of Nebraska, produces a rich blue-green, medium density turf with a quick rate of spread. Stampede, a semi-dwarf, Kelley green turf with a mature height of about four inches, is the densest and exhibits the fastest rate of spread.

How much of your current turf areas are really necessary? Work with nature and reduce the green, hungry, thirsty monster.

TREES AND WHAT GROWS BENEATH

Summers in Texas are brutal! Heat in all regions is compounded with drying wind in the west and north and stifling humidity in the east and south. Trees are often the only relief with cooling shade under spreading branches. Planted on the west, south, and east sides of structures, trees can reduce cooling costs up to 50 percent. Deciduous trees block the sunlight in summer and allow sun to warm the house in the winter. Evergreens on the north side slow winter winds and can reduce heating costs up to 30 percent.

Trees beautify property and the surrounding community, making areas more livable, helping to restore mental health and well-being, and can increase property values as much as 20 percent. Trees act as filters by trapping dust and absorbing air pollutants including excess carbon dioxide while releasing essential oxygen. In all areas, even those with low rainfall, trees help reduce storm runoff and soil erosion by trapping the vital moisture in leaves and root systems. As the top layer of wildlife habitat, trees provide food, shelter, and nesting sites for birds, butterflies, and small animals.

Choosing the Right Tree

Trees are permanent additions to the landscape and form the framework for all other features and plantings; however, not all trees are equal. The importance of the proper tree in the proper location cannot be overstated. Before selecting a tree, determine the functions expected such as forming a windbreak or providing shade in summer and desired qualities such as evergreen, deciduous, flowering, fruiting, fall color, and most important mature size. Trees are categorized as tall (60 feet and above), medium (30 to 60 feet), or small (up to 30 feet) based on mature size. Region and growth conditions may result in differing growth habits and should be taken into consideration when selecting a specific tree.

The wrong tree in the wrong place can cause serious damage to lives and property and incur great expense to remove. Avoid all non-native fast-growing shade trees. The early amount of shade is offset by the cost of removal, damage to property, and loss of wildlife habitat. Two trees to avoid across the state are Chinese tallow *Sapiumse biferum* and the salt cedar *Tamarisk* spp. Both of these trees are invasive exotics that destroy native habitats. More on these and other thieves and robbers in Chapter 10.

Silver maple in the Gulf Coast region is also to be avoided. This tree is soft wooded and prone to disease. No amount of spraying will save the tree. All that is accomplished by trying to save a diseased tree (any tree) is prolonging its life a short time, wasting money, and most important contaminating the environment. These may be considered harsh words, but they are facts. If you have silver maples or similar trees as I do on property I recently purchased, trim as needed to avoid damage from falling limbs and select a native replacement. Plant the replacement and allow it to begin growing as you determine when and how to remove the unwanted tree.

Every region across the state has trees ill suited to the area. Even natives planted in the wrong location can become diseased. Contact tree experts with questions about large trees. Remember the limbs always look smaller on the tree than on the ground. Safety is the first consideration. Contact local Better Business Bureaus, check references, and make sure the company you deal with has liability insurance. Before contracting with a service to spray a diseased tree, get a second opinion. Call your local Cooperative Extension Office for information about the tree and disease. It is a sad fact that a large number of tree

diseases are fatal and the best treatment is the chain saw. No one wants to hear this, and many services take advantage of this fact. By removing a tree early you not only save money and the environment, but you may be able to prevent spread of the disease to healthy trees.

Pine bark beetle damage of pine trees is a prime example. Once the pine tree shows signs of damage, oozing sap, brown needles, it is a goner. No amount of spray will save it. If the tree is allowed to stand, the beetle completes its life cycle and, using the dead tree as a springboard, launches itself to the next victim. If the tree is removed, the cycle of infestation can be stopped.

A few pines were found to be infested with pine bark beetle in a large forested area, a popular park for hiking, camping, and recreation, in Harris County a few years ago. When the public heard several of the trees were to be cut down, they brought lawsuits to stop the cutting. By the time the court proceedings followed their course, what were a few dead trees turned into a few thousand acres of dead trees. Be sure to obtain all facts and make informed decisions. Trees are wonderful products of nature, but the best course to follow may be the chain saw.

Native trees provide optimum value with minimal output. Many genera of trees are native across the state with specific species in each region. Trees grown in the region are the best specimens. Always ask the source of the tree. Trees are available at nurseries as bare root, balled and burlapped, or container grown. Bare root often found with fruit trees should only be planted during their dormant season. Balled and burlapped and container grown can be planted at any time, however during the summer heat is the least favorable time. Transplanting trees from the wild is not recommended. Too often the trees sustain excessive damage to root systems. Starting with seeds, seedlings, or nursery grown stock is best.

Larger is not always better in selecting a tree. Container grown trees have a tendency to overgrow containers, producing roots that grow in circles around the inside of the container. These roots will eventually strangle the tree, causing weakening of the tree, increased susceptibility to disease, and eventually death. Suppress your eagerness for growth, and select small healthy trees—a better investment in the long term—and several studies have shown that taking into consideration transplant shock, after a few years the smaller trees are as large or larger than the original larger ones. Bigger is not necessarily better.

Many nurseries guarantee the trees they plant. This is a good practice; however, if the tree does need to be replaced, and depending on the size of the tree may be up to five years after planting, you have wasted the time in tree growth. A smaller tree would have had the five years to grow, developing a healthy root system and good growth.

The above points should all be considered before purchasing a tree, but what type of tree? Start with the purpose the tree will serve: shade, color, focal point, wildlife habitat, deciduous, evergreen? Once this is determined, where to plant? Determine location of power lines and underground utilities and avoid these areas. Small trees may do under an overhead power line, if necessary, but these spaces are best left bare or used as locations for a wildflower or perennial garden.

Site Selection

Consider location of structures, houses, sheds, workshops, and outbuildings. Recommended minimum distances between the trunk of the mature tree and a structure are small tree—ten feet, medium tree—fifteen feet, and large tree—twenty feet. Trees given adequate space for growth are healthier, require less maintenance, and cause fewer problems, such as broken power lines, buckled driveways, and obstructed traffic views.

Lastly determine soil conditions in the selected site. Soil analysis may be necessary to determine exact composition, pH, structure, and fertility. Since trees should not be fertilized at the time of planting or during the first year, amendments to deficient soil must be made before planting. To ensure a healthy tree growing at its optimum, soil requirements must be met. Trees are long-term investments, and as with all investments it pays to research before investing or in this case planting.

The largest trees in the state, the oaks *Quercus* spp. require the most space. The estimated forty-four species and two varieties found in Texas is the largest number of oaks per state in the United States. These magnificent trees need space to spread, and most species do not belong in urban landscapes. The oaks in the right places are wonderful wildlife habitat. Many animals and birds eat the acorns. The branches and trunks provide homes for birds and small animals. These are wonderful additions to larger landscapes and should be planted, but consider another tree for small urban landscapes.

The maples *Acer* are another large group of native trees with species well suited for specific regions of the state. The fall color of many maples makes them colorful additions to the fall landscape. The scale of the maples, not as tall or as spreading as the oaks, makes them better suited for the urban or smaller landscapes. Be sure to select the species native or adapted to your specific region.

Native conifers are a large group of underutilized trees. Several *Juniperus* spp. and *Pinus* spp. are well adapted to specific regions of the state. Bald cypress *Taxodium distichum* unlike other conifers loses its leaves in the winter and is ideal for poor drainage areas. Sweetgum, pecan, beech, Texas ash, southern magnolia, all have specific uses in the landscape. Even the much maligned hackberry is wonderful for wildlife habitat. Birds and small mammals eat the berries, and at least three species of butterflies use the leaves as a host. Check with the Texas Forest Service, your local Native Plant Society chapter, County Cooperative Extension offices, or local Texas Master Naturalist Chapter for recommended tree varieties and mature sizes.

Planting the Tree

Once a tree and site are selected, proper planting procedures are necessary to ensure a good start for the tree. In the southern half of the state the best time to plant is winter to early spring, in the northern half, as soon as all danger of frost is gone in the spring or in the early fall. The goal is to allow root growth before adverse weather conditions. Prepare the hole before removing the tree from the container. The hole should be two to three times wider than the root ball and slightly shallower. The tree should be planted slightly above the original soil level in the container. Gently remove the tree from the container. Disturb the roots as little as possible. It may be necessary to cut the container down each side to dislodge the root ball.

Set the tree in the hole handling it by the root ball not the trunk. Center the tree in the hole with the trunk straight up. Cut any visible roots that are circling the root ball with pruning shears to encourage roots to grow out into the surrounding soil rather than continue in a circle. Hold the tree and gently backfill around the root ball and tamp soil lightly to eliminate air pockets. Large clods of soil should be broken apart before adding to the hole. Use only soil removed from the hole to backfill. Adding amended soil at this time, especially in clay soil, encourages the roots to continue growing as if they were still in the pot. All you've done is make a larger "clay" pot.

Remove any grass, weeds, or other vegetation within a three-foot minimum diameter around the tree and create a watering saucer by forming a small (about four inches high) dike of soil around the edge. Cover area with three to four inches of mulch composed of bark, woodchips, compost, leaves, or pine needles. Do not use fresh grass clippings.

Adequate water is essential at planting time. Place water hose at base of tree and allow water to slowly trickle until soil is saturated. Root zones should be slow-soaked every seven days for four weeks. Then, reduce watering and adjust for rain as needed for requirements of the tree. Keep soil moist for the first growing season unless the tree requires well-drained soil. Make adjustments accordingly in water schedule. After watering it may be necessary to add more mulch, but keep mulch from direct contact with the trunk.

Stake the tree only if necessary for support in a moderate wind. Do not stake so tightly that the tree cannot sway. Use broad, belt-like materials that won't injure the bark and remove after the first year. Do not wrap the trunk.

Prune only dead, diseased, or damaged branches at time of planting. Wait one year to begin any structural pruning. Chapter 15 covers pruning. Do not remove branches to "balance the root ball."

While the tree is small, the best ground cover is mulch to moderate soil temperatures and moisture. Once the tree is well established, up to five years, and starts to cast shade, other plantings can be added to the landscape. Wildlife habitats consist of three layers. Trees function at their optimum when used as the top layer. A lone tree in the middle of a green turf area may be attractive to humans and a small number of wildlife, but it is really only an island in an inhospitable green sea. Turning the island into a woodland complete with middle or understory and ground cover enhances wildlife habitat, beauty and health of the tree, and reduces maintenance and watering requirements of the landscape.

Creating a Woodland

Woodland areas when planned properly become ecosystems. The area can be any size and take many forms from replicated wilderness to controlled formal. The replicated wilderness requires the largest area and the most natives to work. Very little gardening is required once established. The area consists of native trees of all sizes, vines, leaf litter for ground cover, and what grows, grows. Interesting, but not always practical in urban settings.

The naturalistic woodland is more appropriate to smaller spaces and gardeners' urges to plant and rearrange. The three layers still exist but are planned to provide settings and highlight a

specific plant or focal point. The trees may surround open areas of shorter vegetation duplicating forest glades. Maintenance is minimal in this setting. Trees, understory, vines, and ground covers are allowed to grow and intermingle. Seasonal plantings work in this woodland.

A woodland requiring more maintenance is referred to as nature simplified. Trees are trimmed and managed with accent on the tree structure through interplay with light and motion of the vegetation. This setting usually has less midstory vegetation and is less diverse than the preceding woodlands. Habitat may be reduced and maintenance increased, but the trees are still available as habitat.

The formal approach provides formal lined walkways and paths through managed woodlands. Sculpture and other art forms are often included in the formal woodland. Plants are more manicured and trimmed. Many estate gardens open to the public have formal woodland settings. Small settings with single sculptures between trees can be used in urban settings.

Turf grasses are not part of a woodland setting no matter how wilderness or formal. The best type of woodland is determined by personal preference, but remember maximum wildlife habitat is encouraged with greatest diversity and layers.

Woodlands bring to mind shade, rustling of leaves, shifting shadows with occasional glimpses of color and cooling breezes. With proper plantings, the imaginings can be reality, no matter which type of woodland. The top or canopy layer of a mature woodland is filled with sun-preferring trees. The canopy permits limited light to filter through, allowing only shade tolerant understory and ground cover to survive. Edges of woodlands allow growth of plants preferring partial shade; in-between the two areas are different kinds of shade and different plant genera and species.

Degrees of Shade

Shade is not just an absence of sunlight, but different degrees of sunlight. Bright shade is shade with reflected bright light, no direct sunlight. Filtered or dappled shade is sunlight through thin branches, leaves, or lattice. Partial shade is sunlight for usually four to six hours during the day and is found in areas at the edge of trees or near a structure as sun moves during the day.

Afternoon and morning partial shade are very different in Texas, a fact to remember. Full shade never receives direct or reflected sunlight.

Shade is not only under trees, but near structures. The degree of shade varies with the season. The amount of shade in an area should be determined during each season of the year before planting. Deep or full shade under a deciduous tree in the summer may be filtered shade to full sun during the winter months. Keep a log of sun and shade movement through your landscape. You will be surprised at the different degrees of sun and shade as the seasons pass. The more you understand the interplay between sun and shade the better you are able to work with nature, increase your enjoyment, and reduce the work.

Trees are planted and have grown to produce shade. Time for midstory or understory trees. In small landscapes this layer may be the top layer. Many books and catalogs identify this group of medium and small trees as ornamental trees or shrubs. Many do produce prolific spring blooms and provide fall color. Use the same criteria to select a tree in this category as used for a large tree with one additional criteria, light requirements. By definition an understory tree prefers growing under large trees or in the shade created by tall buildings. Dogwoods require the cooling shade, part to dappled, of a larger tree to flourish. The flowering dogwood *Cornus florida* prefers acid soil found in its native Piney Woods; however, the rough-leaf dogwood *Cornus drummondii* grows in alkaline soil except in the drier areas of the Trans Pecos. Both provide wonderful spring color and fall berries and colorful foliage.

Many Texas natives fill the niche of understory tree. Drive through your region in the spring and note the variety of colors glimpsed through the leaves and branches. Redbuds *Cercis canadensis vars. texensis, canadensis,* and *mexicana*, hawthornes *Crataegus* spp., possomhaw *Ilex decidua*, plums *Prunus* spp., red buckeye *Aesculus pavia*, fringetree *Chionanthus virginicus*, rusty blackhaw viburnum *Viburnum rufidulum*, and farkleberry *Vaccinium arboreum* are a few of the more common ones. These trees all provide nectar for butterflies and/or hummingbirds and fruit for birds and other wildlife and grow in varying degrees of shade. A few will do well in more sun. They are also deciduous.

For evergreen understory yaupon holly *Ilex vomitoria*, wax myrtle *Myrica cerifera* (a dwarf variety with smaller leaves and growth habits is available), brasil or bluewood *Condalia hookeri* are good choices depending on region and soil conditions. All produce berries eaten by birds. The wax myrtle alone attracts over forty different species of birds.

An interesting tree for use away from traffic areas is the devil's walking-stick *Aralia spinosa*. This tree starts life as a tall stick covered with orange spines and a few divided three- to four-inch leaves at the top. The white flowers in the summer are replaced with black fruit in the fall. As the tree matures, suckers are produced, forming a thicket. It prefers rich loam, moist but well drained, and is found growing under sassafras and with eastern red cedar and hawthorns. Worth considering in the right woodland.

The bottom or ground cover layer of the woodland is important and varies depending on the type of woodland. Leaf litter, mulch, and limited plants are found in the wilderness woodland. The more open formal woodland has more area for ground covers. Review the plants requiring shade listed in Chapter 6 for suggestions. In deep shade often the best ground cover is mulch; one created from yard waste trimmings is the ideal, but commercially available mulches will work. Pine bark mulch or pine straw is more acidic than hardwood mulch and is recommended for use in acid preferring woodlands.

Creating interest in a shade garden can be challenging. Shade tends to be dark and mysterious or even forbidding. Woodlands should be inviting with tempting visual effects to entice inspection and wonder about what is around the bend. Use of shades of green and white and differing textures can create dimension. The interplay of light filtering through the upper canopy and striking ferns gently swaying in the breeze creates a dance among the trunks of the trees. Combinations of ground covers with different blooming seasons lend texture and interest to the edges of the path such as pipevines intermingled with violets.

Arching branches can lend continuity to an area. American beautyberry *Callicarpa americana*, larger than the coralberry listed in the ground cover table, is deciduous and produces berries eaten by many bird species. The purple or white berries form large bunches on the stems that can extend as much as nine feet through and over other foliage. Tolerant of most soil conditions, this shrub will grow throughout the state, although in drier areas more watering may be required.

As you plan your woodland or shade area, consider color and texture, size and shape of foliage, as well as flower and seed color. Make your woodland an inviting, exciting place for human visitors as well as wildlife.

HOMEGROWN VEGETABLES AND COMPANIONS

A book on gardening is not complete without vegetables. Homegrown vegetables are often more costly in time and money than commercially available produce, but gardeners still grow or at least try to grow basic crops every year. The widespread commercial use of pesticides, altered seeds, and environmentally detrimental practices spur many to grow their own vegetables. And nothing compares with the taste of a freshly picked ripe tomato, cucumber, squash, other vegetable or fruit or the satisfaction of knowing you grew it!

Vegetable gardening with nature is more difficult but can be done successfully. Diligence is an essential requirement, because many problems can be averted if observed in time. Pest management is a prime example and since the principles are the same as for other parts of the landscape is covered in Chapter 11.

Of the more than 500,000 plant species in the world, only about 1,000 are commonly used for human food, though many more are edible. In the United States only thirty different plant species account for 95 percent of our fruits, vegetables, and grains, and the majority of these are not native to North America. Only nine of the nearly fifty vegetables are even native to the Americas. Corn, white potato, sweet potato, lima bean, common bean, tomato, squash, summer squash, and pepper originated in Central and northern parts of South America.

A few "exotics" and their origins are: eggplant and cucumber from India; spinach and muskmelon from Persia; watermelon and okra from Africa; radishes and Chinese cabbage from China; asparagus, cabbage, kale, and collards from the Mediterranean area; garden peas from Asia; and kohlrabi and Brussels sprouts from Northern Europe.

The early Texas settlers did include native fruits and vegetables in their diets along with plants brought from their homelands. The majority of these natives, which were collected in the wild, have been replaced by commercial varieties gathered in the local supermarket. Many of these early food plants are still found in undisturbed areas, but sadly many have been lost along with their habitats.

Early settlers unable to obtain wheat flour used what the Native Americans used. Flour made from acorns is reputed to be superior to any except some from the seeds of the native grasses. Cattails *Typha* spp. also provided flour along with many other ingredients. Every part of the cattail is edible including the crispy nut-flavored new shoots. A word of caution with collecting any plants from the wild. As with the wildflowers, collect only with permission and do not disturb small isolated colonies of plants. Also if collecting to eat, make sure no pesticides or other contaminants have been used in the area, and use a reliable source for plant identification and preparation. Better yet grow your own "wild vegetables." More later.

The term "truck crops" is commonly used to describe vegetables. This description has nothing to do with transportation but is derived from the French word *troquer* meaning to barter or exchange. The word became

---

The term "truck crops" is derived from the French word troquer *meaning to barter or exchange.*

"truck" and synonymous with vegetables because of the practice of bartering small amounts of vegetables in the marketplace. Vegetable growing and marketing over the years has become big business. A result of this growing form of commerce has led to confusion because of the need to classify whether a product is a fruit or a vegetable.

Botanically speaking the tomato is a fruit, but legally it is a vegetable. The Supreme Court of the United States classified it as such in 1893. An importer argued that tomatoes were fruit and therefore not subject to a duty in effect at that time. The court held that the tomato is a vegetable because it was usually served at dinner in, with, or after the soup or with fish or meats that constitute the main part of the meal. The use of the tomato has changed since 1893 with a much larger part of the crop made into juice, but the tomato remains, legally, a vegetable.

From the botanical standpoint green beans, peppers, okra pods, and many others are fruits, but all are considered vegetables. Cucumbers and muskmelons are closely related fruits, members of the genus Cucurbitaceae with similar growth habits, structure, and nutritional requirements, yet cucumbers are called vegetables and muskmelons are called fruit. Tradition dictates which plants are determined to be vegetables and which fruits. The accepted classification for vegetables is annual plants of which the immature succulent roots, bulbs, stems, blossoms, leaves, seeds, or fruits are eaten and perennial non-woody plants of which the roots, stems, leaf stalks, or leaves are eaten.

Basic Requirements

Food plants, whether technically, botanically, or legally called vegetables, share similar requirements for growth: a minimum of six hours sunlight and nutritive soil with good drainage and even moisture. Meeting these basic requirements is very important for success. Fruiting varieties require more than the minimum six hours of sunlight for optimum production. Many of the root and leaf crops will produce with partial shade conditions, although quality is enhanced with more sunlight.

Raised beds provide the required drainage and are recommended even in low rainfall areas of the state. Soil should be amended before planting to meet the needs of the hungry plants. Soil analysis is recommended to determine deficiencies, although addition of a good compost often meets the needs without knowing the exact deficiencies.

Vegetables do not like to have "wet feet" but require even moisture, best obtained through soil manipulation and irrigation. In heavy rainfall areas the beds should be raised enough to allow drainage of several inches of rain. Plants will wilt after a heavy rain if their roots remain in soggy soil. This is especially true of tomatoes and peppers. Wilting indicates the leaves are not transpiring properly, because the roots have no oxygen. Proper soil drainage is the only solution.

In dry areas a slightly raised bed is also recommended because it is easier to maintain proper soil conditions and even irrigation. Drip irrigation is recommended where the water can be delivered to each plant with a minimum of waste. Check with your local county cooperative extension office and Texas Natural Resource Conservation Commission (TNRCC) for recommended methods in your region.

The size of the bed is determined by the amount of space available, and since the traditional vegetable garden often is not the most attractive spot in the landscape, the space is located behind the garage or a shed or at the back of the landscape. All these sites are acceptable, but before making the final decision, determine how frequently you will check the site in a remote area. Remember "casting your shadow" is the best way to prevent serious problems and work with nature.

Consider the size of the available space before determining which vegetables to plant. The taste of fresh picked corn is unsurpassed, but for corn to produce those wonderful ears, there must be enough plants to allow for proper cross-pollination of the ears. Most home gardens do not have enough space to allow planting of three to four rows in blocks or rectangles. A single row at the back of the garden plot may sound like a good idea but will probably only succeed in producing a screen and empty ears.

Once the site is selected and prepared and types of plants determined, the time to plant is critical and varies across the state. The early Texans used the farmer's almanac and signs of the moon for planting with at times as much or more success than so-called modern methods. Planting charts and seed packages base times to plant on average date of the last freeze in the spring and for fall gardens the average date of the first freeze in the fall. The number of days for a crop to reach maturity is factored in and a date to plant is determined. Table 5 lists forty of the more common vegetables with the number of weeks determined from the average frost dates.

Check the accompanying maps (Figures 4 and 5) for the average date of the first and last freeze for your area. Remember these are

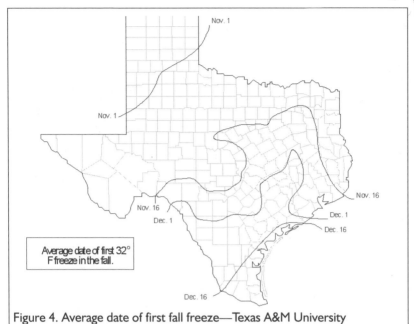

Figure 4. Average date of first fall freeze—Texas A&M University

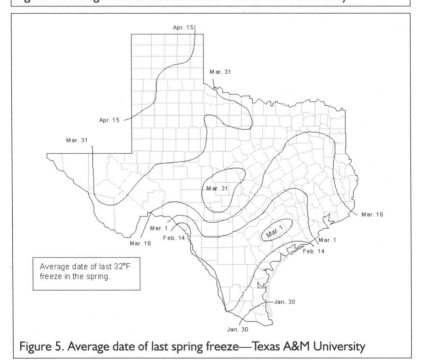

Figure 5. Average date of last spring freeze—Texas A&M University

Table 5: Texas Vegetable Planting Guide

Vegetables	Seed or Plants per 100 feet	Depth of Seed Planting in Inches	Inches Between Rows	Plants	Average Height of Crop in Feet
Asparagus	66 pl., 1 oz.	6-8, 1-1.5	36-48	18	5
Beans, snap bush	1 lb.	1-1.5	30-36	3-4	1.5
Beans, snap pole	1 lb.	1-1.5	36-48	4-6	6
Beans, Lima bush	1 lb.	1-1.5	30-36	3-4	1.5
Beans, Lima pole	1 lb.	1-1.5	36-48	12-18	6
Beets	1 oz.	1	14-24	2	1.5
Broccoli	1 oz.	0.5	24-36	14-24	3
Brussels sprouts	1 oz.	0.5	24-36	14-24	2
Cabbage	1 oz.	0.5	24-36	14-24	1.5
Cabbage, Chinese	1 oz.	0.5	18-30	8-12	1.5
Carrot	1 oz.	0.5	14-24	2	1
Cauliflower	1 oz.	0.5	24-36	14-24	3
Chard, Swiss	2 oz.	1	18-30	6	1.5
Collard (Kale)	1 oz.	0.5	18-36	6-12	2
Corn, sweet	3-4 oz.	1-2	24-36	9-12	6
Cucumber	1 oz.	0.5	48-72	8-12	1
Eggplant	1 oz.	0.5	30-26	18-24	3
Garlic	1 lb.	1-2	14-24	2-4	1
Kohlrabi	1 oz.	0.5	14-24	4-6	1.5
Lettuce	1 oz.	0.5	18-24	2-3	1

Spring Planting in Regard to Average Frost-Free Date*	Fall Planting in Regard to Average Fall-Freeze Date	Number of Days Ready for Use	Average Length of Harvest Season Days
*4 to 6 wks. before	not recommended	730	60
1 to 4 wks. after	8 to 10 wks. before	45-60	14
1 to 4 wks. after	14 to 16 wks. before	60-70	30
1 to 4 wks. after	8 to 10 wks. before	65-80	14
1 to 4 wks. after	14 to 16 wks. before	75-85	40
4 to 6 wks. before	8 to 10 wks. before	50-60	30
4 to 6 wks. before	10 to 16 wks. before	60-80	40
4 to 6 wks. before	10 to 14 wks. before	90-100	21
4 to 6 wks. before	10 to 16 wks. before	60-90	40
4 to 6 wks. before	12 to 14 wks. before	65-70	21
4 to 6 wks. before	12 to 14 wks. before	70-80	21
not recommended	10 to 16 wks. before	70-90	14
2 to 6 wks. before	12 to 16 wks. before	45-55	40
2 to 6 wks. before	8 to 12 wks. before	50-80	60
1 to 6 wks. after	12 to 14 wks. before	70-90	10
1 to 6 wks. after	10 to 12 wks. before	50-70	30
2 to 6 wks. after	12 to 16 wks. before	80-90	90
not recommended	4 to 6 wks. before	140-150	----
2 to 6 wks. before	12 to 16 wks. before	55-75	14
6 wks. before	10 to 14 wks. before	40-80	21

Table 5 Continued

Vegetables	Seed or Plants per 100 feet	Depth of Seed Planting in Inches	Inches Between Rows	Plants	Average Height of Crop in Feet
Muskmelon (Cantaloupe)	1 oz.	1	60-96	24-36	1
Mustard	1 oz.	0.5	14-24	6-12	1.5
Okra	2 oz.	1	36-42	12-24	6
Onion (plants)	400-600 pl.	1-2	14-24	2-3	1.5
Onion (seed)	1 oz.	0.5	14-24	2-3	1.5
Parsley	1 oz.	0.5	14-24	2-4	0.5
Peas, English	1 lb.	2-3	18-36	1	2
Peas, Southern	1 lb.	2-3	24-36	4-6	2.5
Pepper	1 oz.	0.5	30-36	18-24	3
Potato, Irish	6-10 lb.	4	30-36	10-15	2
Potato, sweet	75-100 pl.	3-5	36-48	12-16	1
Pumpkin	1 oz.	1-2	60-96	36-48	1
Radish	1 oz.	0.5	14-24	1	0.5
Spinach	1 oz.	0.5	14-24	3-4	1
Squash, summer	1 oz.	1-2	36-60	18-36	3
Squash, winter	1 oz.	1-2	60-96	24-48	1
Tomato	50 pl.,	4-6, .5	36-48	36-48	3
Turnip, greens	1 oz.	0.5	14-24	2-3	1.5
Turnip, roots	1 oz.	0.5	14-24	2-3	1.5
Watermelon	1 oz.	1-2	72-96	36-72	1

Spring Planting in Regard to Average Frost-Free Date*	Fall Planting in Regard to Average Fall-Freeze Date	Number of Days Ready for Use	Average Length of Harvest Season Days
1 to 6 wks. after	14 to 16 wks. before	85-100	30
1 to 6 wks. after	10 to 16 wks. before	30-40	30
2 to 6 wks. after	12 to 16 wks. before	55-65	90
4 to 10 wks. before	not recommended	80-120	40
6 to 8 wks. before	8 to 10 wks. before	90-120	40
1 to 6 wks. before	6 to 16 wks. before	70-90	90
2 to 8 wks. before	2 to 12 wks. before	55-90	7
2 to 10 wks. after	10-12 wks. before	60-70	30
1 to 8 wks. after	12 to 16 wks. before	60-90	90
4 to 6 wks. before	14 to 16 wks. before	75-100	----
2 to 8 wks. after	not recommended	100-130	----
1 to 4 wks. after	12 to 14 wks. before	75-100	----
6 wks. before/4 wks. after	1 to 8 wks. before	25-40	7
	2 to 16 wks. before	40-60	40
1 to 8 wks. before	12 to 15 wks. before	50-60	40
1 to 4 wks. after	12 to 14 wks. before	85-100	----
1 to 4 wks. after	12 to 14 wks. before	70-90	40
1 to 8 wks. after	2 to 12 wks. before	30	40
2 to 6 wks. before	2 to 12 wks. before	30-60	30
2 to 6 wks. before	14 to 16 wks. before	80-100	30

only averages. With Texas's changing weather patterns, allowances must be made for dates that will fall outside the averages. The number of non-freezing days between the two dates is the average length of the growing season for the area. For instance in the western portion of the Panhandle the last freeze is April 15 with the first freeze November 1. This gives a growing season of approximately 200 days. Any vegetable requiring more than 200 days between planting and ready for use is not recommended. All seed packets include maturation times. Again these are averages, and actual time may vary depending on weather conditions.

Freezes determine only one detrimental weather condition for vegetables. Heat and humidity are also important factors. What appears to be long growing seasons of over 250 days for the regions along the coast and in the southern part of the state are actually two short seasons with parts of July and August as difficult to garden in as the freezing months of the winter in the north. Many crops do not produce when nighttime temperatures exceed 70 degrees for an extended period. Many tomatoes and green bean varieties stop setting fruit and will die during the middle of the summer. Short maturation varieties are recommended under these conditions. A second planting date determined for mature fruit before the first fall frost is recommended. Very seldom is it possible to maintain a tomato plant over the summer and have it produce quality fruit a second time in the fall. For optimum fruit production a second planting of a short maturation variety is suggested.

Vegetables can be divided into warm season and cool season varieties. The warm season vegetables require warm soil temperatures to germinate and high temperatures to mature. Peppers and okra are good examples of warm season vegetables. The cool season vegetables like warm soil to germinate but will not continue to grow and reach maturity if the temperatures are too hot. Many in this group will survive mild freezes once past the seedling stage. Members of the Brassicaceae family (cabbage, broccoli, cauliflower) will grow in the southern half of Texas only as winter crops.

Many Master Gardener chapters across the state offer lists of vegetable varieties recommended for their region. Check the web sites (Appendix B) or call your local County Cooperative

Extension office for more information. The proper variety is an important key to successful vegetable gardening.

Diversify with Companion Plants

Most of the commonly grown vegetables do not have any true wildlife benefit. Many insects that feed on them are considered pest insects, and a large number are exotics that came in with the crop. The green cabbage looper caterpillar that feeds on members of the Brassicaceae and many other families is an example. The caterpillar turns into a small brown moth with several generations produced per growing season.

The traditional vegetable garden tends to promote problems by limiting diversity. Creating diversity is essential to working in harmony with nature. By discarding the concept of the "vegetable plot" and applying principles learned from nature, healthy vegetables and happier gardeners are possible. The sunniest spot in the landscape is usually set aside for the vegetables. Why not use this spot for wildlife friendly plants and intersperse the plantings with the desired vegetables? This concept

of companion planting was used by our ancestors but with the advent of modern agricultural practices has largely disappeared.

Companion plants are plants that share the same requirements for growth and by growing next to each other provide a "service." Successful companions help neighboring plants in one of five ways: provide needed nutrients, protect against disease, repel pest insects, attract beneficial insects, or entice bug-eating birds. Scientific fact cannot explain all successful plantings, and benefits derived may take time to develop.

The fundamental growth requirements, maturation time, and planting dates do not change with companion planting. This information is as critical as in the conventional plot. What does change is planting in groups or rows and separating vegetables from ornamentals. This will not work for all vegetables, such as corn, but will with the majority of the common and some not so common vegetables.

The following companion planting suggestions will not work for all regions of the state because of the above discussed warm and cool season vegetable requirements but with a little planning and ingenuity can be worked out. Consider ornamental varieties of some of the vegetables in areas where the traditional vegetable may be seasonal.

The genus *Allium* in the family Liliaceae is a good example. This genera includes onions and garlic, which are cool season crops in the South, but their ornamental members are perennials in the same regions. *Alliums* protect roses from black spot, mildew, aphids, and red spider. Garlic and onion chives make wonderful border plants in an ornamental bed. Leeks repel carrot flies. Think genera not individual species when considering companion plantings.

The herb dill *Anethum graveolens* in the family Apiaceae (*Umbelliferae*) is a wildlife-friendly cool season annual companion. Dill will increase the health and growth of cabbage; however if allowed to mature near carrots will diminish the crop. Dill attracts bees to increase pollination and is a favorite host plant for the black swallowtail butterfly. Fennel *Foeniculum vulgare*, a member of the same family, is not a good companion plant and should be planted away from any vegetables.

Tomatoes are probably the most commonly grown vegetable in the home garden, but this has not always been the case. Thomas Jefferson suggested using tomatoes as food in 1781, but ornamental only use continued until 1835. Tomatoes originated in South America, but as with so many other plants, Europe intervened and the plants grown in the United States came from Europe. Good companion plants are chives, onion, parsley, marigold, nasturtium, and carrot. Garlic bulbs have been shown to prevent spider mites. Once again many of the companion plants are cool season while tomatoes are warm season. Try non-vegetable genera, such as society garlic, a perennial in most of the state. Garlic chives, more tolerant of heat and humidity than onion chives although they can become aggressive, do make a good companion substitute and an attractive border with purple blooms all summer.

Basil *Ocimum basilicum*, a warm season herb, improves the growth and flavor of tomatoes and aids in overcoming insects and disease. Basil has also been noted to repel flies and mosquitoes. Many different flavored types of basil are available, and the majority thrives in Texas heat and humidity if even moisture is available.

Horehound *Marrubium vulgare* grows well with tomatoes,

improving the quality and quantity of fruit and prolonging growing season. Grasshoppers and other insects have been observed to avoid this herb, making this a good companion for repelling insects. Some sources suggest this is a Texas native found in the Brownwood area of southern Texas but was probably introduced with early settlers. A soothing tea made from the leaves is good for irritated throats from spending too much time talking to your plants.

Tomatoes should be kept away from all members of the Brassicaceae family. In most areas this is not a problem since tomatoes are warm season and the cabbages are cool season.

The herbs marjoram *Origanum* spp. and thyme *Thymus vulgaris* all have beneficial effects on nearby plants, improving both growth and flavor. Both of these herbs do require good drainage and once established are fairly drought tolerant perennials. Consider them for use in borders or as ground covers close to vegetables.

Some of the benefits of companion plantings are derived from planting different plants in the same place. As one plant matures and is harvested, plant the second. Plants that fix nitrogen, such as the lupines, sweet peas, and clover, add nitrogen to the soil for use by other plants. Remember the Texas bluebonnet is a lupine. When the bluebonnets have set seed, interplant with warm season vegetables such as tomatoes or peppers to utilize the nitrogen, a good use of the area to allow completion of the bluebonnet growth cycle hidden among the growing green of the tomatoes.

Radishes are cool season fast growing vegetables that work well to interplant with slower growing carrots. As the radishes mature and are removed, the soil is loosened for better growth of the carrots.

Many other instances of companion plantings exist and are documented in literature. Also many scientific studies have been done discounting the efficacy of companion planting. Patience is required as with all gardening to determine individual success. Diversifying plantings is known to increase success in the garden. Try to think beyond the traditional garden and stick the peppers or tomatoes among the perennials. It works. A bright red or orange habenaro pepper adds color in an otherwise green area in front of the once blooming rose. Tomatoes were once only ornamentals, why not combine ornamental and edible?

For small garden spaces, patio homes, and apartment balconies, containers can be used to successfully grow vegetables. Many varieties will do well in the controlled environment. Almost anything large enough to hold soil and with drain holes will work. If using black nursery pots, consider covering the black or placing the pot inside another to provide an air space to dissipate the heat generated by the sun on the black surface, or remove the bottom of the pot and bury it. A small narrow area can become a successful vegetable garden. Use a good potting soil and change each season to prevent buildup of salts and possible soil borne disease.

Seedlings or Seeds?

Location, variety, and companions have been determined. Now come the plants. Seedlings or seeds, which is best? Many crops are best seeded in the garden, however, the soil temperature must be warm enough for the seeds to germinate or they will rot. Optimum soil temperatures vary for each group but with few exceptions must be at least 50 degrees. In areas where soils are frozen in the winter, seedlings of the warm season crops mature fruit faster. Tomatoes and peppers are traditionally set out as seedlings. Whether you start them yourself or buy commercially available plants is a personal preference. In colder areas eager gardeners plant seeds approximately six weeks before the last freeze in well-prepared soil in pots and tend them on the windowsill, special mats, or small indoor greenhouses. This allows gardeners a chance to garden before the season.

Whether the seedlings are home grown or commercial, the time to plant them out is determined by the date of the last freeze in the spring and soil temperatures. If the soil has not warmed, the transplants will be set back. Better to wait until soil is warm and chances of frost past. Often the urge to plant is too strong and young tomatoes are put in less than desirable conditions. Several methods are available to protect the plants and warm the soil. Hot caps, pieces of plastic coated paper in the shape of a conical hat, plastic jugs with the bottoms cut out, and "Wall-O-Waters," commercially available plastic tubes lined with pockets to hold water have all been used. Anything that will cover the tender plants and protect them from weather extremes will work. Once again observation is important. As soon as the temperatures warm, the covers must be removed or opened to allow passage of air and dissipation of heat. Often taking the chance and putting out tomato seedlings early will reward the gardener with the first ripe tomato on the block, but it is wise to keep a few plants in pots for that sudden surprise that wipes out the early crop.

In warmer parts of the state, protection is still recommended for early transplants. Tomato cages wrapped with row cover allow air movement but prevent drying from harsh winds. Moving from a still greenhouse atmosphere to the extremes of Texas weather is shocking for most plants. Provide at least temporary protection.

Seeding directly is recommended for lettuce, radishes, carrots, beans, beets, peas, and corn. Cucumbers, melons, cabbages, and other members of the family do well either seeded directly or seedlings.

When growing from seed whether sowing directly or starting in pots, fresh seeds are essential. Check dates on all packages before purchase. Seeds can be stored from one season to the next by storing in cool, dry places. Percentage of germination decreases with time, so minimum storage time is recommended. If saving collected seeds, handle as gently as possible and store in a consistent cool, dry place. Temperature fluctuations result in more rapid deterioration than too high or humid conditions. Refrigeration of dry seeds in tightly sealed containers containing desiccants is recommended to maintain quality from one season to the next. If collecting or saving seeds, select the highest quality seeds possible. Remember seeds are living things and should be handled accordingly.

Many heirloom seeds once only available by saving or trading saved seeds are now available commercially. Many of these varieties are more resistant to disease and weather extremes than their modern relatives. Some desired characteristics may vary such as size or shape, but many are well worth the effort taken to find them and are fun to plant among the ornamentals. One of the heirloom tomatoes is purple!

Fertilizing

Fertilization is often required for maximum quality vegetables. Fertilizer types are identified with three numbers, such as 12-24-10. The numbers represent the percentage of nitrogen, phosphorus, and potassium, always in that order. In the above example a 100-pound bag of fertilizer will have twelve pounds nitrogen, twenty-four pounds phosphorus, and ten pounds potassium. The remaining fifty-four pounds in a chemical fertilizer are substances called carriers that allow the product to be easily dispersed but have no nutritional value. In an organic fertilizer the fifty-four pounds are also carriers but contain many different nutrients and micronutrients that are beneficial to plants.

Many vegetable crops are heavy feeders. Fruiting crops such as tomatoes and peppers require high fertility in early stages of growth, but if too much nitrogen is applied later, all the energy will go to stem and leaf production not fruit. Avoid use of high nitrogen fertilizers around mature tomatoes, peppers, and eggplants. Garlic and onion and other root crops prefer consistent fertilizer. Slow release balanced fertilizer is best, and many are available on the market. Use of good compost, cottonseed meal, and other complex organic mixtures are more beneficial than the commercially produced chemical vegetable products because of the presence of essential micronutrients. Foliar feeding is suggested to apply nutrients directly to the plant. Organic sprays such as kelp or fish emulsions are good choices and won't burn leaves as some inorganic sprays will. Apply spray in the morning to allow leaves to dry before night. Cloudy or overcast days under 80 degrees are preferred to prevent burning from the sun even with organics.

Enjoy your vegetables in the garden as well as on the table. Think past the traditional. Plant in the fall instead of the spring, taking advantage of lower temperatures and reduced pests. Create a true cottage garden; mix vegetables with good companion ornamentals. Reap the benefits in time, energy, and taste.

CHAPTER 9

WATER GARDENING
WETLAND ECOSYSTEMS

The major natural resource utilized by man from 50,000 to 4,000 B.C. and through the pre-agricultural ages to 6,000 B.C. was water. With the domestication of grains and animals in the Middle East around 6,000 B.C., man began to control this natural resource and alter the land with agricultural systems such as irrigation. The Sumerian (Babylonian) culture 4,000 to 1,250 B.C., with an economy based on agriculture and trade between east and west, was the earliest culture to control major flooding using dams and canals.

The Assyrian culture 1,250 to 625 B.C. retained the basic elements of the Sumerian culture and records the first formation and use of gardens and hunting parks. The rebirth of the Sumerian culture during the Neo-babylonian 625 to 539 B.C. led to a highly developed material culture with the Hanging Gardens of Babylon an early attempt to re-create nature. The first use of water as a garden in the Middle East is found with the Persian culture 539 to 331 B.C.

In Egypt from 3,300 to 300 B.C., the hot, dry climate led to development of sophisticated methods for water conservation and irrigation. Upper-class residences consisted of combined buildings and gardens called "walled oases" with water used for fish pools and cooling the air.

In the Classical World 900 B.C. to A.D. 412, Rome between 400 B.C. and A.D. 412 contributed to the use of water as a garden feature with development of the peristyle garden. The major characteristics of this classical design consist of a courtyard enclosed by one or more buildings with colonnades, the use of bilateral symmetry, the relationship of the house to the garden with views of the garden, the use of water features, particularly the water basin with one or more fountains, and the use of ornamental as opposed to strictly functional plantings. This era also developed the "villa rusticas," large country homes for the wealthy that included extensive grounds designed for outdoor entertainment on a lavish scale. These gardens shared the characteristics of formal design, use of large impressive water features, sculptures with ornamental plantings, and the integration of indoor and outdoor space. The Romans attempted to dominate the land, but with an appreciation of natural beauty.

During the Middle Ages A.D. 400 to 1300, many changes took place in the world. The Roman Empire collapsed and the climate cooled enough due to volcanic eruptions between A.D. 400 and 800 to cause crop failure and famine. Fortified cities built during the early Medieval period and the enclosed gardens provided the only safe places to experience nature. In these gardens, water features served as focal points with plantings as companions.

In Islamic Europe and the Middle East during the Middle Ages, Islamic-designed gardens developed. The principal characteristics of these gardens are bilateral symmetry; the use of water for aural and visual effect; year-round plant material and climate control; shade for protection; color in tiles and plants; gardens enclosed by buildings and/or walls; and gardens meant for contemplation. The major theme of Islamic use of the land was an appreciation of natural beauty to produce artificial paradises on earth.

During the Renaissance throughout Italy and France, landscapes developed on a grand scale with water features often the major design element. Many of these gardens and water features exist today, among them the gardens of Versailles in Paris.

All these influences along with the English landscape gardening school (1700 to 1860) concept of parks and large open spaces, which influenced the design of many early parks in the United States including Central Park in New York City, are seen in today's landscape designs. However, water features tend to be limited to formal or larger sites, not smaller home landscapes. The time has come to include water features in all gardens no matter the size.

Climate control, pleasing the senses with sight and sound, and providing focal points are all good design concepts, but the importance of water as an essential component of a habitat is reason enough. A well-planned and well-placed water feature can provide all of the above and more. Following the theme of working with nature as in other chapters of this book, the recommended use of chemical additives is minimal to nonexistent. If you are maintaining prize koi, this chapter may not meet your needs. If you want to attract frogs, dragonflies, diving beetles, and other water and land creatures, read on. Once your garden is established, all you have to do is sit back and they will come.

Water gardens by definition are wet areas featuring plants that live with continually wet root systems. Bog gardens are wet areas without constant measurable water depths. Water and bog areas combine in nature to form wetlands, an important ecosystem that can be imitated in the home landscape. In Chapter 5, Texas Wildscapes, different wildlife habitat requirements are listed with water one of the three essential components. Properly planned water gardens provide water for wildlife habitat not only as part of an ecosystem, but as a complete ecosystem.

Understanding the Ecosystem

An ecosystem is a functional unit of nature, any unit of nature with interacting abiotic (nonliving) and biotic (living) components. The abiotic components include climate, sun, wind, air, and moisture. The biotic components include producers, consumers, and decomposers. The producers, or plants, capture the energy from the sun through photosynthesis and make it available as plant material (food) to other organisms. Consumers, or animals, utilize organic material directly by consuming the plant or indirectly by eating the plant eaters. Decomposers break down once living matter (detritus) to obtain energy and in the process release unused components for utilization by plants to complete the cycle.

Water garden plants are those with continually wet root systems.

The interaction of abiotic and biotic components of ecosystems also results in predictable changes in a living community structure (biotic succession). Understanding biotic succession and the interaction of ecosystem components is fundamental to the management of any habitat.

The concept of ecosystems is introduced here because by properly imitating wetland ecosystems, water and bog gardens will maintain themselves. Keep this concept in mind during the planning and implementation of your water garden.

For dry parts of the state, which could include as much as three-fourths of Texas, water gardens are not an impossible dream. Don't flip to the next chapter. Remember that water gardens started as features in the driest, hottest parts of the world. Certain considerations and concessions have to be made, but water as a component of a wildlife habitat and garden feature is possible.

Location, Size, and Type

Location, as with any garden site, is the first consideration. Working with a new landscape design, many of the following considerations will be determined with the overall plan. Adding a pond to an existing landscape requires more work and planning but can be successfully accomplished with the water complementing existing landscape. Consider the plants you intend to grow, the soils on the site, the grade, surface drainage, view of the pond site from the house or viewing structure, the overall fit of the pond in the existing landscape, and anticipated maintenance needs. Importance and significance of these considerations varies depending on the type of water garden. In-ground earthen ponds have different requirements than aboveground or lined in-ground ponds. Recommendations and suggestions are offered for each in descriptions of the different types of water gardens.

Size is determined by the space available to allow the garden to fit into the existing landscape. In small landscapes such as balconies and patios, the scale is small and small container gardens add visual and aural sensations along with movement. The interaction of sun and shade determines plant material. Flowering water plants, including water lilies, require full sun (at least six hours).

Plants are discussed in detail later in this chapter, but since many people want a water garden for water lilies, a few facts are included here in the early stages of planning. Water lilies prefer still water to bloom and thrive. Motion of the water caused by spray from fountains or waterfalls adversely affects the bloom cycle. If you want a water lily container garden, it is possible without a fountain and in full sun.

Any container capable of holding water can function as a water garden. Commercially available water gardens include copies of sugar kettles, barrels, and rain buckets. There are as many as the imagination allows, all with varying prices. A favorite barrel, pot, or galvanized tub can easily be converted to hold water with the addition of a PVC flexible liner (more information later) or waterproof inner liner. The only limit is your imagination. Add desired plants and a fountain and you have a water garden.

Container gardens are also good for drought areas. Fountains provide movement and sound but can be turned off to conserve water. The container can be allowed to dry out and the few plants replaced following severe drought or freezing conditions. The ecosystem concept is harder with the smaller gardens, and alternatives for maintenance are

covered later in the chapter.

A shallow shelf or wet rock used as part of the arrangement in the container garden provides moisture for birds and butterflies. The sound of running water will bring them to your balcony or patio. Once familiar with a water source, and if you have provided other habitat components, wildlife will return even if the fountain is off. To conserve water and on windy days, run the fountain only when you can enjoy the sounds and creatures. Work with the components of nature you have available even in a small space and enjoy the results.

For larger urban and subdivision sites, in-ground lined ponds, either preformed or freeform with a flexible liner, require additional considerations over the container pond. Early in the planning stage, check for local government restrictions and/or regulations concerning ponds. Not all areas do have restrictions, but checking at this stage can save time and trouble. Most do require fences around the yard of any pond 18 inches or deeper. Many municipalities require circulating pumps and/or filtration systems. If garden hoses are used to fill the ponds, an anti-siphon device may be required. Some city and county governments require inspection and/or building permits. Check with local dealers specializing in water gardens. Obtaining a second opinion may be beneficial unless you have access to legal documentation regarding pond construction. Garden ponds are separate entities from swimming pools and are covered by different rules and regulations. Be sure of your information and sources before you start to dig.

Size is very important. The smaller the pond, the greater the impact seasonal and diurnal temperature fluctuations have and the less stable the ecosystem. Minimum size for a healthy balance is considered to be 50 square feet of surface area. Here is math again! An example is a rectangular pond 10 feet long and 5 feet wide. Multiply length by width to obtain 50 square feet. Refer to the formulas in Chapter 6 to determine square footage for oval and round ponds. Commercially available preformed ponds usually list square footage and gallon size.

The depth is also important for the overall health of the pond. Depths should range from 18 to 24 inches. Depths greater than 3 feet are not necessary and could be a maintenance or safety hazard. Double-check regulations. Deepening a pond with less than

50 square feet surface area helps lessen environmental extremes.

The shape should complement existing shapes in the landscape. In formal landscapes, the angles, lines, and smooth curves should be repeated in the shape of the pond. In an informal landscape, the pond should reflect the less geometric, more free flowing patterns. The pond should balance the existing landscape.

Many rigid preformed containers suitable for in-ground ponds are available. Before purchasing a container, verify that it is approved for use by animals. Stock tanks, watering containers for livestock, in oval and round shapes and varying gallon quantities are often less in price than the preformed fiberglass. Preformed fiberglass is available in many different shapes and sizes, many with built-in shelf shapes around the edges for placement of plants. If a preformed does not meet the landscape needs, flexible liners are available for lining holes dug to exact specifications of the site.

While determining size, shape, and location, keep in mind the purpose of your water garden. As a central theme of the landscape, the size should reflect this by taking up a greater portion in a prominent position. If intended as an accent, the size and shape should be adjusted accordingly. Tucked into a corner or around a bend in a path, a water garden creates a pleasant surprise for visitors, adding mystery to the landscape. If fountains or power generated filtration is planned, allow for access to electrical outlets.

A few cautions in water garden placement. Do not place over utility services. Check with local utility companies for location of underground lines before digging. Avoid placing directly under trees to prevent damage to the liner from tree roots, difficulty in digging, and accumulation of leaves and other tree debris in the water. When placing a container garden on a deck or other wooden structure, check structural supports. Water is heavy.

For maximum enjoyment of your water garden and the nature attracted, consider factors seemingly unrelated to the garden. Children and pets are important parts of the family and neighborhood. Small children are fascinated by water and can drown in only a few inches. Lattice screening across the top may be an option.

Many dogs like water, and a water garden becomes a great swimming pool. Aboveground ponds will discourage the dive. My first water garden was an aboveground 100-gallon pond. The boxer we had at the time liked water but not her doghouse. My husband used the base of the doghouse to build a water garden

Picture 4. Aboveground 100-gallon pond

complete with waterfall and fountain. See picture 4. This garden, in too much shade for flowering plants, uses colored leaves and different shaped vegetation to provide color and texture. The sound of the moving water invites visitors.

A final consideration at this stage is the amount of work involved. Soil has to be removed to provide the hole. Most nurseries specializing in water gardens will install their products at a price. Many gardeners prefer to do the work and dig the hole themselves. For every gallon of water in the pond, 0.134 cubic feet of soil must be removed, in addition to soil removed for edging and sand cushioning underneath. For a 100-gallon pond, more than 13.4 cubic feet of soil must be removed. For a 50- to 60-gallon preformed pond, approximately 6 to 8 cubic feet of soil must be removed, equaling about two to three wheelbarrows full. Consider the time and work involved before starting to dig. You want to be around to enjoy your pond.

The time to determine what to do with this excess soil is before removal. In the 100-gallon example above, the removed soil is enough to fill a 5-foot square bed raised 6 inches. The soil can be used for a new bed or to fill in low spots in the existing landscape or hauled away at added expense. However, in many parts of the state the removed soil is clay or fill material added by subdivision builders. Consider using this soil as the base of a berm to complement the pond. The poor soil mixed with other construction debris provides the good drainage required for plants native to the Trans Pecos region.

Size, location, and shape are finally determined. Choice of available materials is the next decision. Cost, life expectancy, installation, availability, and how the material will fit into the landscape all need to be considered. Examples of liners and life expectancy are: PVC polyvinyl chloride depending on grade (20 millimeter or heavier) 7 to 15 years; butyl or rubber (fish grade) 30 years; fiberglass 50 years; and concrete, if installed properly, a lifetime but does require professional installation.

Installing the Pool or Pond

All decisions are made. Time to dig. Lay out the pattern of the hole using the preformed liner or a painted mark on the surface of the soil. Remember, if using an irregular shaped liner, tracing the outline of the liner upside down creates a mirror image of the space. Mark the soil around the liner in the upright position.

Do not dig the hole deeper than the depth of the preformed liner. Allow a couple inches to protrude above the soil's surface. The same applies when using a flexible liner in a freeform hole. Also determine where you want excess water to drain from your pond during a heavy rainstorm. Lined ponds need to be tilted slightly to prevent runoff from entering the pond and to allow excess water to flow into the landscape without damaging plantings. The exposed edge of the liner will be hidden under landscape material. The picture (5) is a 45-gallon stock tank set into the corner of a path to appear as a pool resulting from the overflow of a dry creek bed. The dry creek bed is in actuality the drain from the rain gutter. The pond is tilted to allow overflow to run under the bridge along the creek bed. The rock edging is the same as the stone path and outline for the creek bed.

Before setting the liner, preformed or flexible, make sure no roots, rocks, or other hard mate-

Picture 5. Forty-five-gallon gallon stock tank pond

rial is left in the hole that could damage the liner. Spread a 2- to 3-inch layer of sand in the bottom of the hole to even out the surface under the liner. Add the liner following manufacturers instructions. Make adjustments where needed to allow for drainage. Now is the time to make alterations in placement. Check everything at least twice before adding water.

Liner in place, time to fill with water. Municipal water supplies are treated with chlorine dioxide and/or chloramines. Call your local water supplier for a list of additives used. These compounds are harmful to fish and other aquatic life. If chlorine is the main compound, allowing the water to sit in the pond for twenty-four to forty-eight hours after filling will remove most of the chlorine. Additives are commercially available for removing both the chlorine and chloramines. I recommend their use, especially in smaller ponds, when having to replace a large quantity of water.

Earthen Ponds

The last type of pond is the earthen bottom pond. A larger area than most subdivision lots is required, but where space is available and on acreages this

type provides the most stable wetland ecosystem. Soil composition is important for success with this pond. Heavy, slow draining soils at least 30 percent clay are best. For well draining sandy type soils, treatment of the bottom of the pond with bentonite or similar substances capable of forming nonpermeable surfaces or lining with at least a 6-inch layer of a 30 percent minimum clay soil are viable options. The depth should be at least 2½ feet. Inlets and outlets incorporated into the existing landscape aid in filling and preventing damaging overflow during heavy rainfall.

Pesticides, herbicides, and fertilizers in the surrounding area have more impact on earthen ponds than lined ones. Most earthen ponds rely on drainage for filling. Runoff contaminated with chemicals can easily upset the balance of the wetland ecosystem to the point of destroying the complete system. If contaminated areas border the pond, provide dikes and alternate routes for the runoff to prevent the water from entering the pond.

Large earthen ponds are more work to create, since they are larger and more soil is removed, but once established require minimal maintenance. The fun of observing the diversity of wildlife

Picture 6. Large earthen bottom pond

in the ecosystem is worth the effort. The picture (6) is of our earthen pond, approximately 1,500 square feet surface area with depths up to four feet. The pond covers approximately the same area once occupied by a house. The house burned and my husband and I bought the property, had the slab removed, and he dug the pond. The soil removed was used to form a berm where drought tolerant species thrive even in the seasonally wet weather of the Houston area. My own little corner of the Trans Pecos.

Muddy water that will not clear is a problem in clay soil earthen ponds. This turbidity is caused by suspended clay particles. The particles are so small they are held in suspension between the water molecules. Gypsum, an inert material with no adverse effects to plant or animal life, added to the water in either powder form or gypsum drywall, reacts with the clay particle, forming a particle large enough to settle to the bottom of the pond. The binding of the clay particles is the same principle used to loosen heavy clay soils before planting.

The exact amount to add can be determined by formula, but we found that mixing several cups of the powder to form a slurry with the pond water then adding to the pond worked. Several additions of the slurry over several days were required, and once clear the water remains clear. After a heavy rain with muddy runoff, temporary turbidity returns but quickly clears.

The pond receives runoff from the rain gutters on the front and back corners of our house plus the rain gutter on the back corner of the neighbor's house. Because of the directing of the neighbor's runoff they no longer have standing water in their backyard every time it rains. They do not use any chemicals on the pond side of their yard. The pond's overflow is in the front corner and directs excess water under the front fence around the edge of the bed bordering the fence and disperses it across the front lawn to the street and ultimately to the storm drain. In the process of filling the pond and flowing past the trees and shrubbery and across the grass, the amount of runoff to the storm drain is greatly reduced. In the Houston area this can make a difference in the overall drainage of our flat land.

Good water quality is essential for the health of all water gardens. Water quality factors are dissolved oxygen, temperature, pH, hardness, alkalinity, ammonia, nitrite, carbon dioxide, and contaminates. With proper planning and maintenance this seemingly long list can be easily managed.

Oxygen is dissolved in water from two sources: air and photosynthesis. The amount of dissolved oxygen is very small, measured in parts per million (ppm). In a water garden dissolved oxygen can range from 0 ppm to more than 20 ppm. The concentration is affected by the amount of agitation, the numbers of fish and plants, the time of day, and the water temperature. More oxygen can dissolve in cool water than warm water. As temperatures increase in the summer, fish increase their metabolism, less oxygen can dissolve in the water, and respiration from decomposition is highest. Fish become stressed with dissolved oxygen levels below 3 ppm.

Oxygen dissolves into the pond water from the air as the two are mixed together through wind and wave action. Mechanical aeration using pumps, fountains, and waterfalls can be used to increase the dissolved levels but are not necessary. If you decide to use mechanical forms, many different types are available. Check with your local supplier for proper size and installation require-ments. Three of my ponds do not have any mechanical forms of aeration and all support abundant life. Effective alternatives are available. Continue reading.

During the process of photosynthesis, plants produce oxygen from carbon dioxide and water in the presence of sunlight. This oxygen is available for use by animal life in the pond. A balance of the oxygen procuring plants and oxygen users is required to maintain water quality.

The other water quality factors can also be controlled by properly stocking the pond. Ammonia and nitrites can be reduced by not overfeeding fish or overfertilizing plant material. Mechanical filtration devices are available to remove ammonia and nitrites, and, are required if maintaining koi. Working with nature in the proper balance, artificial filtration is not necessary.

Water Plants

No matter which type pond fits best in your landscape, the same plants will grow. Once the pond is filled and has been allowed to dechlorinate, it is time to plant. Water plants by nature are aggressive and if allowed free reign will soon overgrow a pond.

In all cases, even at times for the earthen bottom ponds, plants should be planted in pots without drain holes and the pots submerged in the water. Use a clay based soil without added nutrients; light soils float out of the pot onto the surface of the pond. The addition of pea gravel over the soil after planting reduces mudding the water and enhances the appearance of the pot under the water.

All water plants vary in amount or depth of water required for growth and are divided into floating, submerged, and marginal. Use of all three types is required to maintain a properly balanced system. Use of native plants is strongly recommended in all water gardens. Many exotic plants have won freedom and now are serious threats to waterways. Chapter 10, Thieves and Robbers, covers the plants and resulting problems. Read this chapter before purchasing plants. Many of the prohibited plants are still found in the nursery trade.

Submerged plants are the oxygenators of the pond and are essential for a healthy pond. Many commercially available plants in this class are imported exotics. Ask before purchasing and don't settle for non-native vegetation. If enough people ask,

suppliers will find the natives. Desirable plants are: najas, naid, southern naida *Najas guadalupensis*; thin-leaf pondweed, baby pondweed *Potamogeton pusillus*; sago pondweed, fennel-leaf pondweed *Potamogeton pectinatus*; water stargrass *Heteranthera dubia*; cabomba, fanwort, Carolina fanwort *Cabomba caroliniana* 'Gray'; Mermaid weed *Proserpinaca palustris*; coontail, hornwort *Ceratophyllum demersum*; and stonewort, nitella *Nitella* spp. Only one variety of submerged plant is necessary, although more varieties may be used to meet the requirements. Submerged plants should be stocked at a rate of one bunch per 2 square feet of surface area in groups of six to twelve bunches per pot. Plants may have to be caged to prevent grazing by fish and other water creatures. Check periodically to ensure growth of these essential plants. In earthen bottom ponds the oxygenators may be placed directly in the bottom.

Floating plants provide color and movement on the surface of the water and should cover 50 to 75 percent of the surface. With few exceptions the floating plants require full sun to flower. Water lilies are the first choice, but other plants do exist and most work nicely with water lilies. Three species of water lilies are native to Texas: *Nymphaea odorata* white water lily, *N. elegans* blue water lily, and *N. mexicana* yellow water lily. Many hybrid, tropical, and hardy water lilies are available. Select the color and size that work best for your garden. None of the exotic species is considered a noxious invasive.

Lotus, *Nelumbo lutea* the native species, are large leaved plants that form colonies and will overgrow an area. These are best in very large earthen ponds or grown in large pots in medium to large ponds. Smaller hybrid varieties are available. Floating heart *Nymphoides aquatica* is a small leafed plant with white blooms and is ideal for small water gardens. This plant will bloom in partial shade.

Use of native plants is strongly recommended in all water gardens.

Marginal plants, also called bog plants, are a large group of plants that like to have wet feet and do well on the edge of any pond, free growing or in a pot. Most do not like deep water, so pots should be placed on shelves or blocks to maintain proper water depth. This group of plants gives dimension to a pond by providing a top layer. When selecting a plant be sure of the mature size. Umbrella palm *Cyperus alternifolius* is large, reaching 5 feet, and is aggressive in and out of the water. Unless you have a very large area you wish covered, I recommend you try the dwarf variety 'Gracilis' or dwarf papyrus *Cyperus isocladus* formerly *haspans*.

Many marginals thrive in shade and provide a good transition between water gardens and other landscape features. The most popular native plants and flower color are white-topped sedge *Dichromena colorata*, grass-like foliage with white bracts; horsetail *Equisetum hyemale*, tall stiff stems, no flower; tuckahoe, arrow arum *Peltandra virginica* prefers shade, attractive eight-inch arrowhead leaves, flowers insignificant; pickerelweed *Pontederia cordata* arrowhead shaped leaves with blue or white flower spikes, favorite of dragonflies; arrowhead, duck-potato, *Sagittaria* spp. nine different species in Texas with varying leaf size and shape, all have white flowers on long stems, favorite food of red-eared slider turtles; lizard's tail *Saururus cernuus* prefers shade, white flowers on long drooping stalk; powdery thalia, water canna *Thalia dealbata* large leaves with long stalks topped with powdery purple flowers, looks exotic, tolerates salts; cattails *Typha* spp. three different species in Texas, however the species cross pollinate, are all aggressive, and should be contained.

Several **insectivorous plants** are native to Texas and are interesting plants to try in a bog garden. The North American or purple pitcher plant *Sarracenia purpurea* prefers shady, damp, organic soil. It requires a winter dormancy and will survive freezes if enough moisture is in the soil. Look for this plant in the houseplant section of your local nursery. The species prefers outside to inside growth.

Several other insectivorous plants are native to Texas. Most are not available in the nursery trade but can be "rescued," with permission of course, or special ordered. The dwarf sundew *Drosera brevifolia* prefers poor soil for growth. Swollen bladderwort *Utricularia inflata* is free-floating, and horned bladderwort *U. cornuta* is most often found on land. All are interesting additions to the ecosystem.

No matter how well you plan, many water plants do overgrow pots and end up in the bottom of the pond. In earthen bottom ponds the plants find ways to grow in the bottom, often producing larger blooms and leaves. Plants will need to be thinned out. Thin out the cattails and try cooking with them. I've been tempted but haven't tried yet. I did try prickly pear pads. Wonderful mixed with scrambled eggs in a flour tortilla. *Sagittaria* spp. are also supposed to be edible, but Lucy the red-eared slider turtle and her mate keep them under control. The time saved outside working with natives can be used in the kitchen to experiment.

Collecting water plants in the wild is acceptable under certain conditions. In continually wet areas many varieties grow in drainage ditches that are periodically cleaned out. It is okay to "rescue" plants from these areas. On private property be sure to obtain permission and do not remove isolated varieties. Remember, just because the plant is growing along the roadside does not make it a native. Carry a guide with you for identification. Several are suggested in Appendix A.

Controlling Pond Algae

Plants are planted according to specific requirements; water quality is good, and suddenly one morning the water looks like pea soup. This is algae bloom and is normal in a new pond. Any sudden change in nutrients or abiotic factors can induce an algae bloom in an established pond. Do not change the water! The new water will also turn green. Once the pond's ecosystem is established, the water will clear. Filtration and aeration will reduce algae blooms but are not a necessity. Still water ponds with proper balance and maintenance can have clear, colorless high-quality water.

Algae are minute single-celled plants that grow together to form filaments, strings, or simple structures. Algae exist in all water and are a source of food for fish and other aquatic species. Because of their small size and rapid growth rates, algae are difficult to control by methods used for other aquatic plants. Cutting and other forms of mechanical control can help to reduce problems but are of very limited use. Many algae are susceptible to appropriate herbicides, but herbicides that control algae also kill higher plants. The herbicide clears the water temporarily of all plants; once gone from the water, the regrowth of algae is not restricted by competition from the higher plants and the problem often ends up worse.

Another consequence of herbicide or algaecide use is that all algae dies at one time instead of the slow, gradual natural process. The ecosystem cannot manage the massive decomposition of the algae by the microbial population, resulting in reduction of the oxygen supply. The reduced levels of oxygen available for animal life can lead to death of fish or other aquatic animals.

With time the balance in the pond will shift away from the green algae. The floating plants will limit sunlight reaching the algae, and the oxygenators will outcompete the algae for the carbon dioxide, thus eliminating the small plants. Time to allow nature to work is the best treatment for the green algae.

Two other forms of algae are common in ponds. One is the long filamentous algae that grows on the bottom and sides of the pond. These are not responsible for any discoloration and are good, giving the pond a more natural appearance by concealing liners, shelves, pots, bricks, and other underwater props. Excess amounts of this slow growing algae can easily be removed by gently scraping the sides of the pond or container.

String algae is common in all ponds and is unsightly although not harmful unless it covers the surface, reducing sunlight. This form often appears in the spring as the water warms up or after a sudden change in nutrients or water in a pond. Again, herbicide and algaecides are available but as above, do not solve the problem and only prolong the resolution or change the form of the problem.

A new method for controlling string algae has been developed by Dr. Jonathan Newman at the Centre for Aquatic Plant Management in England involving the addition of barley straw to water. Tested in a wide range of situations and in many countries throughout the world, the straw has proved to be successful in most situations with no known undesirable side effects. It offers a cheap and environmentally acceptable way of controlling algae in water bodies ranging from garden ponds to large reservoirs, streams, rivers, and lakes. Despite the simplicity of the idea, experience has shown there are a number of basic rules that must be followed to ensure that the straw works successfully.

In order to use straw effectively, it is necessary to understand how the process works. When barley straw is put into water, it starts to rot, producing a chemical that inhibits the growth of algae. Rotting, a microbial process, is temperature dependent, faster in summer than in winter with six to eight weeks for straw to become active with water temperatures below 50 degrees F but only one to two weeks with water above 70 degrees. During this period, algal growth will continue unchecked. Once the straw has started to rot, it will remain active until almost completely decomposed. The time varies with temperature and the form in which the straw is applied but has been shown to remain active for six months, after which activity gradually decreases.

Barley straw works more effectively and for longer periods than wheat or other straws and should always be your first choice. Use only straw, not green material, and make sure no herbicides or pesticides were applied to the growing product. Remember the problems encountered with herbicides and tomatoes in the previous chapter.

The anti-algal chemical released by the straw does not kill algal cells already present but prevents the growth of new algal cells. Thus, algae that die will not be replaced when the straw is present, controlling the algal problem.

Once the straw has become active, the time taken for control to become effective varies with the type of alga. Small, unicellular green algae species usually disappear within six to eight weeks of straw application. The larger filamentous algae, often known as blanket weeds, survive for longer periods and may not be controlled in the first season if the straw is added when algal growth is dense. Adding the straw very early in the spring before algal growth starts is recommended.

Activity is only produced if the straw is rotting under well-oxygenated conditions. Usually, there is adequate dissolved oxygen in water to ensure that the straw produces the chemical. However, if the straw is applied in large compact masses such as bales, or to very sheltered and isolated areas of water, there will be insufficient water movement through the straw, which will progressively become anaerobic (without oxygen). Under these conditions, only surface layers of the straw will produce the chemical and the majority of the straw will have no useful effect.

The most important measurement in calculating the quantity of straw required is the surface area of the water, since the majority of algal growth takes place in this area. The depth of the water or volume of the pond is not necessary when calculating the quantity of straw required. In still waters such as lakes, ponds, and reservoirs, the minimum quantity of straw needed to control algae is 3 to 4 ounces per 100 square feet of water surface. (A firmly packed pint canning jar holds one ounce of straw.) However, when a water body with a history of severe algal problems is first treated, a higher dose of 9 ounces per 100 square feet is recommended. Quantities up to 100 ounces per 100 square feet may be used. Once the algal problem has been controlled, the dose can be reduced to prevent a recurrence. The quantity of straw needed can vary considerably, and it is better to apply too much initially and then reduce the quantity gradually each time straw is added until algal growth starts to increase again. The dose should then be increased to the previously effective level.

Be aware that the chemical is inactivated by mud. In waters with high algal populations and suspended mud, it is necessary to add more straw than in clear waters. If the straw starts to smell, then it is not working and should be removed. Too much straw in too little water is the cause. Reduce the amount of straw in the container and return to the water.

The best way of applying straw varies with the size and type of water body. In small garden ponds where only a few ounces of straw are needed, the straw can be put into a net bag, nylon stocking, or simply tied into a bundle with string. This can be attached to an anchor made of a stone or brick and dropped into the pond. A float should be included to keep the straw suspended in the water. Floats can be made of corks, polystyrene, or small plastic bottles with well-fitting screw tops. Straw works best held near the surface where water movement is greatest. Once the straw has rotted, the net, complete with float and anchor, can be removed and used again. The small packet of straw found at garden centers works best if anchored and attached to a float as described above.

In still or very slow flowing ponds, lakes, or reservoirs, intact bales should not be used but broken up and the loose straw wrapped in some form of netting or wire. The bales are too tightly packed and do not allow adequate water movement through the straw. One of the simpler ways of wrapping large quantities of loose straw is to use one of the various forms of tubular netting normally sold for wrapping Christmas trees, or agricultural use sacks such as ones for onions or citrus.

To improve the distribution of the active factors throughout the water, apply several small quantities of straw rather than one large one. In small ponds where only a single net of straw is required, place in the center of the pond. If there is an incoming flow of water, either as a stream or fountain, place where there is a continuous flow of water over and through the straw. This helps keep the straw oxygenated and spreads the chemical throughout the pond.

Straw is best applied in the autumn, winter, or very early spring when the water temperature is low. Although straw can be applied at any time of year, it is much more effective if applied before algal growth takes place. Monitor the straw's rate of decomposition; additions may be required before the six-month recommended change.

Since it is not always possible to predict an algal problem, it is sometimes necessary to treat an existing bloom. Some algae, the small unicellular species and the cyanobacteria (blue-green algae), can be controlled by adding straw to existing blooms. The time for control depends on water temperature, with water temperatures above 70 degrees F effective within four to five weeks, sometimes faster. Avoid applying straw during prolonged periods of hot weather as the combined effect of the dying algae and the rotting straw increases the risk of deoxygenation. At lower temperatures the process is slower and may take eight to ten weeks to control the algae, but the risk of deoxygenation is less.

Do not wait until all the straw has rotted before making a second application, as there will be an interval when no chemical is being produced and rapid algal growth can take place. The old straw should not be removed for at least one month after the addition of the new straw, allowing time for the new straw to become active.

No adverse effect of straw on aquatic vascular plants has been found in either laboratory or field experiments. However, a noticeable increase in the growth of submerged plants has been observed, likely as a result of the loss of competition from the algae, which has allowed the vascular plants to recolonize in water where previously they were unable to compete with the algae. In some instances the recovery of the vascular plants has been so strong they replaced the algal growth as the dominant plant form, and no subsequent straw treatments were needed.

Loose masses of well-oxygenated straw provide a good habitat for some of the aquatic invertebrate animals such as the water shrimp (*Gammarus* spp.). These invertebrates, mostly detritus eaters, breed and grow rapidly in the safe environment created by the straw, and their numbers can increase by several orders of magnitude within a few months. As the straw gradually rots away and the numbers of invertebrates increases, individuals leave the safety of the straw and become prey to fish and other insect eaters. Invertebrate animals are beneficial to water bodies as decomposers of organic matter on the bottom; some of them graze on algae and aquatic plants, forming an important part of the ecosystem.

There have been a number of observations of improved growth, vigor, and health of fish in waters treated by straw. One reason is the increased food supply in the form of invertebrate animals. Fish may also find it easier to find food in water that is not densely colonized by unicellular or filamentous algae. Another possible explanation is that by controlling the algae, the straw allows better light penetration to occur to deeper levels in the water so that photosynthesis can occur in a greater volume of the water body and provide an improved environment for the fish.

Use of barley straw is a healthy method of working with natural processes to aid in balance of water ecosystems. I have had excellent success in my 200-gallon preformed crescent pond and the top pond on the aboveground feature. The large earthen bottom pond has shown improvement but due to size and lack of water circulation is slower to yield positive results. The stock tank pond is balanced and does not have any algae problems. Friends with varying pond sizes and plantings have all reported success with the barley straw. With patience, barley straw is a safe, economical source of algae control with added benefits.

A reliable source for pesticide and herbicide free barley straw is Natural Solutions Etc. Check their web site at www.natural-solutionsetc.com.

Animal Life

Animal life is an important part of the ecosystem of the pond. Fish, like all other components, must be balanced with the plant and other animal life. Fish are also important in mosquito control; the developing mosquito larval forms are good food sources. If you do not want fish, an alternative for mosquito control is "Mosquito Dunks." This biological mosquito control is a safe and effective way to control mosquitoes without adversely affecting any other part of the ecosystem. The dunks float on the water, releasing a substance derived from bacteria that is ingested by the mosquito larvae. This enzyme blocks the digestive tract and the larvae starve to death. *Bacillus thuringiensis* subspecies *israelensis* is the bacteria used and is related to the *B. thuringiensis* used for caterpillar control. The same principle for action works in both circumstances. BT products are safe and effective controls affecting only targeted stages of development. More in Chapter 11, Integrated Pest Management.

A water garden is suitable for fish only as long as it can supply adequate oxygen and decompose the wastes produced. The number of fish the water garden can support depends on the size of the water garden, size of the fish, temperature, amount of sunlight received, whether or not aeration is provided, and how well the natural or artificial filtration system removes wastes.

Remember the square footage of the surface of the pond (can't seem to get away from math). An unaerated water garden can be stocked at up to one 12-inch fish (not including the tail) or 12 inches total of fish per 4½ square feet of surface area. If aerated with fountains or waterfalls, then 12 inches per 2 to 3 square feet can be stocked. For example for a 9 by 15 unaerated pond (135 square feet): 135 divided by 4.5 equals 30 units of 12 inches or 360 inches of fish. Apply this rule to all water gardens to avoid fish die-off due to stress and poor water quality.

Fish most commonly found in home landscapes are either **goldfish** or **koi**, both exotic, non-native species. References to goldfish are found in Chinese poetry as early as A.D. 1000. The Chinese and Japanese nobility developed many of the varieties seen today from original wild strains.

Koi carp are descendents of the European common carp *Cyprinus carpio*. Koi is a Japanese word meaning love, and koi giving in Japan has much the same meaning as flower giving in the West. Koi, bred in Japan since at least A.D. 300, can grow quite large and live for sixty to seventy years. Special koi are valued at thousands of dollars.

Koi and some goldfish require additional filtration and aeration and may not be suited to the ecosystem concept. I tried goldfish in my aboveground and crescent ponds only to have them provide breakfast for a visiting green-backed heron *Butorides striatus*. In the small stock tank pond I used guppies during the summer and wintered them in a fish tank in the house. With the addition of the large earthen bottom pond to the landscape, I now use **mosquitofish** *Gambusia affinis*. The first fish were rescued from a drainage ditch behind the office building where my husband works. Mosquitofish are live bearers and prolific breeders with a maximum size less than 3 inches. I now have the native fish in all the water gardens. They do not require any special treatment in cold weather or supplemental feeding, eat mosquitoes, and provide ample food to the visiting wildlife.

In determining what fish to

stock, mature size is important. Several small native Texas species can be used such as **sailfin molly** *Poecilia latipinna* which reaches 5 inches. Several colorful varieties are available commercially. **Pirate perch** *Aphredoderus sayanus* with a mature size of 4½ inches is another consideration. The larger, up to 10 inches, **green sunfish** *Lepomis cyanellus*, one of the most common sunfishes, is tolerant of a wide range of environmental conditions. Whichever fish you decide to stock, if it is not a native species, use one that will die if it escapes into the water system. **Guppies** are good because they cannot tolerate prolonged temperatures below sixty degrees.

Proper fish feeding and control is important to maintain water quality. In an established pond, especially with native species, supplemental feeding is not necessary and often even not necessary with goldfish. Feeding promotes faster growth and overpopulation. Excess food builds up in the water, reducing water quality, and provides additional nutrients that often support algae growth. If you do feed the fish, feed only small quantities and what will be consumed in five to fifteen minutes. Fish will eat what is in the pond if supplemental food is not provided. Don't feel guilty if you do not arrange to have someone feed while you are on vacation. It is usually better for the pond if left untended while you are away.

Frogs and **tadpoles** are desirable additions. Bullfrog tadpoles are available commercially and can be added to the pond; however, with a little patience, frogs and resulting tadpoles will come to your garden. In-ground ponds are preferred, but I have found tadpoles in the aboveground pond. Green and gray tree frogs and Gulf Coast toads use the water for breeding only and require areas around the water for shelter during the day. Rock piles, dense ground covers, woodpiles, stone edging on ponds, and paths all provide good cover. Leopard frogs, bullfrogs, and relatives live in the water, emerging at night to sit on the banks to catch prey.

Without adding a single frog or tadpole, I have identified seven different species of frogs and toads: green tree frog *Hyla cinerea*, gray tree frog *H. versicolor* or *H. chrysoscelis*, pig frog *Rana grylio*, eastern narrow mouth toad *Gastrophryne carolinensis*, leopard frog *Rana utriculara*, Gulf Coast toad *Bufo valliceps*, and spring peeper *Pseudacris crucifer* in my four ponds. The tadpoles eat algae, mosquito larvae, and detritus from the pond, performing important duties in the ecosystem. As an added benefit the chorus during the summer and especially during the full moon is wonderful. The resulting eggs and tadpoles are fun to watch, adding extra movement to the water.

A balanced pond with good water quality will attract numerous **water insects**. Most of these insects will never be observed but are performing important functions in the life of the pond. Some are predators of mosquito larva, small fish, and amphibian eggs while others eat the dead organic matter on the bottom of the pond, returning the nutrients to the water. The most frequently found insects are water boatman *Corixa* spp., giant water bug *Lethocerus americanus*, common backswimmer *Notonecta undulata*, giant water scavenger beetle *Hydrophilus* spp., and the large whirligig beetle *Dineutus* spp. None of these or other frequently encountered water insects are poisonous, but several do have painful bites. Several have the common name "toe biter."

> *Use native species to avoid adverse effects on natural water systems in the event of escape during flooding or high water.*

Other detritus eaters are the **mollusks**. Many varieties of snails and clams can be found in ponds. Snails are important to the health of the pond as cleaners. The water snails are water species and will not leave the water to eat land plants. Japanese snails and other varieties are commercially available. Try to use native species to avoid adverse effects on natural water systems in the event of escape during flooding or high water.

Dragonflies and damselflies soon appear around a pond regardless of size. These beautiful delicate creatures are valued jewels with their many colors and sizes. The colors vary from fuchsia purple through neon reds to jet black with many shades of blue and green in between. Not only do these creatures add color and movement to the garden, they are voracious predators of small flying insects including mosquitoes.

Water is essential for all members of the Odonata order of the animal kingdom. Good water quality is necessary for the successful reproduction of both dragonflies and damselflies. The female lays her eggs under floating leaves or among the grasses near the edge of the pond. The eggs hatch within a few days depending on species. The brown or green larval stage called nymph or naiad emerges to spend its cycle among the detritus and floating plants. This predatory stage eats other insects, small fish, tadpoles, and mosquito larvae. Depending on the species, the nymph stage lives in the pond from a few weeks to a few years before climbing out of the water to emerge as the adult dragonfly or damselfly.

Crustaceans such as crawfish, shrimp, copepods, scuds, and isopods all inhabit healthy water ecosystems. Many are added to ponds in purchased potted water plants. Others arrive on the feet of visiting birds. Larval stages have adults that fly as with dragonflies and many insects. The diversity of small animal life in the pond allows a more stable ecosystem.

Arachnids will also soon appear in the pond. Two of the most frequently encountered spiders are the six-spotted fishing spider *Dolomedes triton* and the water mites *Limnochares americana*. The greenish brown 3/8- to 3/4-inch fishing spider with white lengthwise stripes along its thorax and abdomen is often seen sitting on floating leaves or skimming across the surface of the water. The spider eats tadpoles, fish, and small frogs and in turn is eaten by fish and visitors to the pond.

Water mites are small, usually red, pinhead-sized spiders. They eat plant and animal life in the pond. Neither of these two or any other frequently encountered water spider is considered poisonous to man. Like all other parts of the ecosystem, the arachnids have their important functions.

Water and wetland ecosystems are also home to **snakes**. Of the numerous genera of snakes in Texas only four are poisonous: rattlesnakes *Sistrurus*, copperheads *Crotalus*, cottonmouths *Agkistrodon* spp., and coral snakes *Micrurus fulvius fulvius*. The most frequently encountered snakes around and in a pond are garter and ribbon snakes both *Thamnophis* spp. and water snakes *Nerodia* spp. Take time to learn to identify the various snakes and welcome them into the landscape. All snakes are beneficial and are an important part of the ecosystem. They aid in rodent control and keeping the number of frogs, fish, and crawfish in check.

Turtles are popular and fun

additions to a pond. Usually these have to be added, although if the landscape is near a natural water source, one may arrive. My pair of red-eared sliders *Trachemys scripta elegans* were rescued from the middle of a busy highway near Houston. Several other native species are found in Texas, and I strongly suggest you purchase only native species at the pet store or rescue local ones. Turtles do require large ponds and like logs or rocks for basking. Supplemental feeding is not necessary if plants and fish are in the pond. Young red-eared sliders eat fish but as they mature prefer vegetation.

Maintenance

Many pond maintenance guides recommend cleaning the bottom of the pond yearly and removing the detritus to maintain a clear pond with good water quality. If the pond is thriving, with healthy fish and plants, this messy job is not necessary. By working with nature to supply and maintain the balanced ecosystem there is no need. In fact, cleaning the bottom will upset the balance, killing all water insects, crustaceans, and mollusks, including the dragonfly and damselfly nymphs, tadpoles, and eggs. You will probably end up starting all over again, algae blooms included.

Aggressive plant material should be removed and divided when the pots are overgrown. The smaller the pond the more often the plants need dividing. Many blooming water plants in pots, especially water lilies, do require fertilization. Use a slow release tablet form specifically for water plants. Follow label directions and take all precautions to avoid excess fertilizer leaching into the water. Increased nitrogen promotes algae bloom and reduces water quality.

Establish your ecosystem, sit back, watch nature, and enjoy your work. Keep a journal or log of visitors. The variety and numbers will amaze you even in a small garden. Suggested field guides are listed in Appendix A to aid you in identification, although you do not have to know the name of a visitor to enjoy it.

CHAPTER 10

THIEVES AND ROBBERS

BANNED, ILLEGAL, AND AGGRESSIVE PLANTS

Gardening literature concentrates on descriptions, uses, and virtues of plants. Occasional reference is made to a plant as aggressive or to call it a "weed." This book stresses the use of native plants, if not native to a specific ecoregion, at least native to Texas or bordering states. I'm sure many of you are thinking, "What's the harm with a few exotic species? Natives just don't quite give the look I want." The harm can be minimal to serious and in the extreme result in a fine and/or jail for the gardener and extinction of a plant or animal species. A bit extreme for planting the wrong plant? Not really.

Millions of dollars are lost in agricultural, recreational, and sport land use each year as a result of invasive exotic plants. Farmers have always tried to control invasive plants or weeds, since these plants reduce crop yields and interfere with harvest operations. In recent years the invasive problem has escalated with the cost passed on to the consumer through higher food costs and reduced quality.

Control of invasive plants in parks, refuges, forests, grasslands, and other natural areas is passed on to the user through increased taxes or decreased services. The invasive water plants discussed in this chapter clog waterways and blanket lakes, disrupting recreational and sport use. The funds to fight the invaders could and should be put to better use.

Exotic plant and animal life poses a serious threat to native plant and animal species that have natural predators. When allowed to grow in an ecosystem, the normal checks and balances take place and invasive growth is controlled. Large stands of one species of plant attract caterpillars or other leaf eating insects that reduce the population. With exotic species this does not happen. The natural predators, with a few exceptions, were not imported along with the plants. Without the predators the exotics outcompete the natives, reducing or completely eliminating the plants and wildlife dependent on the plant. Exotic invasives present a long-term threat to biodiversity, ecosystem stability, and the balance of nature important to all species including man.

Since the first European settlers landed, thousands of plants have been introduced into the United States. According to the U.S. Congressional Office of Technology Assessment, there are at least 4,500 species of foreign plants and animals that have established free-living populations in the United States. Of that total, at least 675 species (15 percent) cause severe harm. In economic terms, 70 species, or 12 percent of the total harmful species, caused documented losses of $97 billion from 1906 to 1991. By 1950 the number of plant introductions into the United States was estimated to be at least 180,000. In 1975 it was estimated that at least 1,800 introduced plant species had escaped into the wild, with a large proportion establishing free-living populations. The numbers continue to increase.

Biological invasions are a seriously underestimated problem. Unlike chemical pollutants that tend to degrade over time and permit an ecosystem to recover, biological invasions tend to multiply and spread, causing ever-worsening problems. Insidious effects of invasive non-native species include displacement or replacement of native plants and animals, disruptions in nutrient and fire cycles, and changes in the pattern of plant succession. Adequate surveys and reliable monitoring data are not available for many of these invaders.

How can we as gardeners solve the problem started by our ancestors and perpetuated by commerce? Planting native plants is only part of the solution. Understanding, identifying, and educating are all possibly long-term aids. At this stage there is probably no real solution.

Sometimes exotics are planted on purpose with good intentions, at least at the time. Kudzu *Pueraria montana var. lobata* planted in the South is a well-documented, well-known example. Planted in the early twentieth century as a control for erosion, it soon showed limited ability to control erosion but great ability to cover everything in its path. Despite extensive research and millions of dollars, the problem continues and will probably get worse. Kudzu, thought to spread only by runners (vegetatively) producing clones, has now been discovered to set seeds in North Carolina and Illinois. This not only allows for wider spread of the plant but also increases genetic diversity, allowing development of resistance to chemical controls. To my knowledge Texas is not affected; however, with the discovery that kudzu has set seeds, can Texas be far behind?

Not all invasive exotics are good ideas gone terribly wrong. The majority of the damage is caused by "escapees." These are plants that have moved from landscapes into the wild, either through floods, animal transfer, or dumping. Once a plant is added to a home landscape, the gardener has essentially lost control of where that plant will go. Many

parts of Texas have flooding—flash floods in the desert to tropical storm and hurricane floods along the coast. During a flood plants are uprooted and moved and seeds are dispersed in the wind and water. Many of the plants will die, but not all. Once the plant material lands on dry soil, growth occurs. In the case of water plants, growth continues often in unwanted areas.

"No person may import, possess, sell, or place into water of this state exotic, harmful, or potentially harmful fish, shellfish, or aquatic plants except as authorized by rule of permit issued by Texas Parks and Wildlife Department." Texas Parks and Wildlife and the state take this statement seriously and so should you. The 76th Texas State Legislature delegated the Texas Parks and Wildlife Department to develop a statewide management plan to assist water management authorities in the safe practices available for controlling nuisance aquatic vegetation.

Texas Parks and Wildlife Illegal Plants

Twelve water plants are listed on the Texas Parks and Wildlife Department little-known list of "Harmful or Potentially Harmful

Exotic Aquatic Plants." This list comprises plants that have been shown or have the potential to damage waterways and wildlife habitat. The current list includes all species of salvinia *Salvinia* spp., giant duckweed *Spirodela polyrhiza*, water hyacinth *Eichhornia crassipes*, hydrilla *Hydrilla verticillata*, Eurasian water milfoil *Myriophyllum spicatum*, rooted water hyacinth *Eichhornia azurea*, torpedograss *Panicum repens*, water lettuce *Pistia stratiotes*, lagarosiphon *Lagarosiphon major*, alligatorweed *Alternanthera philoxeroides*, paperbark *Melaleuca quinquenervia*, and water spinach *Ipomoea aquatica*.

Of the twelve listed plants the biggest threat is from the salvinias especially giant salvinia *S. molesta*. All members of the family Salvinaceae are small, aquatic ferns that float at the surface of the water with a "hairy" root-like leaf dangling below. Floating leaves are in twos, oblong to nearly round, about .4-.8 inches long (giant salvinia leaves are up to 2 inches); a third leaf is positioned below the water surface in place of roots. The plant has no true roots. Floating leaves are bluish-green and covered with stiff hairs and bump-like projections. A crease usually runs down the center of each leaf. Multiple sets of three leaves may be connected along a common axis. Differentiating between salvinia species is difficult, especially if the plants are immature. See Figure 6.

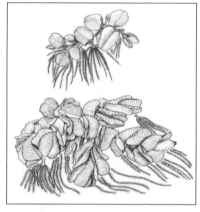

Figure 6. *Salvinia molesta*

Common names for this family include water fern, Kariba weed *S. molesta*, butterfly fern, watermoss *S. auriculata*, and water spangles *S. minima*. The family includes eleven species all native to tropical climates with the exception of *S. natans* from Europe, North Africa, and Java.

Salvinias are found in quiet water areas in ponds, lakes, and bayous. Reproduction by spores occurs only in *S. natans*; all others reproduce by asexual budding. Fragmented leaf clusters can also produce new plants.

Most have limited if any value to fish or wildlife. The fern is a tropical plant; however, especially with the giant salvinia, once established, cold will only damage, not kill. The mat of leaves is too thick to be destroyed by freezing temperatures or ice, resulting in potential for it to become established throughout the state.

Giant salvinia (*S. molesta*), the most noxious of the salvinias, was first found in Texas in 1997-98. With the ability to double in size every four to six days, it has continued to spread. By March 2001 the plant had been found in four public reservoirs (Toledo Bend, Conroe, Texana, and Sheldon), twenty-seven private lakes, five streams, two rivers, and six river basins. The Texana salvinia infestations entered Sandy Creek after autumn floods in 1998 overflowed a private pond holding the plant. Infestations have also been reported in ten other states in the South and West.

This alien water fern *S. molesta* is an import from southern Brazil and has already caused ecological, economic, and social impact in other countries. Lake Kiraba in Africa has solid mats of salvinia covering more than 250,000 acres of the reservoir's surface, forcing shoreline communities to relocate because of destroyed fishing.

It has also wreaked havoc in Australia, New Zealand, and Papua New Guinea. One of the major causes of the spread is release or escape after sale in plant nurseries and aquarium-related businesses. One nursery in Oklahoma actually gave it away!

The plant at first rings a lake with velvet-like leaves, creating a kind of skirt on the water, after a couple of months it covers nearly every inch of the surface. The mat of vegetation blocks sunlight, uses up all suspended nutrients, and prevents oxygen from mixing with the water. It essentially kills the lake, destroying all life.

At the present time there is no effective means of control. The fine hairs covering the thick leaves as well as the thickness of the mats prevent good coverage of herbicides. Mechanically removing the plant will not destroy it since a new plant can grow from only a portion of a leaf.

A Brazilian weevil *Cyrtobagous salviniae,* the natural predator of the fern in Brazil, appears to be the best chance for control. The insect feeds on the leaves and stems as larvae and adult, keeping the population in check in its natural waters, and has been used successfully to remove tens of thousands of acres of the weed on the Sepik River and Australian reservoirs.

Years of research have shown the weevils feed only on salvinia, not any other type of vegetation; however, a problem has been encountered in finding the one of at least three or four subspecies that will eat *S. molesta*. Currently several different weevils are in quarantine waiting to be tested in the U.S. The clearance will probably take until mid-2002 or longer. It is hoped that the beetle in combination with herbicides may be the answer.

For now the best control is education. People need to be aware of what the plant looks like and report any sightings to Texas Parks and Wildlife and if on private property properly destroy all plants. Lake Conroe formed an "adopt a shoreline" group. An infestation was found, money was raised for treatment, and at least for now the spread of the plant has been stopped.

Vigilance is required by all. Check boats and other watercraft, even tackle and fishing gear, for fragments of the plant. Watch for these plants at water-garden centers and inform the owners of the illegal status of the plants. If questioned, suggest contacting TPWD.

Texas is not the only state in the U.S. to recognize the impact of the giant salvinia. U.S. federal regulations and others in several states prohibit its importation, cultivation, and transportation. This plant has been termed the "World's Worst Weed."

The **floating water hyacinth** *Eichhornia crassipes*, the plant that formerly carried the distinction of being the worst water weed, is also a native of South America. This *Eichhornia* species has rounded leaves to 8 inches on inflated stems that may stand 3 feet or more above the water. Leaves and stems are thick, spongy, dark green, and glossy (not hairy). Dense, fibrous, branched root masses hang from beneath the plant. Flowers are purple and produced in upright clusters.

water hyacinth

E. crassipes is believed to have been introduced in the U.S. at the World's Industrial and Cotton Centennial Exposition of 1884-1885 in New Orleans, Louisiana, and may have been cultivated in the U.S. as early as the 1860s. By the late 1890s *E. crassipes* had become such a problem for navigation that Congress was prompted to pass the River and Harbor Act of 1899, which authorized the U.S. Army Corps of Engineers to begin major aquatic plant control programs.

Water hyacinth reproduces by budding daughter plants or by producing seeds. Populations may double in size every one to eighteen days. The Army Corps of Engineers was unable to control water hyacinth, and populations expanded to over 125,000 acres in Florida by the late 1950s. Dense growths of water hyacinth reduce light and oxygen diffusion as well as water movement and can smother beds of submerged vegetation and eliminate plants that are important to waterfowl. Low oxygen concentrations under water hyacinth mats can cause fish kills and have been reported to have completely eliminated resident fish populations in some small Louisiana lakes. The combination of the large leaves and hanging roots can produce evapotranspiration rates in excess of twice normal evaporation, leading to significant water loss in West Texas water supply systems.

Rooted water hyacinth *Eichhornia azurea* is similar to floating water hyacinth but lacks the strongly inflated stems. Additionally, completely submerged leaves may divide and appear ladder-like. Floating water hyacinth, which has rooted to the bottom while growing in shallow water, may become atypically elongated if water levels rise and therefore resemble this species. This *Eichhornia* species has the same detrimental effects as *E. crassipes*. If you really like water hyacinth, remarkably real looking plastic plants are available.

Water lettuce *Pistia stratiotes* is one of the most cosmopolitan aquatic plants in the world found on every continent except Europe and Antarctica. The plant is easily recognized by its lettuce-like leaves. The individual rosettes reach 8 inches in diameter, but often grow in clusters. Leaves are hairy, spongy, and have numerous veins. Each rosette also has a dense, fibrous cluster of feather-like roots dangling below. Flowers are small, green, and nearly hidden in the center of the rosette. It is a floating plant but is capable of rooting in wet soil for prolonged periods.

water lettuce

Origins of the plant are unclear, but based on the abundance of associated insects, it is believed to have come from South America. The problems associated with water lettuce are similar to that of its South American neighbor water hyacinth.

Another non-native aquatic invasive is **hydrilla** *Hydrilla verticillata*. Hydrilla grows in long, often branching stems with leaves in whorls of five (two to eight). Leaves are .8 inch long or less, have toothed edges and a toothed lower midrib, making the plant rough to the touch. It produces small, insignificant flowers to .17 inch across with three white petals. Coloration is usually dark green; leaf midrib may be reddish.

Hydrilla was introduced into Florida in the early 1950s through the aquarium trade and initially marketed as Indian star-vine. Since then the plant has spread through Florida, as far north as the eastern seaboard states and west into California and Washington. This plant exhibits rapid growth under a wide range of environmental conditions. Hydrilla can grow up to one inch per day until it nears the surface of the water. Once near the surface it forms a thick mat of branches and leaves that intercept sunlight, often preventing native plants from growing beneath. The ability to grow and photosynthesize at light levels below those required for native submerged species allows hydrilla to colonize deeper water, frequently growing in water 10-15 feet deep. The thick mats not only kill native species, they clog waterways.

hydrilla

Hydrilla's ability to reproduce by fragmentation, tubers, and seeds results in rapid spread within and from one lake or reservoir to another. Nearly 50 percent of fragments with a single leaf whorl can sprout a new plant, resulting in a new population. For fragments with three or more leaf whorls, the success rate is over 50 percent. The tubers can remain dry for several days and still remain viable. Viability has been shown to survive over four years buried in undisturbed wet sediment. The tubers also survive herbicide treatment and ingestion and regurgitation by waterfowl. The tubers allow hydrilla to remain established even during an aggressive treatment program. A single tuber can potentially produce approximately 6,000 new tubers per square yard.

Hydrilla can reproduce sexually by seed formation, but viability is low and importance in spread is believed to be insignificant at this time. In Texas only female plants have been found, so seed productions in the state are unknown.

Eurasian water milfoil *Myriophyllum spicatum* is an aquatic plant native to Europe and Asia first introduced into North America in the late nineteenth century. Only recently has it been added to the list of invasive exotics. *M. spicatum* is similar to the North American native water milfoil *M. exalbescens* but can be differentiated on the basis of leaf morphology. In general, *M. spicatum* produces five to twenty-four pairs of leaflets per leaf, whereas *M. exalbescens* produces four to fourteen. About 70 percent accuracy can be obtained by characterizing everything with fourteen or more pairs of leaflets as *M. spicatum*.

Eurasian water milfoil

M. spicatum produces long, branching stems with feather-like leaves usually in whorls of five to twenty-four. Whorls are usually more than .24 inch apart with rather thin and relatively long leaves less than 1 inch and short leaflets less than .6 inch. Stems are often reddish or reddish-brown; leaves are usually green. Terminal flower clusters are produced above the water line in mid-June through late summer. In addition to flowering, the plant reproduces asexually by producing vegetative buds and by fragmentation. Eurasian water milfoil may survive winter as a whole plant or a root mass, or by producing buds.

Eurasian water milfoil is a strong competitor capable of displacing native submerged plant species, reducing both habitat diversity and plant species diversity. When excessive growth occurs, many of the same problems are created as with hydrilla.

Giant duckweed *Spirodela oligorhiza*, a small (to .2 inch leaves) plant, has flattened, rounded leaves that are light green above and often reddish tinted below. Each leaf has five to eleven veins or nerves. It has multiple, unbranched, filament-like roots below. Common duckweed *Spirodela polyrhiza*, a legal native, has only two to four leaf veins. The related *Lemna*, smaller with only a single unbranched root, are also not prohibited.

Lagarosiphon *Lagarosiphon major* has fairly long to .8 inch, lance-shaped leaves, that are either smooth edged or are only slightly toothed. Leaves may be alternate, opposite, or whorled and usually curl backwards. Coloration is green with a green midrib. It produces small, three-petaled flowers.

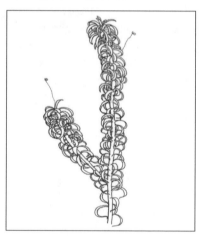

Lagarosiphon major

Alligatorweed *Alternathera philoxeroides* has been described as an amphibious plant because it grows in a wide range of habitat types including both terrestrial and aquatic. The aquatic floating

giant duckweed

form usually has hollow stems while the rooted terrestrial form does not. Both forms grow in long, tangled mats with upright stems, which rise to about two feet above the water line. Leaves are green, opposite, oval to lance-shaped, and smooth edged up to 4 inches long. Small .05-inch white flowers are produced in clusters of six to twenty on stems that arise from the leaf bases from April through October.

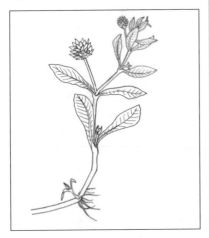

alligatorweed

A. philoxeroides originated in the Parana River region of South America but has since spread to other areas of South America, North America, Asia, and Australia. Problems resulting from excessive growth are similar to those caused by water hyacinth and water lettuce.

Paperbark or melaleuca *Melaleuca quinquenervia*, an Australian tree that grows in water, reaches 50 feet in height but may grow as a shrub or smaller tree. Leaves are dark green, alternate, elliptical, to 4 inches long with short stems and parallel veins. Flowers are white and form a bottle-brush shape about 4 inches long. Seed capsules may be present on thinner branches.

Torpedograss *Panicum repens* is typical of many grasses with stems rising to about 28 inches in height from nodes or horizontal rhizomes. Blades are .08-.28 inch wide, flattened or folded, and green in color with occasional purple tints. Flower spikes are 2.8-4.7 inches tall with widely spaced spikelets .09-.10 inch long.

torpedograss

Grasses are often extremely difficult to identify. Similar but not prohibited grasses may have spikelets shorter than .09 inch in length or longer than .10, blades wider than .28 inches, closely spaced spikelets, or have very large and branching flower spikes.

Water spinach *Ipomoea aquatica* is actually an aquatic morning glory. It is a vine but is not twining or climbing; hollow stems float or trail over muddy banks. Leaf shape varies from oval to lance- or arrow-shaped, and leaves are positioned alternately on the stem. Roots may appear at the nodes. Flowers are pink to purple and typical of other morning glories. This plant has been found in herb gardens labeled as an edible. Check scientific names before buying and planting.

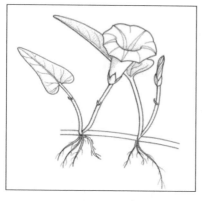

water spinach

The United States Geological Survey maintains a toll-free number for reporting suspected non-indigenous aquatic species, including salvinia. The number is 877-STOP-ANS or 877-786-7276. For more information contact TPWD aquatic vegetation control headquarters in Jasper at 409-384-9965. Report any sightings of suspected salvinia to TPWD's Randy Helton at 409-384-9965 or by e-mail to salvinia@sra.dst.tx.us.

Purchase, possession, or sale of any of the listed plants is a Parks and Wildlife Code Class B misdemeanor. Penalty for those found guilty is a $200-$2,000 fine and as much as 180 days in jail, and each individual plant can count as a separate offense. A second offense of possessing plants on the prohibited list is a Class A misdemeanor and carries a penalty of $500-$4,000 and as much as a year in jail. Running down individuals or businesses possessing or distributing plants hasn't been a top priority of TPWD game wardens, but the giant salvinia may change that. Remember state and federal laws prohibit possession of giant salvinia.

Some of you may have these plants in your garden and feel they are doing no harm and as long as Texas Parks and Wildlife stays out of your yard, no problem. An acquaintance of mine grows water hyacinth to help clear his ponds. He tells me he composts excess and never gives any away. Can an individual successfully control plants? What happens when it rains hard and high water washes through your yard? Flooding is a major way plants are moved from one location to another. Remove all illegal plants and fragments; allow them to dry out or desiccate for several days, then compost or dispose of in a sanitary landfill. Incinerate if possible to ensure complete destruction. Do not place green plants in a plastic bag and throw in the trash. Bags are broken open, and the fragments could end up anywhere. Be ruthless and remove!

Invasive Trees

Not all exotic invasive plants are illegal or water plants. The Chinese tallow *Sapium sebiferum* in the eastern and southern parts of Texas and the salt cedar *Tamarix* spp. found all across the west including Texas are two trees creating environmental havoc.

Chinese tallow trees are promoted for fall color and the berries for crafts. I recently heard somewhere in the Northeast a small bundle of branches with berries sold for $25. Fall color and craft use seems okay, harmless at least, but this brilliantly colored tree with the white berries has a sinister side. It is displacing native plant species and associated wildlife at an alarming rate. The Nature Conservancy has placed tallow on its "Dirty Dozen" list of the twelve worst exotic invasive species in the United States.

The Chinese tallow *S. sebiferum* also known as popcorn tree, chicken tree, or Chinese tallowberry is an exotic species introduced from China into Charleston, South Carolina, in the late 1700s and into the Texas Gulf Coast between 1900 and 1910 by the Department of Agriculture. Another "good" idea gone terribly wrong. The purpose was to investigate the economic possibility of tallow production for soap industries in Houston and Jacksonville, Florida. The industry never became economically feasible but provided the origin of the tallow expansion. Tallows have spread from North Carolina to Florida, throughout the Gulf Coast states, and into Southern California. At last estimate, southeast Texas supported

234,000 acres of the trees.

In Texas the invasion of the tallow has degraded the prairies, wetlands, and habitat for many migratory and ground nesting birds. The Attwater's prairie chicken and the whooping crane, both on the federally endangered list, are the most well known, however many other species of birds and other animals are affected.

Chinese tallow tree is a moderate-sized tree, 30 to 40 feet, with leaves resembling a poplar. The leaves are deciduous, alternate, and simple; with ovate blades from 1½ to 3 inches long and from 1¼ to 2¾ inches wide, broadly pointed at the base, abruptly long-pointed at the tip, entire on the margin, and smooth on both surfaces. The fragrant greenish-yellow flowers are borne on erect terminal spikes and are popular with beekeepers. The fruits are round three-lobed capsules about ½ inch in diameter. At maturity the outer part splits and falls away, leaving the three white and waxy-coated seeds hanging from a central column. The milky sap of the tree is poisonous. Picture 7 shows Chinese tallow leaves and fruit.

Tallow trees start producing seeds after only two to three years and the rootstock may be

Picture 7. Chinese tallow leaves and fruit.

viable for more than one hundred years. Mature trees may produce up to 4,500 pounds of seeds per acre per year, allowing expansion by flooding and birds. They thrive on poorly drained, intermittently flooded, saline soils. Once germinated, the seeds and small trees are not bothered by standing water.

Chinese tallow is difficult to control. It has been shown to be toxic to cattle and is not preferred by any domestic or native herbivore. The tree is controlled in its native China by population and is not considered invasive. The tree grows rapidly, establishes easily, can resprout, and is a prolific seed producer. Removal of existing trees is relatively easy, but maintaining the effects of the removal is difficult and costly. Currently, the situation appears to be that the Chinese tallow forests will maintain themselves indefinitely, continually expanding and replacing native wetlands, prairies, and forests unless management practices are implemented. Mechanical and chemical methods along with prescribed fire have been used with limited success, depending on the combination and the age of the trees.

Control is expensive and labor intensive. Gardeners should use knowledge and influence to help the agencies trying to control the tallow trees by removing trees in home landscape and encouraging communities to destroy existing trees and not plant new ones. Live oak, southern red maple, sweet gum, and other native trees are far superior landscape trees. By not planting tallow, preventing new establishment, and working to reduce present tallow acreage, we can stem this bioinvasion and help save our diverse ecosystems. For tips on removing Chinese tallow, contact Texas Parks and Wildlife's Urban Wildlife Program at 512-912-7011 or The Nature Conservancy of Texas at 210-224-8774.

Salt cedar or tamarisk tree *Tamarix* spp. has been called a tree with a drinking problem. The tree takes over the area near a spring or other body of water and pushes out the native species of willows and cottonwoods. Once established, the invader soaks up so much water it may leave the place high and dry. Salt cedar trees have been shown to soak up over five million acre feet of water every year in the already parched Southwest. Some estimates have the plant using ten to twenty times more water than the native displaced species.

Tamarix spp. are native to Eurasia and Africa and were

introduced into the western U.S. as an ornamental in the early 1800s. Most species are deciduous shrubs or small trees growing to 12-15 feet and forming dense thickets. *T. aphylla* is an evergreen tree that can grow to 50 feet and flowers during the winter. Salt cedars are characterized by slender branches and gray-green foliage. The bark of young branches is smooth and reddish-brown. As the plants age, the bark becomes brownish-purple, ridged, and furrowed. Leaves are scale-like, about 1 1/16 inch long, and overlap each other along the stem often encrusted with salt secretions. From March to September large numbers of pink to white flowers appear in dense masses on 2-inch-long spikes at branch tips. See Picture 8.

The salt cedar are fire-adapted species whose presence increases the frequency, intensity, and effect of fires and floods. While growing, the trees absorb salt in their tissues. When a tree dies and remains in place, the salt is added back to soil, increasing salinity and reducing growth of other species until the salt can be dispersed. They steal the water then make the soil unfit for other species. True thieves and robbers of the plant world.

The tree has been shown to stabilize sand dunes and grows along Galveston Bay, but this is a small virtue. With several means of dispersal, the trees do not stay where planted. Plants spread vegetatively, by roots, submerged stems, and sexually. Each flower can produce thousands of tiny seeds contained in a small capsule usually adorned with a tuft of hair that aids in wind dispersal. Seeds can also be dispersed by water.

A variety of methods have been used in the management of

Picture 8. Salt cedar *Tamarix* spp.

salt cedar, including mechanical, chemical, and biological. The most effective management involves a combination of the three. Many factors must be considered for the safe, effective removal of the salt cedar. For information on management of salt cedar, contact Curt Deuser, U.S. National Park Service, Lake Mead National Recreation Area, curtdeuser@nps.gov.

Other Undesirable Plants

Many other non-native invasive species can be harmful to individual species without impacting an entire ecosystem. Researchers in Chicago found that songbird nests in Japanese honeysuckle *Lonicera japonica* were preyed upon more often than nests built in native shrubs and vines. *L. japonica*, the yellow and white honeysuckle seen along the roadsides throughout the state and readily available in nurseries, is an escaped exotic from Japan, not a native. This is an example of an escaped exotic that has naturalized, leading people to believe it is a native species. The native coral honeysuckle *L. sempervirens* may not be fragrant, but it is more colorful, attracts butterflies and hummingbirds, and is not as aggressive as the exotic.

I recently picked up two different water garden magazines at the grocery store, and one recommended water hyacinth and the other water lettuce. Neither magazine even hinted at the aggressive or possibly illegal status of these two thieves and robbers. Both magazines were printed in the Northeast where I'm sure these plants are kept under control by freezing. I have trouble imagining someone carefully removing water hyacinth to a basement to spend the winter.

Many books and plant lists even in Texas include the tallow and *Tamarix* as suggested trees and shrubs and the Japanese honeysuckle as a "good" vine. The latest list from A&M for shrubs includes the *Tamarix*. Just because the plant is in a list does not mean it should be planted.

Not all exotic non-native plants are invasive. It is important to learn which plants to avoid planting and to inform your communities of the long-term dangers of invasive exotics. Working with nature to maintain the ecosystems is much easier than trying to remove invasive exotics and reestablish habitat. For more information on exotic invasive plants, check the Plant Conservation Alliance Alien Plant

Working Group at http://www.nps .gov/plants/alien/.

Invasive Birds

Plants are not the only thieves and robbers. Among birds there are also exotic, invasive species destroying native birds and upsetting ecosystems. The English house sparrow *Passer domesticus* and the European starling *Sternus vulgaris* are two common birds that do not belong.

The **English house sparrow** is so common people have given it many names. One of my non-birding friends calls it a "che-che." When asked he told me that is what his father called it. For those of you who may not recognize this bird, it is small, six inches, with a brownish-gray body and white wing stripe. The male has a black throat with white cheeks and a chestnut nape. The female and young lack the black throat; they have a plain dingy breast and a dull eye ring. City birds are often dingy with soot, obscuring distinguishing markings. Figure 8 is a male house sparrow.

This sparrow, actually a finch unrelated to our native sparrows, arrived in the United States for the first time in 1850. Eight pairs

were brought in from England by a group of men in Brooklyn who believed the bird would help control insect problems such as span worms and the caterpillar of the snow-white linden that was stripping trees and leaving droppings on passersby. The thinking was since everyone had trouble with bugs, one more bird would help in control. They also believed sparrows were attractive and would be a worthwhile addition to the existing birds.

The first pairs did not survive, but three years later a larger group was released in Greenwood Cemetery. These did survive and reproduced. Within ten years, with additional imports, the birds inhabited many Eastern cities. Popularity of the birds increased and a lucrative trade developed with it often cheaper to import more birds than to buy from existing breeders. By 1875 it had become clear that the enterprise had been a bad idea. They had eaten the linden moth caterpillars but discovered grain, consuming up to eight pounds each per year. They attacked and drove out native species, including more efficient insect eaters, infested buildings, and polluted parks. Gardeners found them nipping buds, mutilating fruit, and pecking newly planted flower and

Figure 8. Male house sparrow

vegetable seeds as soon as they were planted. They were accused of a variety of crimes, including murder and arson. Sparks from a foundry in Pottsville, Pennsylvania, set fire to a large nest and to the buildings containing it.

Many attempts have been made to kill the sparrow, but today they remain the commonest bird in the United States. Their numbers have dropped from the days when horse droppings on city streets provided them with a regular diet of grains. Although more frequently found in urban areas than rural, they continue to reduce the number of native bird species. Control is difficult because of limited options.

The chief means of control is elimination of nesting sites. All bird houses should periodically be checked and any sparrow nests removed and discarded. The nest is a messy structure made of dry grass, string, weeds, plastic, or anything else small, readily available, and easily transported. The pieces are piled into a rounded mass with a hole in the middle. Don't just drop the materials on the ground. Sparrows can rebuild the nest in a matter of a few hours. The eggs are speckled with light brown spots. Don't be hesitant to destroy the eggs.

Purple martin houses are prime nesting sites for the sparrow. They not only take over needed sites for the martins but infest the houses with mites that are lethal to newly hatched martins. Prompt removal of all sparrow nests and yearly treatment of all cleaned sites in the spring with diatomaceous earth will help prevent mite infestation. Sparrows nest from early spring into early fall. You must remain vigilant; don't stop when the martins leave their nests in early summer. By continuing to remove nests and eggs, you can reduce the number of birds.

After martins depart in the fall, clean all nests and plug the holes until the martin scouts arrive in the spring, generally early February. At this time remove the plugs, add the diatomaceous earth, and check every week for sparrow nests. Martins are not disturbed by periodic checks and removals of their neighbors. Purple martins *Progne subis* are more and more dependent on man for their survival. We all need to work to remove as many obstacles as possible.

Another bird affected by the house sparrow is the Eastern bluebird *Sialia sialis*. Not only are nest boxes taken over, but the sparrow will destroy a nest with young to take over the box. With the bluebird's habitat decreasing, care must be taken to reduce unnatural predation by the house sparrow. Once you have watched a pair of bluebirds, you know the importance of saving their nesting sites.

Another invasive exotic is the **European starling** *Sternus vulgaris*. This bird may not be as well known or as common as the house sparrow, but it creates as much or more damage to crops and native songbirds. *S. vulgaris* is a short-tailed, blackbird-like bird, eight inches long, with a sharp bill. In flight it has a triangular look and flies swiftly and directly, not rising and falling like most blackbirds. In spring the feathers appear glossy purple and green and the bill is yellow. In winter the feathers are heavily speckled with light dots and the bill is dark, changing to yellow as spring approaches. No other "blackbird" has a yellow bill. Young starlings are dusky gray, a little like the female cowbird, but the tail is shorter and the bill longer and more spike-like. See Figure 9.

A group known as the American Acclimatization Society introduced this exotic, also native to Europe, into New York City in 1890-1891. Eugene Scheiffelin, the head of the organization, was a Shakespeare enthusiast whose goal was to introduce all birds referred to in

Figure 9. European starling in winter plumage

Shakespeare's writings. In *Henry IV*: "Nay, I'll have a starling shall be taught to speak nothing but 'Mortimer'...."

This introduction succeeded whereas earlier ones had not. For the first ten years the descendents remained in the greater New York area. With their ability to adapt to a variety of habitats, produce two nestings a year, and diverse diet, they soon expanded their range. By the 1930s they were reported in Tennessee and Wyoming, reaching Oregon by the 1950s and upper Alaska by 1970. In 1994 an estimated population of 140 million birds resulted from the original 100 birds.

Is it only coincidence that the invasion of the starling coincided with the decline and extinction of the Carolina parakeet *Conuropsis carolinensis* in Florida and the passenger pigeon *Ectopistes migratorius*? Food for thought.

The European starlings' diet is varied. Approximately half consists of insects, especially moths and butterflies and caterpillars, beetles including their larvae and grubs, crickets and grasshoppers, and earthworms. Their aggressive nature allows them first choice at the insects, greatly reducing available food for native birds. They eat a wide range of seeds, grains, and fruits, both natural and cultivated, resulting in measurable losses in agricultural regions.

Nests are bulky collections of sticks, dried grasses, and other plant fibers, paper, feathers, and similar debris built in both natural and artificial cavities. Breeding pairs will commandeer woodpecker holes and birdhouses and nest in cavities, displacing native songbirds. Starlings commonly nest in manmade structures, entering attics through torn or missing soffit or attic vents, openings where wires or plumbing enter the building, and even under loose siding. A clutch normally consists of four to six blue-green eggs. The incubation period is eleven to thirteen days, and the fledglings leave the nest at about twenty-one days of age.

The large, gregarious, and noisy flocks of thousands of birds generally roost in traditional roosts each night, damaging trees by the sheer numbers of birds. Not only is the loud noise from these flocks disturbing, but the unsightly acidic droppings can cause damage.

The most common problem associated with starlings nesting in buildings is bird mites, which will bite humans and cause a small pustule, similar to a chigger bite. Starlings have been associated with numerous bacterial and parasitic disease organisms transmissible to humans and livestock. Avoid areas covered with droppings.

Control is similar to sparrow control, only generally on a larger scale. Exclusion is always the best option to a nuisance wildlife situation since it prevents most situations from developing. Seal all openings larger than 1-inch wide where starlings might nest. Be sure the starlings have been flushed from the nest site before closing the opening. Ensure all wall openings for pipes or wires are properly sealed or caulked. Make sure all attic and soffit vents are properly screened. This not only keeps out birds but other pests such as rats, mice, and squirrels. In large open structures, like barns and warehouses, close off the space above the rafters where starlings roost and nest with industrial bird netting. In areas that cannot easily be sealed, persistent removal of the nests will eventually discourage the birds from nesting.

When putting up birdhouses for native birds, use smaller holes for smaller species and do not put perches at the entrance holes. With purple martin houses, treat the starlings as you do the sparrows, although the starlings do become discouraged more quickly than the sparrows. Depending on available material, the starling nest in the early stages may resemble a martin nest. Observe the site to make sure it is used by a starling before discarding material. The finished starling nest has a dome of nesting material similar to the sparrow nest while the martin nests never have a dome. Starlings are very aggressive around martin houses. I have watched them remove eggs and young from a nest box. Many martin houses now come with optional moon shaped openings in doors to exclude starlings.

Flocks of starlings and blackbirds often congregate in large numbers in improperly pruned trees, especially in parking lots. Trees that are trimmed to form a dense round crown become an ideal roost. Avoid this by pruning the tree to create a more natural and open growth form. Proper pruning techniques are covered in Chapter 15.

Use of traps is another option. The sieve trap and the nest box traps are effective for taking a few nuisance individuals. It is also possible to flush the starlings from the nest into a bait or insect net held in front of the nest opening. Several martin house manufacturers list appropriate traps. When starlings are trapped, dispose of in a humane fashion, such as suffocation in a plastic bag or drowning. Supply water in your trap to avoid stressing captured non-target birds and to act as an added enticement to enter the trap.

When using traps of any kind, check at least once every 24 hours and immediately release any trapped non-target birds. Native songbirds are protected by various state and federal laws and may not be killed, taken from the nest, picked up, or possessed for any reason, and their feathers may not be possessed or sold. Arts and crafts may not include these protected species under any circumstances.

Shooting is not an effective way to control a pest bird situation. In most cities the discharge of a firearm is illegal. Some municipalities even consider pellet rifles and BB guns as firearms. Before considering shooting as a control method, contact your local law enforcement agency to find out the laws in your area. Many localities have ordinances protecting birds, including such pest species as starlings, house sparrows, and pigeons. If you are legally able to use a weapon and local ordinances do not protect

starlings, use a pellet rifle or shot cartridges rather than solid bullets. The bullet from a .22 long rifle can travel over 1.5 miles. Be absolutely sure what you are shooting at and identify your back stop. A .22 bullet will go through corrugated tin, drywall, and plywood to hit anyone or anything behind it. It is prudent for anyone who plans on using a firearm to receive some type of firearm safety training.

Poisons are not a good option in an urban landscape and should be used with extreme caution at any time. Check with local authorities and local Texas cooperative extension offices for current types and usage.

Sound has been tried in many ways to scare away birds, but unless the noises are randomly discharged, birds quickly learn to ignore the sound. People have tried to get around this problem by using ultrasonic devices that produce sounds above the human threshold of hearing. Ultrasonic devices have their problems: Ultrasonic waves reflect off objects, rather than going around them, producing sound "shadows" where the birds can avoid the sound. Research at Purdue University has shown that some ultrasonic devices have caused hearing loss in dogs. In general, ultrasonic devices rarely drive pest birds from established home ranges.

Another use of sound is using recorded distress calls of the target bird species. Originally accomplished by recording calls on tape, now calls can be digitally stored on a chip and programmed to be played in a random pattern. While birds may eventually learn to recognize that particular call over time and ignore it, this type of auditory scare device may prove effective longer than previous startle device technology.

Effigies ("scarecrows") have been used to control starling damage. Models of owls, hawks, snakes, and cats have all been used. To keep these "scarecrows" effective they must appear life-like and be moved often so the birds do not become accustomed to seeing them in the same spot every day. The use of balloons with eye-spots, kites with hawk silhouettes, and streamers are more effective because they are in constant motion. Mylar streamers are especially effective near roost sites: The lightweight streamers blow around in the slightest wind and make birds very nervous, especially when the long streamers reach out toward or touch the roosting birds.

Roosting flocks of starlings and blackbirds can be driven from roost sites where they are creating a nuisance by harassing the flock at dusk for three or four consecutive nights or until they find a different roost. Spraying the birds with water from a hose or by mounting a sprinkler in the roost tree will encourage the birds to move on. Shaking the tree, if it is small, using fireworks, or beating on metal pans can also be used. Start harassment as soon as the birds begin roosting. Don't wait until the roost is well established and the birds develop a strong attachment for the site. Be persistent until the problem is solved.

The starling and the house sparrow are exotic, non-native species in North America, listed as unprotected species by the U.S. Fish & Wildlife Service. The birds, their eggs, and nests may be removed by any method except by poison, steel traps, or with guns and lights at night. Some municipalities have issued local ordinances that protect all birds, both exotic and native. Be sure to check with local authorities before starting any bird control activities.

Working with nature effectively often will require being ruthless and appearing hard hearted. Man, for one reason or another, has caused environmental harm, and sometimes seemingly drastic actions are required to undo the damage. Exotic species whether plant or animal, do not have natural predators to control their numbers. Man has to take on the role of predator if the native species are to survive. Whenever I feel squeamish about dispatching a starling or emptying a sparrow nest, all I have to do is look at the sun glistening off the purple martin's feathers as he gracefully glides to catch a mosquito. I perform my duty without another thought.

CHAPTER 11

INTEGRATED PEST MANAGEMENT
GOOD vs. BAD

eginning with the first agricultural practices, Texans have dealt with pests. The differing ecoregions and varying climate have enabled exotic pests along with native species to reach disastrous numbers at times. An estimated 25,000 to 30,000 insect species live in Texas, and experts believe there are several yet unidentified species. This number includes 6,000 beetles and 5,000 moths and butterflies but does not include other pests such as fungus and plant viruses and bacteria. The majority of these insects are not harmful but are beneficial to the ecosystems they inhabit.

The few true pests do impact agriculture and other areas of the economy. An estimated one-third of agricultural crops worth ten million dollars are lost to pests yearly. Insects also damage forest lands and can carry disease to man and livestock. To counter these losses man has created an estimated 35,000 products to control insects, fungi, weeds, and other pests.

The first and best know synthetic pesticide is DDT dichlorodiphenyltrichloroethane. DDT was first isolated in Germany in 1874, but it took until 1939 for Paul Muller, Swiss Nobel Prize winner, to discover it was a potent nerve poison on insects. Cheap, easy to use, and potent long after application, DDT was labeled "the Atomic bomb of the insect world." Used widely and indiscriminately during and after

World War II, it did at first show positive results. In Sri Lanka malaria cases dropped from three million to 7,300 in the decade between 1946 and 1956. American farmers converted from lead arsenate, the leading insecticide before the war, to DDT.

As early as 1946 DDT started to show its sinister side. Insects began to show resistance to the chemicals. The slow-to-degrade chemicals accumulated to lethal levels in the food chain, killing fish and birds and, most ominously, began to concentrate in mothers' milk and human fat.

In 1962 *Silent Spring* by Rachel Carson galvanized the world, calling attention to the damage and long-term effects of the indiscriminate use of all synthetic pesticides primarily DDT. Federal pesticide regulations were toughened, and in 1970 enforcement was taken from the Department of Agriculture and given to the new Environmental Protection Agency. DDT was banned in the United States in 1972, but many countries still use it. Proponents of DDT claim the harmful effects are far outweighed by the number of lives saved from malaria and other insect borne diseases. This controversy continues today and is beyond the scope of this book.

Many other synthetic pesticides followed DDT and are now banned in the United States. To reduce the use of the remaining synthetic pesticides, the use of "organic" pesticides has been encouraged. Organic or natural pesticides defined as ones derived from once living matter are often considered "safe" but are not necessarily. Some of the most potent poisons in the world are organic. Nicotine, used commonly until replaced by the synthetics in popularity, is one of the most toxic of all poisons and acts quickly. Marketed under the label "Black Leaf 40" it was advertised as "An Effective and Economical Insecticide for Plants-Animals-Poultry." Many deaths were reported yearly due to nicotine poisoning. Yes, this is the same nicotine found in cigarettes. And yes, cigarettes are poisonous. Several documented deaths have resulted from children eating cigarette butts. Another topic for another time.

Other natural pesticides are also toxic to humans including rotenone. The pyrethrins derived from chrysanthemums can cause allergic reactions. Many organics do not differentiate harmful from helpful insects, destroying natural predators. Organics are safer for the environment because they will degrade rapidly and be recycled. Return to organic pesticides is not the complete answer.

Insect resistance to pesticides is increasing. Over 400 species of insects and mites are resistant to pesticides, more than twice as many as in 1965. Harvest yields have almost doubled, and use of insect poisons has grown ten-fold since 1945. However, insects annually eat twice as much crop as in 1945. Ninety percent of American households use pesticides in house, yard, or garden, but even scrubbing with soapy water may not remove skin absorption of some of these chemicals.

The World Health Organization estimates three million acute pesticide poisonings occur yearly worldwide, resulting in about 220,000 deaths. In the United States, the poison control centers compile statistics annually and show pesticide exposures as a separate category but did not differentiate agricultural and nonagricultural exposures until the establishment of the Food Quality Protection Act (FQPA) in August 1996. The summarized reports for 1991-1995 show pesticides responsible for about 4 percent of all reported poisonings and fertilizers implicated in 8,000 to 10,000 reported exposures per year. The FQPA not only differentiates agricultural and nonagricultural uses but also looks at total exposure due to similar families of pesticides, i.e., organophosphates, carbamals, etc. This additional information is the reason dursban, diazanon, and acephate are no longer available.

Total use of all agrochemicals is difficult to estimate because nonagricultural use is poorly quantified. The U.S. EPA determines pesticide usage to be about 1.2 billion pounds of conventional pesticides used annually in the U.S. with an estimated 77 percent used in agriculture. In Texas homeowners pour about four million of these pounds on lawns and gardens. More pesticides and fertilizers, an estimated eight to ten times as much, per square inch are applied to a typical yard than to the most intensely sprayed farmland. An estimated one-third of the home-use pesticides are wasted through improper use.

Overused pesticides and fertilizers in the Houston home landscape run off into the storm drains, creeks, bayous, and rivers, ending up in Galveston Bay. This runoff pollution is the number one source of water pollution in most of the state's watershed. Every year the amount of runoff is equal to one half of the total spill of the Exxon

Valdez in Alaska! This "non-point source" pollution is insidious. No one source can be found and stopped.

The prolonged and improper use of pesticides creates a counterproductive cycle that destroys beneficial insects and microorganisms, requiring more chemicals to kill. This cycle wastes time and money, is self perpetuating, and should be stopped.

Three Principles of IPM

Integrated Pest Management (IPM) is a viable solution to the hazards and problems created by pesticides of all kinds. IPM began as a named system in 1972 as a result of cotton producers in the state working with Texas A&M University to solve the dilemma of pesticide resistant cotton insects. The use of the synthetic pesticides had created voracious populations of boll weevil and tobacco budworms. IPM has had a significant impact on the agricultural practices in the state with reduction of up to 70 percent in pesticide use on some crops.

IPM principles have been shown to work in agriculture and can and should be applied to all home landscapes. IPM is an approach to pest control that utilizes regular monitoring to determine if and when treatments are needed and uses physical, mechanical, cultural, biological, and educational tactics to keep pest numbers low enough to prevent intolerable damage or annoyance. IPM has increased in importance with the establishment of FQPA and the loss of additional chemicals.

IPM means different things to different people. Environmentalists refer to it as a system that uses no chemicals; gardeners tend to use it in its original context; and some pest control operators use it loosely to cover their routine application of chemicals. Unlike conventional pest control methods where pesticides are applied on a rigid schedule, IPM applies only those controls needed, when needed, to control identified pests that cause damage above the acceptance level. Ask questions before hiring someone to apply IPM methods to your landscape.

Monitoring is the most important and individual step. Each gardener has his own idea of how much damage is tolerable. When pest damage (insect, weed, fungal, bacterial, etc.) is observed, it is important to identify the pest and stage of development before deciding a course of treatment.

Early identification is essential.

Insects are the most diverse terrestrial animals on earth, found in all terrestrial ecosystems and freshwater habitats in the world. In ecological communities they fill the roles of predators, herbivores, scavengers, and detritivores. They are essential components of all ecosystems. Only a relative few are considered true pests, making proper identification very important. However, even with the large number of insects, the plant damage may not be due to insects. Fungus, bacteria, viruses, and environmental conditions can all cause damage.

Finding the cause of the yellow leaf, strange spot, or hole is the first step. Observing the offender is the best way. Identify before using any elimination process. The insect may be a predator and not the one who ate the leaf. Several good identification books (see Appendix A) are available.

With only a relatively few harmful insects in an area, soon the worst can easily be identified. Before removing, look for predators. All the native and most of the exotics do have predators. If predators are present, consider leaving a few of the pest insects to keep predators around. Once predators such as assassin bugs, lady beetles, lacewings, praying mantis, and wasps are attracted to one insect population, they will remain in the area as long as prey is available.

This is where the second principle of IPM applies and the individual variations occur. A few holes in leaves can be tolerated to maintain a pest population to control a large range of insects. Individuals set the amount of damage tolerated. When the level of damage exceeds the set limit, then is the time to consider the third IPM principle.

Appropriate strategies and steps to reduce the offenders require not only identification of the pest, but also the stage of development and the time of year. Aphid infestation resulting in sooty mold on crepe myrtles should not be treated in the fall when trees will soon drop leaves naturally. To treat with anything is a waste of time and money. The aphids will die over the winter, and new leaves will appear in the spring.

Caterpillar damage is common on many native species of plants and trees. Remember, caterpillars are one stage of the butterfly and will soon be gone. If the plant is a native, it will recover without your help and produce new leaves and blossoms for the butterflies.

By leaving the caterpillars, you promote the beautiful butterflies to add color and movement to your landscape.

Weeds are a major concern, especially before a landscape is established. Many of the worst weeds are exotics and should be removed; however, remember that a weed is only a plant in the wrong place. Identification again is key, and the stage of development is important. Herbicides need to be applied when the weed is actively growing, drawing nutrients into the leaves and roots. Once the plant blooms and starts to set seeds, the herbicides only hasten seed formation. The weed will die after setting seeds with or without the herbicide, and the herbicide will not kill the seeds. The best method at this stage is digging before seeds have a chance to disperse. Prevention with heavy mulches and good soil preparation is the best weed treatment.

If the damage is determined to not be insects, the level of damage and treatments vary. Viral diseases are difficult to treat, and usually the best method is to remove the infected plant and discard to prevent spread of the disease. Most viruses are specific to a plant family and will only spread within that family. Do not replant a member of the same family in a spot previously infected with virus.

Bacteria are easier to treat than viruses but do require identification. Texas A&M has a plant disease identification lab. Samples can be submitted for identification. Contact local Texas Cooperative Extension offices for additional information.

Fungal diseases can be confused with environmental problems but are usually more symmetrical in spot formation. Plant disease labs are the best method of identification. Good "housekeeping" is necessary to reduce fungal spread. Spores transmitted by air and water droplets are methods of spreading fungus. By keeping infected leaves and plant debris away from the base of the plants, this spread can be reduced.

Red tip photinia *Photinia fraseri* is often infected with fungal leaf spot, causing spots on the leaves, yellowing, and finally leaf drop. This disease is difficult to treat with fungicides, requiring repeated sprayings that often only slow down the infection. This is an exotic from China not adapted to any part of Texas, although it is heavily promoted. Keeping dead leaves removed from under the shrub, watering without splashing, and not stressing can reduce the disease, but the best treatment is removal and replacement with a native. Wax myrtle *Myricaceae cerifera* has about the same size leaf and is evergreen; although it does not have red leaves, it also does not have leaves that turn yellow and fall off. Once again natives avoid a pest management situation.

Environmental damage requires a little detective work. Wilting, yellow leaves can be caused by too much or too little water. Yellow leaves with green veins may be due to lack of iron in the soil. Roots growing around the plant and strangling it may cause stunted growth and leaf drop. Misapplication or drift from herbicides can mimic disease or environmental damage. Examine all possibilities before spraying with anything. A soil analysis may be helpful. Relocating the plant or modifying the soil may be the best solution.

A healthy garden and landscape is the primary way to utilize nature and implement IPM. Diversity is nature's way to prevent intolerable predator damage. The more varieties of plants the less likely for a pest to reach damaging proportions. The diversity encourages and promotes the natural predators. Healthy "happy"

plants, like healthy humans, are more capable of combating disease with built-in defense mechanisms. A plant struggling to survive does not have this capability.

Eliminating Pests

When a pest problem is observed and identified, use the least toxic method of elimination first. Mechanical and physical methods are the first course of action. A strong spray of water will reduce numbers of aphids and other soft-bodied insects and spider mites to tolerable levels. The insects are displaced from the safety of the leaves to be eaten by predators or desiccated by the sun. The spraying may have to be repeated several times but will work.

Hand picking large insects such as tomato hornworms, slugs, and snails and dropping into a container of soapy water or vegetable oil works well. Wearing gloves is recommended because many insects have spines or secret oily substances that can cause injury or allergic reactions. The "two-brick" method is an alternate method. This classic procedure involves centering the insect between two bricks or blocks of wood and squishing. A certain satisfaction can be gained from forcibly eliminating the offender. I find this works well with leaf-footed stink bugs, both adults and nymphs.

Small vacuums can be used to suck up the pest. Models specific for this use are available commercially. **Traps** are available; the ones using pheromones, naturally occurring sex-based chemicals produced by the insects, are species specific. This type of trap may attract more pests so, although very effective, it is recommended that the trap not be placed too close to the infested plant. The more generic sticky traps attract numerous species. Check the traps to be sure they are not entrapping beneficial insects. The sticky traps are also a good method of monitoring, especially in small, enclosed gardens or greenhouses.

Do not use the "bug zappers." These kill many more beneficial, harmless insects and small night creatures than mosquitoes or other pests.

Barriers can prevent infestation. Row cover, a white spun polyester fabric, works well in vegetable gardens. Applied in the early spring, the cover blocks pests such as leaf miners, cabbage loopers, some vine borers, and insects that transmit viral and bacterial diseases. The cover does need to be removed when the vegetables start to bloom to allow pollination to occur. By this time the plants should be large enough to combat some of the pests.

Diatomaceous earth (DE) can be used as a barrier around gardens or plants. DE is made from the shells of single-celled algae called diatoms that lived more than 25 million years ago. These ancient aquatic creatures built protective shells around themselves from silica in seawater. When the diatoms died, their shells fell to the ocean floor. Over millions of years these shells formed large deposits now mined to produce diatomaceous earth. The mined product is ground into a fine talc-like powder or dust containing approximately 85 percent silica. These needles spear the bodies of pests, causing dehydration. If eaten by a pest, the needles interfere with breathing, digestion, and reproduction. The material is not harmful to people or animals unless inhaled in large quantities. A mask should be worn when handling. The material is most effective when dry and should be reapplied when it becomes wet. Diatomaceous earth is effective against slugs, snails, and soft-bodied insects.

Beer traps are also effective for slugs and snails; however, due to the size of the slugs and snails in the southern regions, a deep dish at least 2-3 inches is recommended to hold the beer. Shallow dishes only allow the happy creatures to slither away and return the next night. A true Texan may want to use a long-neck beer bottle with a small amount left in the bottom. Place the bottle on its side in an area frequented by slugs. After imbibing, even the large ones have difficulty finding their way home.

Pathogens are naturally occurring bacteria that attack specific host pests. *Bacillus thuringiensis* (BT) products are the most common and fastest growing pathogen based products. This bacteria found commonly in the soil and harmless to man is a stomach poison that paralyzes the digestive tract of the host organism. The first BT created affects caterpillars including cabbage worms, cabbage loopers, tent caterpillars, and hornworms. The caterpillars need to eat only small amounts of a treated leaf for the dose to be fatal. Within a few hours of ingestion the caterpillar stops eating and dies within one to three days. Death is not instantaneous, but the damage will stop. Monitor

before reapplying. This product does not discriminate among caterpillars. Be sure you want to eliminate the caterpillar you are spraying. Identify that caterpillar!

Bacillus thuringiensis "San Diego" is specific for young larvae of the Colorado potato beetle, and *Bacillus thuringiensis israelensis* (BTI) is toxic to mosquito larvae and is the main ingredient in the mosquito dunks discussed in Chapter 9. Other BT products are also available.

Predators and Parasites

Predators and parasites are nature's defense force and are present in most gardens where pesticides have not been heavily used. Once pesticide usage is stopped in an area, it will take time for the normal population of predators and parasites to return. Monitoring during this transition time is even more important. Every time a harsh treatment is applied, the time to recover is lengthened.

The most common beneficial or "good bugs" are the parasitic wasps, praying mantis, lady beetles, assassin and wheel bugs, lacewings, and parasitic nematodes. Many beneficials are available through mail order or at

Beneficial Bugs

parasitic wasps
praying mantis
lady beetles
assassin and wheel bugs
lacewings
parasitic nematodes

your local garden supply. Since these insects are mobile, once released there is no guarantee they will remain in your yard. Learning about the beneficial before release may help it to remain longer in your landscape.

Numerous tiny **wasps** parasitize different stages of other insects by developing larval stages inside and outside the host insect, resulting in the death of the host. Many wasps are host specific, developing in one or a limited number of related species. The *Trichogramma* wasps are very tiny (1/25 inch) wasps that attack eggs of over 200 different pests. This tiny wasp will never be noticed in the garden but is there. To promote growth avoid sprays containing pyrethrum and electric bug zappers.

Praying mantids are one of the best-known predators with several species found in Texas. They are cannibalistic, feeding heavily on their own kind, so very few survive. The survivors prefer slow-moving prey like crickets, bees, and grasshoppers, which tend to be minor pests in much of the state. They are not effective for aphids, mites, or caterpillars, making them of minor benefit to the gardener.

Lady beetles, ladybugs, or ladybird beetles are one of the most beneficial insects. The larvae is a voracious eater of aphids, scale, and insect eggs. The larvae looks nothing like the adult but is a small, approximately ¼-inch long, ridged caterpillar-looking creature, sometimes referred to as an "alligator," usually darkly colored interspersed with differing patterns and color depending on species. Release purchased adult insects at night into a recently watered garden to retain a higher percentage of these highly mobile beetles.

Assassin and **wheel bugs** are medium to large ferocious-looking insects with long "beaks" that are used to spear insects and suck out the juices. These insects occur naturally when aphids are present and insecticides are not used. A resident population of aphids helps keep the insects once they arrive. Avoid handling these predators as "spearing" can be painful.

Green **lacewings** are voracious predators both as adults and larvae, attacking any soft-bodied insect encountered. Favorite foods are small worms, insect eggs, mites, immature whitefly, and aphids. The adults are light green about ¼ inch long with prominent paired lacey wings. The larvae are similar to lady beetle larvae and gray-green in color. Several species are native to Texas. Lacewings are common where pesticides are not in use.

Parasitic nematodes are microscopic roundworms similar to the pest nematodes, but they feed on insect larvae, soft-bodied insects, and almost any living creature found in the soil. Beneficial nematodes are available by mail or in garden centers and are easy to apply following label instructions. Moisture is very important for their survival, so it is important to keep soil moist after their release. When the nematodes no longer have a food source, they will die off without leaving any harmful residue in the soil or water supply.

Don't forget the birds. Attract bug-eating birds to your garden by providing plants to meet their needs. Habitat requirements are covered in Chapter 5, Texas Wildscapes. By planting specific plants to provide food and shelter for birds like wrens, vireos, warblers, swallows, martins, finches, chickadees, and bluebirds, you can encourage the birds to remain in your landscape dining on your pests. The birds may also eat beneficial insects as sometimes one "good bug" will eat another "good bug," but in the end the pest population will remain within tolerable limits, and you have the added enjoyment of watching the increased activity.

Biological Controls

The next line of defense are the organic, natural, or biological controls. The least toxic of this group are the insecticidal soaps. These are mild contact pesticides made from potassium salts of fatty acids. They control a wide range of soft-bodied pests such as aphids, whiteflies, and spider mites by destroying their membranes and nervous systems. They are biodegradable and harmless to humans and most beneficial insects. The soap sprays may burn leaves and should never be applied in the sun. Read labels to make sure they are appropriate for infected plant.

Sulfur and copper are naturally occurring soil elements and have been used as fungicides for centuries. They control many common plant diseases, including powdery mildew, rusts, rose black spot, and anthracnose. High levels of sulfur and copper can be harmful to plants and soil life. These fungicides are preventatives and will not cure a disease problem once it appears. As with all substances, carefully follow label directions.

Botanical sprays are plant derived extracts with proven insecticidal properties. The most common sprays are pyrethrum, sabadilla, rotenone, ryania, nicotine sulfate, citrus oil, and neem oil.

Pyrethrum derived from the flowers of several chrysanthemum species causes rapid paralysis of most insects. Some people do have allergic reactions to this product. Pyrethrins are toxic to fish. Be careful around water.

Sabadilla is obtained from the seed of a lily-like plant and works as both a contact and a stomach poison for a wide variety of insects. Although not particularly toxic to mammals, the dust can irritate the eyes and respiratory tract. A mask should be worn when applying this pesticide.

Rotenone is made from the roots of derris plants from Asia and cube plants from South America. It is a broad-spectrum insecticide considered moderately toxic to man and most animals, causing respiratory irritation and allergic reactions, and highly toxic to fish and birds. Residues remain on plant parts for approximately one week.

Ryania from the stems of a woody South American shrub, *Ryania speciosa*, is a broad-spectrum stomach poison moderately toxic to man and water life.

Nicotine sulfate is a highly toxic alkaloid extract from tobacco used to control most soft-bodied insects. Because of high toxicity to man, it is not recommended for routine use.

Neem oil is from the tropical neem tree *Azadirachta indica* found widely distributed in Asia and Africa and closely related to the chinaberry tree *Melia azadarach* in Texas. It acts as a broad-spectrum repellant, growth regulator, and insect poison with both contact and systemic action by making plants unpalatable to insects, but it is considered almost nontoxic to mammals. If pests still attack, it inhibits their ability to molt and lay eggs.

Citrus oil, d-limonene, a naturally occurring substance found in citrus, has been shown to be non-toxic to man, but slightly toxic to aquatic life. The substance is

Botanical Sprays

pyrethrum
sabadilla
rotenone
ryania
nicotine sulfate
citrus oil
neem oil

used in many compounds as either an inert or an active ingredient with broad-spectrum action.

When selecting a pesticide, avoid the urge to buy the larger container because it is cheaper by the ounce. Buy only what is needed for the current infestation. Read the label of all commercial products very carefully, and follow them completely. This is not the time or place to apply the adage "if a little is good, more is better." Following this is a waste of time and money, and leads to destruction of the ecosystem. Remember, just because a product is organic does not mean it is "safe." Use safety precautions when applying any pesticide.

Follow the IPM system. Know your insects. Place a field guide next to the spray bottle for quick, easy reference to be sure you are not intending to kill a "friend." The dead bug is *not* the only good bug!

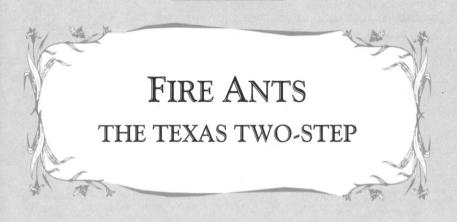

FIRE ANTS
THE TEXAS TWO-STEP

The red imported fire ant *Solenopsis invicta*, an important pest across much of the state, affects agriculture, humans, and the environment. Texans spend hundreds of millions of dollars to control this exotic escapee in home landscapes, recreation areas, and agriculture each year.

Suggestions have been made that the imported fire ants are not all bad. Studies have shown they feed on boll weevils, cotton bollworms, and fleas. But these "benefits" are far outweighed by the damage created. A 1998 study showed average costs of $151 to each homeowner and over $525 million to the five major urban areas in Texas (San Antonio, Houston, Fort Worth, Dallas, and Austin) to control fire ants in lawns, gardens, and homes. This figure includes money lost on repairs and medical treatments due to fire ant stings. Fire ants also cause reduced property values, structural damage, and indirectly contaminated water systems due to pesticide overuse or misuse. Fire ants infest electrical equipment, such as air conditioners, traffic boxes, and airport runway lights. Stinging incidents can result in costly tort liability claims.

An agricultural survey between 1997 and 1999 showed losses of over $90 million. Fire ants sting calves and other domestic animals, resulting in increased veterinary expenses, decreased animal quality, blindness, or death. A recent cattle producers' survey found that the beef cattle industry alone suffered losses of around $67 million annually. Fire ants feed on seeds, young plants, fruits, and other plant parts of crops, affect harvesting equipment, damage electrical and irrigation systems, and deter hand labor harvesting. Insecticides available to prevent these problems are limited and often too costly to use.

Fire ants alter the ecological balance by damaging plants and reducing food sources for native ant species, other insects, seed eating birds, and amphibians. Hazards to wildlife due to predation by the insect include loss of quail and other ground nesting birds and death of fawns and other newly born animals. Damage to natural resources increases due to people applying their own pesticides in public places without authorization.

Fire ants have altered the behavior patterns and activities of hunters, ranchers, and participants of other outdoor activities. In some areas, it is impossible to sit in the grass or stand on a shoreline to fish without being stung. This situation discourages tourism and poses liability concerns to owners and managers of public areas. For example, an estimated $545,400 is spent annually on controlling fire ant-infested golf courses.

Dr. William F. Buren, an entomologist at the University of Florida who named the ant *S. invicta*, believed the fire ant could not be eradicated—only controlled. *Invicta* means unconquered. In 1995 the correct name for the red imported fire ant was discovered to be *Solenopsis wagneri*. A taxonomist discovered the name *wagneri* on a museum specimen dated earlier than the *S. invicta* designation. By international rules of nomenclature, the earlier name has priority. However, with the characteristics of the imported fire ant, the name *invicta* will probably be retained and is used in this book to refer to the red imported fire ant.

Several species of native fire ants live in Texas. The native fire ants are very similar to the imported pest but actually help slow the spread of the imported species and should be spared if possible. Both native and imported fire ants are small, dark orange/brown ants with workers of various sizes that quickly mobilize and sting *en masse* when their mound is disturbed. Other than the much larger "red harvester" or "Texas red ant," which has no variation in worker size and is conspicuous on its trails and around its flat open mound entrance, most other stinging, ground-dwelling ants in Texas are encountered as solitary individuals.

Ants that resemble the imported pest, *Solenopsis invicta*, include *Solenopsis geminata* and *S. xyloni*. The latter species is found near rivers, creeks, and stock tanks in drier parts of the state. Workers that boil out from disturbed mounds of the native *geminata* are generally the same range of sizes as the pest species of fire ants, *S. invicta*, but the large workers have heads that are considerably wider than their abdomens. This distinction is less pronounced in *S. xyloni*. Because not all fire ants are the pest species, distinguishing native from imported is an important first step before proceeding with chemical treatment.

The imported exotic from Brazil is believed to have arrived on a freighter in Mobil, Alabama, before 1930, probably as part of the ballast. Beginning soon after the Second World War and in conjunction with the housing boom of

Fire ants alter the ecological balance by damaging plants and reducing food sources for native ant species, other insects, seed eating birds, and amphibians.

the period, the imported fire ant began its march across the South, the spread due largely to the movement of grass sod and woody ornamental plants used in landscaping. This inadvertent movement was noted by the U.S. Department of Agriculture in 1953 when a direct link was established between commercial plant nurseries and the spread of imported fire ants. In response to mounting public pressure, the U.S. Congress appropriated $2.4 million in 1957 for control and eradication efforts. As part of an overall plan a quarantine was imposed to retard or prevent the artificial dissemination of these now notorious pests.

On May 6, 1958, regulations governing the movement of nursery stock, grass sod, and other items were instituted through the Federal Quarantine 301.81. By that time, however, imported fire ants had moved into eight southern states. By 1980 the fire ants had infected 200 million acres from Texas to the Carolinas. By 1996 the infected acres had increased to 300 million across the South. In Texas by

Figure 9. Fire ant distribution in Texas—Texas A&M University

1997, 56 million acres were determined to be home to the stinging pest. See Figure 9.

This spread, although slowed considerably by federal regulations and climatic conditions, continues today. In recent years isolated infestations of imported fire ants have been found as far west as California and as far north as Kansas and Maryland. This increase occurred in spite of diligent efforts to, if not eliminate, at least reduce the numbers.

To achieve control of the fire ant, the first step is to understand how it lives, forages, and reproduces. Fire ants live and do most of their foraging for food through underground tunnels. A nest consists of a network of tunnels and chambers that occupy a vertical column 12-18 inches in diameter and approximately 36 inches deep. The tunnels can extend several feet from the main column before reaching the surface. After cool, rainy weather in spring and fall, the ants clear blocked tunnels and expand chambers to create a conspicuous mound of loose soil above the nest. The colony dwells in this aboveground extension when the temperature there is optimal for brood development. Though aboveground mounds harden and persist in some soil types, their absence does not mean fire ants are not present or receding. A colony can exist for several months before visible signs appear on the surface.

Imported fire ant queens produce new queens year round, and in Texas mounds often contain multiple queens. Imported fire ants disperse naturally through mating flights, colony movement, or by rafting to new sites during periodic floods. All are strategies to ensure survival.

Out of distrust, revenge, desperation, or a hope for quick profits, countless remedies have been used in attempts to eradicate fire ants. Encouraging a few fire ant colonies to abandon mounds in a yard is relatively easy. Even regular watering can cause a colony to move. However, safely and economically eliminating hundreds or thousands of fire ant colonies from parks, farms, and ranches has proved to be nearly impossible. Remedies against fire ants that are effective in a backyard will not solve the overall problem across the countryside because no effective and safe measure has proved to be economically feasible or sustainable on the grander scale.

Mirex was the first insecticide used until banned by the EPA in 1978 after fifteen years of use. The chemical, discovered to cause cancer and birth defects in laboratory mice, had been found in human tissue samples collected in the South. Mirex did kill fire ants but also destroyed the native predatory ants *Solenopsis geminata*, enabling the prolific fire ants to reinfest a sprayed area as the predominate species.

A second product, Ferriamicide, lasted only two weeks in 1979 before being removed as more toxic than Mirex. With the establishment of the Food Quality Protection Act, increased testing, and environmental awareness, chemical products effective for control are constantly being removed from the market. The banning of these chemicals is good for the environment and has increased testing of safer and in the long run more effective treatments for the fire ant.

In 1997 the Texas legislature approved a fire ant research and management plan using IPM methods. The plan spends $2.5 million annually on research, education, and community-wide controls and coordinates efforts of institutions and agencies such as the Texas Agricultural Experiment Station, the Texas Cooperative Extension, the Texas Department of Agriculture, Texas Tech University, the University of Texas, and the Texas Parks and Wildlife Department. The goal is to provide both short-term and long-term solutions to the fire ant problem.

Biological control methods using parasitic flies and other insects, mating disruption, and genetic solutions are all being studied as possible long-term solutions. Short-term solutions have been developed using community-wide IPM methods with the "The Texas Two-Step Method."

Two-Step Fire Ant Control

The "Do-It-Yourself Fire Ant Control for Homes & Neighborhoods" program is a result of the Texas Imported Fire Ant Research and Management Plan. The Texas Two-Step Method is the right plan, and with a little persistence and patience fire ants can be controlled. Step one requires broadcasting a bait over the area. Step two is to treat the individual mounds.

Step 1

A bait is an insecticide that insects sense to be food. In the case of ants, workers find the bait particles and carry them back to the colony, where the fourth instar larval stage ingests the bait. This stage of development is the only one to eat solid food. All other members of the colony including the queen eat the "nutritious" fluid excreted by this stage. This fluid contains the active ingredients of the bait and by various means of action, breaks the life cycle of the colony, which eventually dies out. Fast acting types of insecticides kill queens and some workers. Insect growth regulator types do not kill workers but disrupt the colony life cycle, so that workers die of natural causes and are not replaced.

Baits work slowly compared to individual mound treatments. If baits kill fire ants too fast, the foragers might not make it back to the mound and sick workers would be removed before the active ingredient reached the queens—the ultimate target for colony elimination.

Baits have advantages and disadvantages. The slow speed is both. The advantage is that the active ingredient reaches most of the ants and many of the colonies in a treated area before it noticeably affects them. Even the smallest colonies will probably pick up an effective dose even if the mound is not visible. Baits have many advantages over contact poisons—cost, in most cases. Baits are the least expensive method both for product and labor to distribute. Fire ants are controlled in an area for a longer period. Toxicity is minimal to humans and to the environment. And maybe most important, baits work more with nature by catering to the voracious omnivorous appetite of the foreign ant. The

The Texas Two-Step Method is the right plan, and with a little persistence and patience fire ants can be controlled.

bait base is preferred food for the fire ant. The workers will select the bait over other available food. The native fire ant species will check out the bait but leave it until the last to carry back to the nest. However, the bait will kill native fire ants. This characteristic allows less disruption of the native mounds and provides them an advantage over the imported species.

Fire ant bait is a product containing a food plus an insecticide. A number of fire ant baits are commercially available for broadcast treatments. Conventionally formulated baits are composed of an inert pregelled corn carrier and soybean oil with the incorporated toxicant (either a slow-acting insecticide or an insect growth regulator). Less pesticide is needed with baits because of the efficiency of delivery. Baits work best when scattered lightly over the whole yard. Push-type spreaders put out baits too quickly. Hand-held spreaders are ideal set on the smallest opening. Make one or more passes to obtain even distribution over the area to be treated. Read the product label for exact rate to apply, usually 1 to 1½ pounds per acre or 1 to 1½ ounces per 13,000 square feet. This light distribution allows the particles to fall into and under leaves, hiding them from birds and other possibly interested feeders. The toxicity is low for any creature other than ants, and the widely spread particles aid in preventing possible contamination.

Baits require patience. Products containing hydramethylnon or spinosad work the fastest, controlling fire ants within two to four weeks. Insect growth regulator baits such as fenoxycarb, pyriproxifen, and methoprene usually require two to six months. New baits are being formulated all the time with some of the newest fermentation products of bacteria and fungus that qualify as natural or organic baits. Read the labels carefully to determine which toxicant or insecticide is used in the formulation.

Apply baits at the right time for maximum effectiveness, only when ants are foraging. Fire ants search for food when the soil surface temperature is between 70 and 90 degrees F., generally April-May and September-October in most of Texas. To determine if fire ants are active, place a small amount of suitable food—potato chip or a few grains of bait—next to a mound without disturbing the mound. If fire ants begin removing the food within 30 minutes, they are feeding and it is a good time to spread bait. Fall applications work well to reduce numbers the following spring; however, baits are rarely picked up during the winter months or mid-summer July and August.

A few tips to make baits more effective: In summer apply in the evening. During the day in extreme heat, baits quickly lose their effectiveness and fire ants do not forage. Use only fresh bait. Once opened, baits should be used quickly. Opened baits may last only a few weeks; unopened containers stay fresh up to two years. To test baits for freshness, sprinkle a small amount next to an active mound. If the bait is fresh, fire ants will begin removing within 30 minutes. Lastly, apply baits when no rain is forecast for at least eight hours to reduce the risk of the bait being washed away.

Step 2

One week to ten days after baiting, treat fire ant colonies needing immediate attention i.e., many workers left, by treating individual mounds. This is the fastest way to eliminate a mound and is suggested for mounds located next to house foundations, in high traffic areas, or other trouble spots. Several options are available for this step: shoveling, boiling water, organic products, dry powders, liquid drenches, and granular products.

Shoveling, literally removing by digging out, can be used to disturb or move colonies from gardens, compost piles, or other areas where pesticides cannot be used. Wear rubber gloves and liberally dust the gloves and shovel with talcum powder. The powder creates a slippery surface that ants cannot climb. The captured colony can be destroyed by carefully dousing with soapy water. Do not pile on top of another mound. This will only increase the size of the mound. After a slight disturbance the workers will accept the new queen or queens and continue on with life.

Boiling water at the rate of three gallons per mound will eliminate colonies. Caution needs to be used with this method to prevent burns to the person carrying the water and damage to surrounding vegetation. Boiling water poured on grass or over plant roots can be lethal.

Several organic or plant derived products are available for fire ant control. Some contain citrus oil (d-limonene), pyrethrins, rotenone, or pine oil. Mix with water according to label directions and pour on mounds. Some organic products act more slowly than "chemical" pesticides.

Baits as used in Step 1 can also be used for mound treatments but are slower acting than other treatments. For nests located next to sidewalks and curbs where the colony extends under the concrete, baits are often more effective.

Dry dust treatments containing various active ingredients do not require addition of water; however, a light watering to settle the dust will prevent the powder from dispersing in the air or coming in contact with passing feet. Sprinkle the dust lightly and evenly over the mound without disturbing the mound. Any disturbance can cause the ants to move without coming in contact with the poison. This is a chemical pesticide, and it is best to keep pets and children away from the site until the dust is gone.

Liquid drenches are pesticides mixed with water first and then applied directly to the mound. One to two gallons of water is recommended per mound. Always wear chemical resistant, unlined gloves to protect skin when handling liquid concentrates and follow label directions.

Granular products contain an insecticide that releases into the soil, usually when drenched with water. Sprinkle the recommended amount of product around and on top of the mound. According to label directions, sprinkle one to two gallons of water over the granules with a watering can. Sprinkle gently to avoid disturbing the colony and washing the granules off the mound. Add water slowly starting at the outside edge of the colony in a circular motion until the center of the colony is reached.

Be Responsible with Pesticides

Whichever products you choose to control fire ants—respect the environment! Never use gasoline or other petroleum products for fire ant control. Although gasoline will kill fire ants, it is extremely flammable and dangerous to you and to the environment. Don't leave insecticide granules on streets or sidewalks after application. They will be washed into the storm drains. Follow label directions when disposing of extra pesticides and containers. Never pour leftovers down the drain. This can cause contamination of

streams and endanger aquatic life. Use all insecticides according to label directions before discarding the container.

In urban areas, working with neighbors to reduce fire ant populations is more effective than individuals alone. This reduces movement between yards and slows reinfestation. Fire ants will probably never be eliminated, but by understanding the most effective treatments and with patience and persistence, the numbers and damage created can be reduced. For more information on fire ants check out http://fireant.tamu.edu, or http://insects.tamu.edu or http://agcomwww.tamu.edu or contact your local county Texas Cooperative Extension office.

Fire Ant Predators

All fire ants have natural predators, however the imported fire ant predators other than the armadillo did not arrive with the insects. Armadillos dig into fire ant mounds and eat the ants, primarily the developing brood. They also dig into mounds in droughts when more favored foods are hard to find. The impact is probably small, but the disruption of the colony may aid the phorid flies; since some phorid flies attack fire ants when mounds are disturbed, armadillos and phorid flies could be a winning combination.

Phorid flies are known to be parasitic on a number of ant species. Some are thought to be host specific to imported fire ants. The adult flies lay eggs on foraging fire ant workers outside the mound; the maggots migrate into the fire ant's head capsule where they feed. This eventually leads to decapitation of the fire ant. As interesting as this phenomena is, the major effect of these flies is to cause the fire ants to cease foraging. In the presence of the fly, workers will retreat into the colony to prevent egg laying by the phorid. This disruptive response to the fly restricts the ability of the colony to feed itself and may "even the playing field" so that other ant species can become more competitive with the imported fire ants. This more indirect and subtle effect has only recently been identified as the mechanism by which phorids might reduce the impact of fire ants.

For the first time the federal government has provided funds ($100,000) to the USDA Red Imported Fire Ant Research Lab in Gainesville, Florida, to grow phorids specific to the imported fire ant in large enough numbers to determine if they are truly the control of the future.

Other biological studies are being conducted on the microsporidian disease *Thelohania solenopsae*, an obligate intracellular pathogen of fire ants. Preliminary field studies on populations of the black imported fire ant, *S. richteri*, carried out in Argentina indicated that decreasing densities of fire ants were associated with increasing presence of this pathogen. These data suggest that this pathogen may be an important factor in reducing fire ant numbers by weakening the colonies. Although the vertical transmission of this disease is understood, the horizontal transmission is not.

Solenopsis (Labauchena) dagerrei is a parasitic ant that attaches to the fire ant queen and redirects fire ant workers to tend the brood of the parasite to the detriment of the colony's own larvae. *S. dagerrei* is intriguing because it lacks a worker caste; only queens and males are produced. The presence of this parasitic ant has a debilitating effect on colony growth and the proportion of sexual reproductives produced in the colony. Queens of *S. dagerrei* enter fire ant colonies and attach themselves to the mother queen.

Previous studies have demonstrated that this parasite inhibits the fire ant queen and her egg production, thus causing the fire ant colony to collapse and eventually die out.

To date, none of these natural enemies has been sufficiently evaluated to determine if, in and of themselves, they might produce any true suppression of fire ant populations. In all likelihood, parasites, predators, and pathogens will be used in combinations to reduce colony fitness. Reduction in colony vitality could cause greater mortality under stress conditions and allow for better competition from native ant species.

Work continues in finding a control. The best options appear to be working with nature. In the meantime, everyone needs to be aware of the danger of the fire ant to ecosystems and inhabitants of the ecosystem including man. Know the enemy and be prepared to do battle. Be observant, especially after drastic environmental changes such as flooding or droughts. Wear gloves when working outside around discarded material even if it has only been sitting a few days.

Employing the principles of IPM, common sense, and working with nature, the imported fire ants can be conquered!

COMPOST GARDENER'S GOLD

The wonderful rich soil on the forest floor, the fertile soil on the alluvial plain are all the result of nature recycling organic matter. Man calls this process composting. Records indicate early civilizations including ancient Rome and Greece practiced this form of recycling. Farmers deliberately piled animal manure and soil or muck in ways to promote decomposition and then used the resulting product to fertilize crops. These practices continued through the Dark Ages and the Renaissance. In the New World, both native Indian tribes and early settlers relied on composting to provide a nutrient source for their crops.

The practice remained basically the same from its inception until the early twentieth century when Sir Albert Howard, a British colonist in India, invented the layering method of compost pile construction. A scientist at the 300-acre farm of the Indore Institute of Plant Industry, Howard developed large-scale composting based on Indian and Chinese folk techniques. He devised a system in which layers of plant material alternated with layers of manure, in a ratio of at least three parts plant debris to one part manure. His ideal compost pile was freestanding and measured five feet high and ten feet wide. In the early 1930s Howard returned to England to spread the word. The Indore method soon became the standard by which experts built their compost heaps.

Howard and other early proponents of home composting praised the value of manure in the pile. Unfortunately the implication that manure is critical to successful compost has deterred many. Any organic waste matter will work. Since Howard popularized composting, researchers have refined techniques and developed new products to make the process easier.

With the introduction of synthetic, chemical fertilizers and the old concepts of composting being malodorous, composting was discouraged. Many areas have laws prohibiting composting! These laws need to be reviewed, revised, or removed. Composting, nature's method of recycling, is the answer to many urban and suburban problems, the most crucial being what to do when the landfills are full. This problem is covered in Chapter 14, Don't Bag It! Use It!

Compost is defined as "a mixture of various decaying organic substances, such as dead leaves or manure, used for fertilizing soil." This dictionary definition covers only a small portion of the benefits. Compost does increase fertility by adding nitrogen, phosphorus, and potassium, the same elements found in all chemical (synthetic) fertilizers, but in smaller slow release amounts, making them available over a longer period.

In order to maximize use of the nitrogen, phosphorus, and potassium, other elements are needed. The significance of compost is the addition of these needed elements called major and minor micronutrients and the soil organisms to process them into usable forms. The major micronutrients are magnesium, essential to chlorophyll production, calcium, and sulfur. The minor micronutrients are iron, manganese, zinc, boron, copper, molybdenum, and chlorine. These micronutrients are needed only in small quantities and can be added in chemical form, but too high a concentration of any one can be deterimental. Nature's way is the most dependable.

The soil microorganisms, bacteria, fungi, microscopic worms, and insect larvae in the compost process all the elements into usable forms for the plants. During this process the organisms produce complex sugars that help hold soil particles together into clumps, creating air spaces and improving soil quality.

All these components work together to provide good friable soil. Heavy clay soils are loosened and sandy soils are held

together, improving moisture retention. This restructering of the soil helps reduce soil loss due to erosion. The increased aeration helps plant roots penetrate more deeply into the soil. The composition of the compost helps to maintain the pH of the soil near neutral. All these benefits promote growth. Compost supplies not only fertility but also environmental factors with all the nutrients in the proper quanties for healthy growth.

Composting is an easy, cheap way to promote plant health. Through regular use of compost the need to use chemical fertilizers, pesticides, and herbicides can be greatly reduced or even eliminated, saving even more money and time and reducing the potential for contamination of waterways and drinking water.

Composting is easy! The methods, recipes, and procedures to successfully compost are as plentiful as the benefits derived. The Indore method is good but not necessary. Manure from livestock animals can be added but is not necessary. Available space, time, and materials accessible determine the best method.

> *Compost is "a mixture of various decaying organic substances, such as dead leaves or manure, used for fertilizing soil."*

Items to Avoid

A few items should never be added to a compost pile. Avoid meat, fish, dairy foods, oils, grease, and fatty foods. These items can disrupt the decomposition part of composting, cause odors, and may attract rodents. Pet feces and used kitty litter may eventually break down but also may contain bacteria, viruses, and parasites that can be transmitted through the compost to humans and pets.

Fireplace ashes can be added with caution. Only use ashes from burned wood and then only in limited quantities. Ash increases the alkalinity of the compost and ultimately your soil. Ash from burned paper and pressed logs contains potentially harmful residues and should be avoided. Coal ashes and ashes from charcoal barbecues contain sulfur oxide and other compounds toxic to the soil and should never be added.

Sawdust or wood chips from painted, treated, or pressurized wood should never be added to the compost. The chemical residue does not break down and can be harmful to humans and pets.

Do not add noxious weed seeds or runners to the pile unless the internal temperature is known to be hot enough to destroy the material. This is the same for diseased or infected plant material. To avoid transmitting a disease, discard the infected plant; do not compost it.

Exclude any pesticide treated material. Most insecticides and herbicides will break down in the compost pile but not all. Assume the residual effect of the pesticide will last as long in the compost pile as it would on the targeted plant.

Non-organic materials such as plastic, metal, glass, etc., will not decompose and should not be added to the pile.

Creating a Compost "Pile"

Keeping the items to avoid in mind, it is time to create the "pile." The best way is to keep it simple. The passive method involves the least amount of work and little or no maintenance. Pile organic ingredients into a mound and let them decompose. Stack additions on top and remove completed compost from the bottom. This method does take longer but yields compost of high quality

once or twice a year. The pile can be freestanding or contained in a bin. The only advantage to a bin is to neaten the appearance of the pile, and size is not important. Woody materials such as large stems and branches can turn the passive pile into a brush pile. To avoid this all material of any size should be cut up with pruners, a machete, or a chipper-shredder.

An active compost pile requires management. The concept of management reflects more accurately the potential for varying degrees of participation in the process. The individual who decides to manage a compost pile for any reason, be it speed of production, efficiency of composting, or obtaining exercise, the ways to intervene are numerous.

Whether a freestanding or container held pile, decomposition requires four factors: an adequate mix of carbon and nitrogen materials, plenty of air, sufficient moisture, and organisms. These components can be manipulated in many ways to influence the process. Altering any of the factors qualifies as management and will speed up the process.

Mixing or turning the pile can result in finished product in as little as three to four weeks; however, under ideal conditions the pile can produce compost as

quickly without being turned. Using only some of the management techniques but never turning the pile, finished compost can be formed in eight to ten weeks. Determine the technique best suited and the one most likely to be followed for successful composting.

Location is important. Place the pile out of sight lines from the used areas of your landscape and your neighbors. Even neat piles are not always attractive.

Consider wind and sun. Microorganisms generate and maintain the heat in the pile. Wind and sun can influence heat loss from the exterior of the pile. The more rapid the loss the less active the microorganisms near the edges of the pile. Hot, dry air also dehydrates the pile, slowing the biological processes in the middle. In hot, dry climates keep the pile shaded all day. Piles in hot, moist climates often work best with morning sun to dry some of the excess moisture and afternoon shade to protect from the intense heat. Morning sun and afternoon shade is also suitable for compost piles in dry, cool-summer climates. In cool-summer areas with plenty of moisture, a pile benefits from a sunny location to help reduce heat loss and to dry the outside of the pile slightly.

A windy location can provide air to a pile, but too much air can dry the material, slowing the process. Compensate for the drying effect by adding water or placing the pile in a more protected spot.

The best base for a compost pile is bare soil. This allows for drainage and migration of earthworms in and out of the pile. Tree roots can be a problem, but if the pile is turned frequently, roots will not be allowed to establish long enough to pull the nutrients from the pile. Concrete pads can be used as bases but should be tilted slightly to the back to allow for drainage. Scrap metal sheets or wooden bases are also possibilities. Wooden bases should be untreated wood and will decompose over time and need to be replaced.

Many different styles and composition compost bins are available commercially. Each has good and bad features. No real advantages have been documented over simple wooden sided or screen bins. If space allows, a series of two to three bins provides more composting action. When one bin is full add to the next, allowing the first to decompose. When the second is full, move to the third. By the time the third is in use the first should contain finished product ready for use. When selecting a bin or structure, determine available space and location before making the selection. Use what is easiest for you to meet your needs.

Whatever the location or final structure of the bin or pile, allow a working space. A minimum access of six to eight feet on at least two sides is recommended to allow room for a long-handled pitchfork and wheelbarrow or cart.

Compost Recipe

Managing materials added determines the speed of the finished product. A simple recipe is to start with a layer of coarse material, like twigs, straw, or leaves. Add a layer of grass clippings and leaves, mixed with eggshells, coffee grounds, tea bags, and fruit and vegetable scraps from the kitchen, along with water and soil or old compost. Always bury or cover food waste when it is added to a pile to decrease the likelihood of attracting rodents or flies. Add more leaves, grass clippings, and kitchen scraps as they become available. Turn the mixture on a regular basis to provide spaces for air to circulate. Be sure it stays

moist but not soggy. For best results try to build the pile at least three feet wide and three feet deep. If it's smaller, composting will take longer. The compost will naturally heat up and decrease in volume as it breaks down.

The above recipe is only a suggestion. Many commercial composters come complete with recipes. No single formula provides effective decomposition. Assorted ingredients and varying amounts of management will all result in compost. If you are interested in fairly rapid decomposition and high internal temperatures (130 to 160 degrees F.) then design the pile with deliberate attention to the carbon-nitrogen ratio. Achieving roughly equal amounts of carbon and nitrogen is easier if the pile is built all at one time and mixed, or materials are arranged in tiers between two and six inches thick. However the pile is built, do not compact it. Air is essential to the decomposition process. Compressing reduces air and significantly slows decomposition.

Roughly equal volumes of carbon in the form of leaves and other brown material mixed with nitrogen material such as kitchen wastes and green matter will yield compost with a nitrogen content between ½ and 1 percent. Adding manure as the nitrogen source will increase nitrogen to about 2 percent.

Manure is a key ingredient in commercial compost. In the Hill Country, turkey manure is mixed with leaves and grass to make a very rich compost. In San Antonio, manure, food waste, wood waste, and leaves and stems are used. In Denton, Belton, Austin, and Bryan/College Station "night soil" is mixed with leaves and stems for compost. "Night soil" in use today is human waste that has been cleaned, sterilized, and pelletized for use as a fertilizer. Several companies bag this material and sell it in the retail trade.

Many of these same sources of manure are available to the home composter. When looking for a manure source, consider the value of feed the animal has eaten. A diet rich in alfalfa balanced with trace minerals produces higher quality manure than a diet of low protein hay. Good sources of manure are riding stables or places that board horses. Feed lots, auction barns, poultry farms, rabbit raisers, zoos, or a visiting circus are all sources for manure. Remember all fresh manures are too hot (nitrogen content too high) to use straight and must be composted.

Manure is valuable because it returns to the soil that which came from the soil, another form of nature's grand recycling plan.

Another factor in managing the compost pile is particle size. The rate of decomposition increases as the size of the organic materials decrease. Take the time to cut or chop large fibrous materials before adding to the pile. Exclude woody materials if unable to chop or shred. Shredded organic material heats up rapidly, decomposes quickly, and produces a uniform compost.

Compost is "finished" when it is a deep rich homogenous brown, sweet smelling, and produces a "smear." The smear test is to rub a small amount between thumb and forefinger. If a brown residue is left on your finger, the compost is ready and of good quality. Unfinished compost is still usable as mulch where it will continue to decompose and add nutrients back to the soil. When using a manure-based compost, make sure the manure is mixed with brown material and cool before spreading.

Commercially available "compost starters" and "activators" are not necessary. The organic materials added to the pile will include all that is necessary to get the pile going. Chemical

CHAPTER 13

fertilizers are also not necessary. Old compost, garden soil, blood meal, and manures are better sources. Keeping all additions to the pile organic or natural is the best way to work with nature.

Problems and Solutions

Composting is simple, but a few problems may be encountered. A bad odor may indicate anaerobic conditions, not enough air or too wet. Correct by turning and adding dry material. If too much green grass has been added, turn and mix in dry leaves. Turning may add enough air to promote aerobic decomposition.

If the center of the pile is dry, moisten materials while turning the pile. The pile should be moist but not soggy. If warm and damp in the middle but nowhere else, the pile is probably too small. Collect more material and mix the old ingredients into a new pile.

If damp and sweet-smelling but not heating up, mix more nitrogen source such as green material, blood meal, or manure into the pile.

Flies can be unwelcome visitors to the pile. Although the larval stages of many flies won't hurt and may speed up the process, the adults are nuisances.

The easiest prevention is to bury food scraps in the pile. Keeping a pile of leaves or other clippings handy for this purpose is a good idea.

Fire ants around or in a compost pile indicate the pile is not working properly. Increase the size or mix in more material. When the pile is large and/or hot enough the ants will leave and not return. Adjust the pile before adding pesticide. You do not want to kill the beneficial soil microbes by adding pesticides.

Composting for the Apartment Dweller

Even apartment dwellers can compost kitchen scraps indoors using vermi-culture, the term for composting with earthworms. Either brown-nose or red worms work best. Do not use night crawlers or other large, soil-burrowing worms. Composting worms are available commercially complete with instructions.

A portable bin, almost any sturdy container with a secure lid, can be used year round and kept in a cool place such as under the kitchen sink or on the patio or balcony. A six-cubic-foot box (length x width x height) or an eight-gallon garbage can will handle about six pounds of food per week. To start, mix food scraps with torn up newspapers, add the red worms, then let them work. Do not add fish, meat, dairy products, bones, fatty or acidic foods, or grease to the bins. A pound of red worms for every pound of food scraps you plan to compost each week is recommended.

Bury food waste throughout the bin, and worms will gradually eat it and turn it into rich compost. Two or three times a year, when most of the contents have become dark "worm castings," the compost may be harvested. The finished product will be greatly reduced from the original volume and should only fill one half or less of the bin. The compost may be harvested by moving it all to one side and adding fresh bedding to the empty side. Bury waste in the new bedding and the worms will move from the old to the new, allowing finished compost to be harvested. Your plants, whether in the house or on the patio, will thrive.

Many areas of the state have Master Composter Programs. The times and locations of classes vary. Check with your local office of the Texas Natural Resource Conservation Commission or www.mastercomposter.com for up-to-date information.

Compost is available commercially, but not all compost is equal. The most commonly available is often low quality and may tie up nutrients. Use the "smear and smell" test before buying, and don't settle for low-quality products. Ask about the source of the product and what went into it; after all it is your money.

In the Middle Ages alchemists tried to turn metal into gold. Little did they realize that the farmers had learned the secret. Composting is the art of turning organic waste matter into brown gold. Compost and make your own gold. Your habitats will thank you.

DON'T BAG IT! USE IT!

LEAF AND GRASS MANAGEMENT

Brown gold, described in the last chapter, is made from yard wastes, a natural consequence of gardening and a good indication of a thriving landscape. But if not composted what becomes of the leaves, grass clippings, spent blooms, and trimmed branches, large and small? The traditional method of disposal has been to gather it all up, place it in a plastic bag or garbage can, and set it out for the garbage collector. No more thought is given to the leaves, weeds, and grass clippings. They are gone!

But are they really gone? What happens to the bags and contents of the cans? The landfill. The place no one wants in "their backyard." What happens to the yard wastes? Nothing happens to them. The bags and piles stack up with household garbage, filling landfills.

A study begun by garbage archaeologists from the University of Arizona in 1973 and continued into 1987 revealed the truth about garbage and dispelled many misconceptions. An entire steak—bone, fat, meat, everything—was found next to an old but legible paper dated April 23, 1973. The year of the find was 1987! The steak and newspaper had lain buried in the landfill for fourteen years with very little if any decomposition.

Digs in eleven landfills in 1988-1989 revealed the same facts. So-called perishables survived surprisingly long times; a mound of guacamole thrown out in 1967, leaves raked up in 1964, and lumber from 1952. The most common food found preserved in landfills was hot dogs. Preservatives at work!

Landfills are not big compost piles. In landfills refuse is rarely shredded, large quantities of fluids are prohibited, and little air circulates around the waste material. In these closely compacted environments only the anaerobic microorganisms survive. As James Noble of Tufts University's Center for Environmental Management says, "It is not surprising that everything doesn't biodegrade rapidly; the miracle is that anything biodegrades at all!"

The landfill study found that 20-50 percent of food and yard waste biodegrades in the first fifteen years. This means that 50-80 percent remains in the landfill longer than fifteen years.

The garbage studies conducted in New York and Arizona revealed similar results. Plastics made up 10 percent of the total volume. In 1970 paper occupied 35 percent with an increase to 50 percent in 1989. Telephone directories were the fastest growing paper component taking up 18 percent of the space. Copies buried for forty years were still legible.

Texas is the second largest generator of garbage in the United States with 33.8 million tons per year in 1998. California is first with 56 million, New York third with 30.2 million tons. Texas is a large state, but this is not an excuse. The highest percentage of waste continues to be paper at 41.4 followed by yard wastes at 14.8. In Houston yard waste at 32.6 percent makes up the largest component of waste with paper second at 31.3 percent.

All states, Texas included, continue to run out of acceptable landfill space. Disposing of organic materials in Texas landfills costs more than $150 million a year and consumes more than 15 million cubic yards of space. To slow down the need for new landfills many states have instituted yard waste bans—no yard wastes are picked up with the trash for addition to landfills. See Figure 10. Note that Texas is not included yet. These states along with many communities in other states do provide yard waste composting programs.

Austin area citizens produce enough garbage to fill the Erwin Special Events Center every four months. In 1991 the city instituted a "Pay-As-You-Throw" garbage collection system to reduce waste. The system works. From October 1998 to October 1999, solid waste services

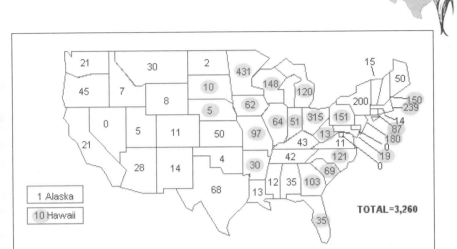

Figure 10. States with shaded numbers prohibit yard waste in landfills.
Numbers indicate the number of yard waste composting programs in the state.
Compiled from the Municipal Solid Waste Factbook, US EPA, August 1997

diverted 27.81 percent of its regular residential garbage from the landfill; up from 9.77 percent when the program began. With this system residents are provided instructions on what can and cannot go into trash collection and are charged only for what is collected. Yard wastes placed in approved containers do not carry any additional fee. The material is collected separately and composted. The composted material called "Dillo Dirt" is used in landscaping city parks and is sold to the public through local nurseries.

Dallas each spring from the middle of March to middle of April collects specially tagged yard wastes during a "scalping collec-tion" period. A small fee is charged for the special bags that are available in early March at area recreation centers. In Dallas call 3-1-1 or 214-670-8613 for more information.

The city of Plano diverts 100 percent of its collected landscape waste and corrugated cardboard from the landfill. Residents place these materials in biodegradable bags, which are collected by the city on designated days and processed at the city's municipal composting site in Melissa and returned to the citizens as compost or mulch.

The above systems are good and should be expanded to all communities, but they are only a partial solution. Gardeners have the capability of reducing yard wastes in landfills and using the nutrients nature provides to enhance the landscape. Lawn clippings are rich in needed components and by dry weight contain 4 percent nitrogen (higher if recently fertilized), ½ percent phosphorus, 2 percent potassium, and an abundance of micronutrients not attainable in commercial fertilizers. Mowing and leaving the clippings on the lawn is the easiest way to recycle the nutrients and does not contribute to thatch buildup.

Thatch is a layer of material that develops between the base of the grass plant and the soil's surface. A thatchy lawn is very spongy to walk on and is usually a result of application of too much nitrogen, too much water, poor soil drainage, or soil compaction. All are results of poor maintenance practices. Refer to Chapters 3 and 6 for proper maintenance.

If you feel you must catch the clippings, use them in compost or as mulch. They are too valuable to discard. To save time and energy you might as well place the bag of fertilizer directly into the garbage, saving the time it takes to spread it on the lawn. This is essentially what you are doing by sending the clippings to the landfill.

Leaves are nature's way of returning nutrients to the soil. Leaves contain 50-80 percent of the nutrients a plant extracts from the soil and air during the growing season. In time they decompose, supplying plants with a natural, slow release form of nutrients. A covering of leaf litter in a forest is an indication of a healthy forest ecosystem.

Each year Texans spend millions of dollars on various products of the forest industry to enhance the growth and beauty of their landscapes, at the same time throwing out leaves, grass clippings, and other yard waste materials that could be used in place of the commercial products.

Three ways to utilize the valuable yard wastes are mowing, mulching, and composting (Chapter 13). Mowing during the summer months is a weekly routine for most homeowners. In parts of Texas it is almost a year-round job. The time spent mowing can be reduced, yield a healthier greener lawn, and allow time for other activities by following a few simple steps.

Don't bag the clippings!

Sounds simple, but it works. Avoid scalping in the early spring. This practice does not harm the lawn, but is not necessary to the health of the lawn. Good mowing techniques involve cutting the grass when it reaches one third higher than the mower setting (dependent on type of turf). The type of mower is not important. Mulching mowers are ideal, but regular bagging rotary mowers work well. For safety be sure the chute is blocked when the bag is removed. Mowing at the proper interval is more important than the type of mower.

When clippings are allowed to remain on the lawn, the need for synthetic fertilizer is reduced. Lawn clipping can supply at least one quarter of the fertilizer needed. Applying a 1/4-inch layer of screened good compost in the spring along with leaving the clippings uses nature's way to promote turf health and allows for even distribution of nitrogen over the growing season, avoiding sudden growth spurts that can lead to stress during times of heat and or drought.

Proper watering of turf areas (Chapter 3) is also important in the Don't Bag It program. Water the lawn only when it needs watering and then long enough to wet the soil to a depth of four to six inches. Do not water again until it needs it. During dry spells, if this system is followed, mowing and watering will be reduced. That's time you can spend watching nature enjoy the habitat you have provided.

Mowing can also be used in the fall to manage a light leaf litter. The leaves shredded by the mower can be left on the turf along with the grass blades to decompose and add nutrients back into the soil. This works best with a mulching lawn mower but can be used with a regular mower. If the clippings are collected, the resulting mix of green and brown makes an excellent addition to the compost pile.

Raking or using a lawn mower with a bag to shred and collect the leaves can collect heavier leaf accumulations; the collected leaves can be used as mulch in vegetable gardens, flowerbeds, and around tree and shrubs. Mulches reduce evaporation from the soil's surface, inhibit weed growth, moderate soil temperatures, keep soil from eroding and crusting, and reduce soil compaction. A three- to six-inch layer of shredded leaves around the base of trees and shrubs helps prevent damage from the extremes in temperature during the summer and winter months. In annual and perennial flowerbeds, a two- to three-inch layer is sufficient to inhibit weed growth. One of the arguments used against using leaf mulch is that it harbors "bugs." Insects do live in leaf litter, but the majority of the insects are beneficial and do more good by breaking down the litter to release nutrients than harm to the plant.

A thick layer of leaves makes an excellent all-weather garden walkway. If you have pet paths, the leaves form a barrier between the paws and the mud or dust.

One important exception to recycling leaves and other trimmings is disease. If a serious infestation of fungal disease, bacterial or viral infections, or insect pests is noticed, the waste should be disposed of immediately in a way to prevent spread. If you have a "hot compost," it is acceptable to compost; otherwise place in appropriate container for curbside trash pickup. As natural nutrients are added back to the plants, they will become healthier and fewer pest problems will develop.

Leaves and trimmings should be shredded to work the most efficiently. Many types of equipment are available for this purpose. One of the best Valentine presents I ever received was a chipper/shredder. It chips branches up to three inches in diameter and shreds leaves through another chute. I recycle all my yard wastes. The branches larger than three inches are cut into firewood or used as borders or accents in the landscape. Not everyone has the need for a large chipper/shredder. Smaller machines on the market are also effective. A string trimmer inserted into a heavy duty garbage can filled with leaves will shred the leaves nicely.

When working with any kind of chipper/shredder, it is essential to follow all safety precautions—glasses and gloves are mandatory. I've had chips kick out and hit me and branches knock my hands. I also never work alone. Use common sense and enjoy the feeling of utilizing your old wastes to make new treasures.

As population increases and home landscapes become a larger part of the Texas environment, it is increasingly important to manage them responsibly. Working with and maintaining nature and our natural resources all work together by keeping all yard wastes collected in a spot on the site.

Remember the three R's— Recycle, Reduce, and Reuse!

CHAPTER 15

PROPER PRUNING
PREVENT CREPE MURDER AND OTHER ATROCITIES

Nature shapes trees and shrubs by wind, available sunlight through branches, and soil conditions. Observing trees and shrubs in their native habitats allows an appreciation of the beauty resulting from this seemingly random system. Man in his infinite wisdom generally does more harm than good with his shaping, killing or ruining more trees each year from improper pruning than from pests. Observing nature's methods and applying them to the home landscape can prevent "Crepe Murder," "Texas Chain Saw Massacres," and other atrocities.

Pruning is the removal or reduction of certain plant parts not required, no longer effective, or of no use to the plant. Reasons to prune are to direct or correct growth in shade trees to avoid later problems; maintain the natural shape or limit the size; remove undesirable growth that detracts from the plant such as broken, unsightly, diseased, or insect-damaged growth, suckers, or water sprouts, rubbing branches, and existing stubs that allow disease and insects to enter the plant; develop a particular form such as a hedge, produce compact growth, and prevent legginess; maintain maximum coloration on plants selected for twig or stem color; improve or maintain flowering by selectively removing branches; allow light to penetrate to the interior of the plant; rejuvenate old or declining plants by removing older wood so young growth can develop; and increase safety to humans or property by removing large branches that are weak, broken, or interfering with the house or other landscape features. Pruning can be reduced or eliminated by selecting the proper plant for the location; however, even experts often misjudge the size or growth habit of a mature tree or shrub. The most suitable landscape plants sometimes do require pruning.

Pruning can be done any time of the year; however, recommended times vary with different plants. In general the best time is during late winter or early spring before growth begins. The least desirable time is immediately after new growth develops in the spring. Trimming new growth at this time uses up needed nutrients and may cause dwarfing. Limit amount of pruning in the late summer to prevent possible frost damage of new growth not hardened enough to survive. Damaged, dead, or diseased branches should be removed as soon as possible to avoid additional insect and disease problems. Prune spring flowering plants such as azaleas, dogwoods, and red bud after blooming in the spring; if pruned earlier, the flowers will be removed. Live oaks

and red oaks should be pruned late June through September and January through early February to lessen risk of oak wilt disease.

Most woody plants (trees and shrubs) fall into two categories based on the arrangement of the buds on twigs and branches. The bud arrangements, either alternate or opposite, indicate the plant's typical growth habit. A plant with alternate buds usually has a rounded, pyramidal, or columnar growth habit. Plants with opposite buds rarely assume any form other than one with a rounded crown. The position of the last pair of buds determines the growth direction of the new shoot. Buds on top of the twig will grow upward at an angle and to the side on which directed. Cutting back to a bud or branch is recommended with preference to buds that point to the outside of the plant rather than buds pointing to the inside. New shoots from outside pointing buds grow out and not through the interior of the plant crossing other branches that will eventually have to be removed.

To shorten a branch or twig, cut back to a side branch and make the cut ½ inch above the bud. If the cut is too close to the bud, the bud may die; if too far from the bud, the wood above the bud dies, causing dead tips on the end of the branches. When the pruning cut is made, the bud or buds nearest the cut become the new growing point. When a terminal or end bud is removed, the nearest side buds grow more than they normally would since apical dominance has been removed. The bud nearest the pruning cut becomes the new terminal bud. If more side branches are desired, remove the tip.

Removing the tip applies only to branches and twigs. Do not dehorn or cut back mature trees —known as "topping the tree." Topping, sometimes called Texas Chain Saw Massacre, and leaving large stubs cause weakened trees with shorter life spans. Thinning is the recommended method for landscape trees. Thinning removes unwanted branches by cutting them back to their point of origin, conforms to the tree's natural branching habit, and results in a more open tree, emphasizing the branches' internal structure. Thinning also strengthens the tree by forcing diameter growth of the remaining branches.

When thinning, remove an unwanted branch at its point of origin or a strong lateral branch, careful not to prune into the branch collar or leave a pronounced stub. The branch collar is the swelled area near the base of the limb. To avoid peeling bark, remove larger branches with a saw utilizing the three-cut method. Undercut 12 to 24 inches up from the branch collar. Make the second cut from the top all the way through the branch, two to three inches above cut one. The final cut should be just beyond the branch collar. Support the stub so it does not tear the bark.

Avoid costly problems by using correct pruning methods. Always make a clean cut to accelerate wound closure. Wound dressings are not recommended since they do not prevent rot. Trees' natural defense mechanisms work well to heal cuts if the cuts are done properly. One exception to wound paint or dressing is on oak trees in areas with oak wilt. The dressing will help to prevent spread of the disease. For large mature trees, experienced arborists should be consulted before cutting. Trees are valuable landscape assets and should be treated as such.

Shrubs and small trees are easier for the homeowner to prune. The three methods used are thinning, renewal or rejuvenation, and heading back or shearing. Most deciduous shrubs should be thinned rather than sheared. **Thinning** prevents excessive or unsightly branch formation at the top of the plant and maintains the natural growth habit. Follow the same procedures as for thinning mature trees. Thin the oldest and tallest canes first, allowing for growth and development of side branches. Plants can be maintained at a given height and spread for years by thinning with a recommended removal of no more than one third of the branches per year. Nandinas are best pruned this way.

Rejuvenate shrubs that have become too large or contain undesirable unproductive wood by cutting off the oldest branches at the ground, leaving only the newest stems. If there are not many younger stems, remove the older wood over a three-year period to maintain the overall shape of the plant. New developing shoots can be cut back to various lengths by thinning to encourage strong branch development.

Heading back or shearing refers to cutting back a branch anywhere along the length of the stem. This method concentrates vigorous, upright growth below the cut and is frequently done with hedge shears without regard to the natural form of the plant. If every branch or twig is headed back, more growth develops than was removed by the pruning and the natural form is altered by extra growth. Hedges are pruned to a definite size and shape with this method.

Heading back or shearing is the most commonly used and the most improperly used method. Crepe murder is a prime example. No one source can be found for this atrocity. One early reference is from Europe where small trees were planted along a river in front of a hotel balcony. As the trees matured, the view of the river was obscured. The owners of the hotel, to accommodate the visitors, yearly sheared the tops of the trees. This practice has gone on through the years, without regard to the growth habits of the trees.

One excuse for this butchery is to promote flower growth. No documentation can be found to substantiate this claim. Crepe myrtles left to grow naturally still produce many blooms. Removing only the spent blooms can increase a second flowering but is not essential. Allowing the small trees to maintain normal shapes promotes healthy trees more resistant to powdery mildew and aphids. The peeling bark trunks of crepe myrtles, one of their attractions, can be accented by thinning. The crepe myrtles are not a native Texas tree but if

Picture 9. Properly pruned crepe myrtle,
allowing highlighting of distinctive trunk.

allowed to grow naturally are attractive additions to the landscape. The accompanying illustrations are for crepe myrtles but apply to all small trees and shrubs. See Figure 11.

Pruning Tools and Techniques

To know and follow the rules of pruning is important, but of equal importance is using the correct tools. Equipment can be limited to a few items if the proper ones are selected. Select tools that will do the job, keep a sharp edge, and are relatively easy to sharpen and handle. When pruning diseased plants, disinfect all pruners, shears, and saw blades after each cut to prevent spreading disease to healthy plants. Use alcohol or bleach mixed at the rate of one part to nine parts water. At the end of the day, oil all equipment well to avoid rusting. Take proper care of the tools and they will last longer.

Hand pruners come in two styles, anvil and bypass, and are designed for cutting stems up to

Figure 11. Proper crepe myrtle pruning procedure

Improper method of pruning

1. Cutting on the dotted line as shown is known as hedging.

Proper method of pruning

1. Shrub before pruning. Remove all weak and dead branches and suckers.

2. Same plant after being pruned as above. All sucker growth remains.

2. Same shrub after pruning as above.

3. The final result: The natural shape and beauty of the shrub is lost and blooms will be sparse.

3. The final result reveals the natural and distinctive form of the shrub with vigorous and prolific flowering.

½ inch in diameter. Attempting to cut larger branches risks making a poor cut and/or damaging the pruners. When razor sharp, anvil style pruners, the ones where the blade comes to rest against a flat piece of metal when the handles are squeezed shut, will do most pruning jobs on green or hardwood stems or shoots. When even slightly dull, the anvil has a tendency to crush soft, green tissue. Crushing opens the plant tissue to infection and makes it harder for the plant to callous over the wound, so use anvil pruners for hard, old, or dead wood no thicker than a pencil. Anvil pruners are also good for trimming long roots and the tips of bareroot planting stock.

The blades of bypass pruners cross like scissors, making clean cuts and are the pruners of choice for new, green growth and are best for pruning dormant canes of grapevines and for winter pruning of the slender, sappy growth of conifers. Avoid using bypass pruners on thick, hard limbs or stems over ½ inch as too much squeezing pressure exerts a twisting action that can loosen the bolt that holds them together and can ruin the metal spring that keeps the handles apart when the pressure is applied.

Lopping shears or loppers have long handles that are operated by both hands. Even the least expensive can cut material ½ inch in diameter. Better ones can cut through branches 2 inches or more, depending on the species of plant and condition. Loppers can be found in both anvil and bypass styles. The bypass, rated on the label by capacity for cutting limbs of various sizes, usually from 1 to 2 inches in diameter, is the most useful tool for general pruning jobs. This is the right tool for all hard, woody growth thicker than ½ inch, but avoid cutting limbs thicker than the rating or the damaging twisting force will result.

Pruning saws are recommended for limbs larger than 2 inches and up to 6 or seven 7 in diameter but work best on limbs between 2 and 5 inches. Do not use a carpenter's saw, which tends to bind and get sticky from accumulated sap. Either a D-type handle and blade in a single unit or a folding saw where the blade folds into the handle when not in use is recommended. Models that produce a "turbo" cut have teeth that are sharpened three ways, increasing the cutting power. Other useful models have hardened teeth that need no sharpening. Almost all pruning saws cut on the pull stoke.

Bow saws are recommended for branches too large for a pruning saw with room around them to work. Bow saws come in two configurations, a 21-inch triangular shape with the short leg forming the handle and a 24-inch rectangular shape. The thin blades have larger cutting teeth than pruning saws and are easily replaceable. Bow saws are not for work in thick tangles of close limbs. When cutting limbs over 8 inches, the blade may twist and bind in the cut. This indicates the need for a chain saw.

Chain saws are for the largest limbs and are useful for removing overgrown trees and shrubs completely. Chain saws can be dangerous and should only be used by knowledgeable individuals taking all safety precautions. If the trimming job requires a chain saw, it may also require a professional. Remember the branches always appear smaller from the ground than they actually are. When hiring a tree care company, seek out professionals who can provide references and proof of insurance.

Pole pruners, a combination of lopper and saw on a telescoping handle, allow removal of branches from the safety of the ground. A pulley system at the top operates a lever that closes bypass lopper blades when a nylon rope is pulled from below. Some models have an extra pulley or gear to increase cutting power with little extra effort. The usual cutting rating is for limbs from 1 to 2 inches, similar to regular loppers.

Hedge shears have long handles and blades ordinarily 8 or 9 inches long. The sole use is to trim back ragged new growth on hedges. Most trees and shrubs should not be hedged.

Once the reasons to prune are determined, the basic principles understood, and the proper tool selected, pruning is primarily a matter of common sense. To maintain tree and shrub health, carefully select branches and limbs to enhance the natural beauty and shape. Consider the use of the tree or shrub in your landscape and the importance to the habitat. Think before cutting! Only you can prevent trimming atrocities.

INCLUDE NATURE
TIPS TO UPDATE LANDSCAPING

Landscapes are living growing entities and therefore constantly changing. Some changes are planned, others not. Even the most carefully designed and instituted designs do not always evolve as anticipated, and eventually every garden no matter the size, formal, informal, or cottage, needs alteration. Take this perfect time to modify, adjust, and welcome nature with all the benefits into your landscape.

Evaluation and Planning

Making a sketch or a detailed plan of the existing landscape and incorporating modifications is helpful but is not absolutely necessary. Observation is more important. Ideally the observations should be made during every season, even when the plants are dormant. A gardening journal is an excellent way to document changes and record what worked and what didn't and why. No two years are exactly the same, but with careful observation, trends and patterns can be determined. The modifications do not need to be extreme.

Landscape books and magazines abound and are good for basic ideas, but the majority do not understand or encourage the concept of working with nature. Use the available literature for ideas and suggestions, but also walk through native areas and observe how the trees and shrubs grow. Often the simplest solutions are the best.

Before making any changes, walk around your landscape and mark any exotic invasive plants such as Chinese tallow or salt cedar that need to be removed. Also consider removing any problem or often diseased tree or shrub such as red-tipped photinia. Reexamine need for turf areas. Maybe children are grown or the family pets have changed. Consider changing to a friendlier grass such as buffalo.

Check all existing trees and shrubbery around roofs and eaves. Remove all branches and limbs touching or possibly touching during a wind storm. Remove the offending limbs properly as described in Chapter 15 to avoid future problems. Make these major changes before continuing with additional modifications.

Water Drainage Issues

The next consideration is drainage. Proper drainage is important and should be corrected before proceeding. Low areas where water collects and remain damp or even soggy are perfect for bog or water gardens. Digging a little deeper may be all that is needed to insert a preformed liner or

shape a freeform pond. Be sure to allow for drainage in and around the pond.

A stone lined dry creek bed is ideally suited to attractively channel runoff from areas where ponds are not appropriate and work well near a structure in narrow spaces. A creek bed or gravel path is better than trying to build up small areas. Houses and other buildings built on slabs must have the brick or siding above the soil level to prevent possible damage from too much moisture and/or insects. Native plantings can easily be worked in among the stones lining the creek bed on the side away from the structure. In narrow areas think "up" and use vines on trellises and lattices.

For high areas either level them or take advantage of the well-drained soil and plant natives that require good drainage. A cactus garden or a favorite West Texas native will work well and require less care and watering.

Overgrown Plants

Don't remove trees and shrubs that have grown across turf areas, weakening or killing turf and blocking pathways, but prune. Observe the offending tree or shrub from all sides. Most shrubs and small trees can be "limbed" up to reveal the trunk. By removing the lower branches, the blocked pathways and shaded areas are reduced. Picture 10 illustrates an American holly overgrown at the corner of the house limbed to accent the multi-trunks and provide space for additional plantings.

Picture 10. American holly limbed to allow easy passage along path provides planting area for toad lily.

If the plant has been sheared to reduce size in the past, the limbing may take a year or more to complete. To maintain the health of the plant, never remove more than one-third of the growth. The time spent to properly prune and train the shrub is well spent and will increase the middle level of habitat for wildlife.

Many trees and shrubs have peeling or textured bark; use the bare trunk as part of the garden structure. Compliment this feature with ground covers or small plants.

Proper pruning also sets a completely wild landscape apart from a native garden. Isolating and pruning one small tree makes it stand out clearly against the backdrop of an unpruned area, instantly and easily creating the feel of a maintained garden in front of a wild habitat area.

Many large trees produce roots growing above the soil, resulting in unsightly areas and making mowing difficult. Surface roots meet the needs of the tree for oxygen, moisture, and nutrients. Deep roots are for anchoring and moisture when the top few inches of soil are dry. Trees that are watered lightly and frequently develop more surface roots than deep roots, making them more vulnerable to drought and windstorms.

Removal of the surface roots is not recommended. The best option for these situations is to accept the growth habit of the tree, work with it, and alter watering patterns gradually to encourage development of deep roots. Chapter 7 describes proper watering for trees. If the trees have been watered shallowly over a long period, start with a mixture of deep and shallow watering to allow the tree to grow new deep roots. Avoid sudden drastic changes which could result in damage to the tree.

Even with pruning or thinning, the damaged turf under trees may not receive enough light to recover. Think ground covers to replace or reduce the turf area and cover exposed root systems, another way to increase habitat and reduce maintenance. Shade-loving ground covers are the best solution. Soil can be added to aid in planting, but never add more than 1-2 inches of soil around a tree per year. Work around the surface roots; do not cover them. Add mulch to moderate soil conditions after planting the ground cover. If too shady for ground covers, a layer of mulch provides an attractive, easy-to-care-for cover. Remember trees growing in their native habitats are heavily mulched with leaf litter. A layer of up to four inches of leaves can safely be added because they trap air and will decompose.

Shade and sun patterns can change due to factors beyond your control: new buildings, neighbors' trees, etc., in your surrounding area. Growths of neighboring trees are slow and result in the gradual decline of sun-loving plants in the landscape. Adjust to these changes by replacing plants with shade tolerant native species. Some species will tolerate less sun if soil nutrients are high. Consider adding good compost and mulching to save favorite plants.

Rejuvenating Planting Beds

A common problem in landscapes is depth (distance from back to front) of the planting beds. Foundation plantings should be in beds a minimum of three to four feet deep to allow for growth of the shrubbery. Deepening existing beds often gives a new look to old plantings. Limb-up the old shrubbery and plant a new row of border plants. In subdivisions with "lawn police," deepening the bed is a good way to gradually reduce the amount of turf.

When adjusting depth consider altering the shape of the border. Lay a garden hose to determine shape. Slight curves add a more relaxed informal feel to an area, although some formal plantings also benefit from curves. Avoid too wavy a line, which creates a busy feeling and sharp angles that make maintenance difficult. Now is your chance to be creative.

Trees and shrubs planted singly with small planting beds surrounding them in turf areas soon grow too large for the planting bed and look like overbalanced islands in the midst of a green ocean. Remove additional turf and increase the underplantings. Consider incorporating the planting area into other planting areas in the yard, avoiding several separate "islands." The goal of incorporating is to avoid small strips or corners of turf that are difficult to mow and water. The larger groupings also increase available habitat providing the three layers.

Adding Pathways and Structures

Replace turf areas used frequently as paths with materials such as pavers, flagstone, pea gravel, or heavy mulch. All provide a more stable, useable, lower maintenance path. Addition of paths throughout the landscape encourages visitors to examine all areas of the garden, reduces turf areas, and increases accessibility. Create "rooms" of different plantings or habitats along the paths with seating areas to stop and enjoy the butterflies and birds attracted by the native plantings. Increasing planting beds at first is more work but if done properly reduces maintenance and increases habitat, leaving more time to enjoy nature.

Include structures, arbors, trellises, and statues to add points of interest. Draw the visitor along the paths to see what is around the corner. Bird feeders, baths, and houses all increase the interest and catch the eye. Think of adding a little whimsy in the form of yard art. Picture 11 reveals a large concrete horny toad hiding under a Texas sage. The non-plant additions are a good way to express personality. Every gardener is different and instead of trying to express individuality with the latest, greatest exotic plant on the market, be original and create your own garden art. Much easier to take care of and friendlier to the environment.

Work with nature and the natural growth habit of the plantings to enhance landscapes, provide habitat, and reduce maintenance. Healthy, happy plants always reward the gardener.

Picture 11. Whimsy. Horny toad under Texas sage.

CATS, DOGS, ARMADILLOS, AND OTHER CRITTERS
DEALING WITH NEIGHBORS' PETS

Wild animals are increasingly found in urban and suburban settings. Green spaces along rivers, creeks, and bayous provide corridors for movement. As these corridors decrease along with loss of habitat, the creatures are trapped on islands surrounded by man's developments, moving the animals into cities. In San Antonio raccoons, opossums, rabbits, squirrels, deer, coyotes, and fox have been seen. In Houston beavers, bobcats, and alligators are added to the list. In Austin Mexican free-tail bats live under the Congress Avenue bridge—the largest urban bat colony in the world.

The wild creatures are only trying to survive in an increasingly hostile environment.

Several species including raccoons and opossums have adapted to live around humans. As man encroaches into their space they adjust, eating pet food instead of normal diets, sleeping under decks and houses instead of burrowing into river banks or tree cavities.

With increased contact with man come increased dangers. The Texas Wildlife Rehabilitation Coalition located in Houston reports between 5,000 and 6,000 injured animals are seen by the center's volunteers annually. To help wildlife survive man's intervention, it is essential to recognize and work with the critters.

The first impulse of many homeowners is "How do I get rid

of it!?" Thinking needs to change. Wildlife habitats provide a friendly environment, and the majority of these wild creatures do not cause harm to humans, pets, or gardens. Most are night creatures and go about their lives actually benefiting the environment while man sleeps. A little knowledge and tolerance is all they need.

Snakes are considered by many as unwanted visitors to a landscape; however, the majority of snakes in the state are nonpoisonous and beneficial, helping to control rodent and insect populations. Only rattlesnakes, copperheads, cottonmouths, and coral snakes are poisonous. A good field guide provides quick and easy-to-learn information to identify the pit vipers and the coral snake. State law protects many snakes, making indiscriminate killing or any other control illegal. Contact local Texas Parks and Wildlife Departments before using any control measures.

Bats, frequently misunderstood and persecuted, play a vital role in nature's balance, consuming vast numbers of night-flying insects, pollinating flowers, and dispersing seeds. In North America their primary prey includes pests that cost farmers and foresters billions of dollars annually.

While bat populations are in decline worldwide, in North America they are the most endangered land mammals; more than half of all species are listed as endangered or are official candidates. Bats suffer from habitat loss and environmental pollution, but the primary cause is wanton destruction by humans. A new Texas law states: Bats "may not be hunted, killed, possessed, purchased or sold; however, bats may be moved, trapped, or killed if inside or on a building occupied by people. A person may transport a bat for the purpose of laboratory testing if there is a rabies concern." Help dispel the myths. Learn more about these interesting, beneficial mammals and welcome them into your landscape. Contact Bat Conservation International, Inc. and visit the website at http://www.batcon.org.

When a visitor is suspected of causing damage in the home landscape, follow the basic IPM principles; monitor, determine tolerable levels of damage, and apply appropriate strategies and tactics. The first step, to monitor, is to identify the culprit. Check for tracks in mud or loose soil and observe any scat (droppings) in the area. Visit your garden after dark with a flashlight. With the exception of wild cats, the visitors are not aggressive. They are more afraid of you than you are of them; however, avoid cornering any wild animal. Observe from a safe distance. Several field guides are available to help in identification. Check Appendix A.

Just because plants are disturbed does not mean the visitor is a plant eater. An **opossum**'s diet is varied and includes insects, slugs, and snails, making them beneficial visitors. Their presence is often not noticed unless caught in the porch light eating the pet food or disturbing the dog during nightly visits.

Raccoons may upset pots and disturb water gardens in search of frogs, fish, and snails. This animal, like the opossum, is omnivorous and may be found eating pet food. They too are providing a service and are beneficial to the landscape.

Armadillos also eat insects, primarily grubs. While searching for these insects, they often uproot plants and leave holes in turf areas. My visitor last fall left the front lawn well aerated and grub free—no insect or disease problems even with the heat and humidity of a typical Houston

Picture 13. Opossum in author's backyard.

summer. Another beneficial visitor and interesting to watch.

Once the visitor is identified, determine how much damage to tolerate in exchange for the benefits. A few upset pots are easier to deal with than the slimy trails and destroyed plants from slug and snail damage. Filling a few holes is cheaper, easier, and more environmentally friendly than waging chemical warfare on turf insects.

Controlling the Invaders

To control, tailor the method to the habits of the culprit, and as with insect pests use the least toxic method first. Simply removing available pet food often will send the visitor to other areas. Other strategies include fencing, caging, repellents, plants, raised beds, and traps.

Picture 14. An armadillo, usually a night visitor, out in the daytime.

Fencing is the best deterrent. An eight-foot fence will usually keep deer out while a four-foot fence works for smaller visitors. Bury a portion of the fence to prevent burrowing animals such as rabbits from entering. Leaving the top foot hanging loose or attaching sheets of slippery plastic to the outside deters climbers. Electric fences also work well. Many types are available from simple solar powered units to more expensive timered units. Be sure to select one that delivers current in pulses so that any animal or human touching the wire can react before getting a second shock. Before installing any fence type or height, check zoning and/or deed restrictions.

Caging is a good system for individual plants. One-inch mesh fencing cut into three-foot sections and formed into cylinders make easy-to-handle cages. As plants grow they will fill the cages, making them less visible. Cages are also good for protecting woody plants in the winter from nibblers—rabbits, moles, or porcupines. Plastic pop bottles with the top and bottom removed and held down with a stake are effective. One-quarter-inch mesh cages work on larger specimens. The taller cages can also help prevent deer nibbling. Do check cages periodically and remove in the spring to prevent damage to the growing bark. Netting covers over shrubs or vines work to limit damage from browsers such as deer.

Repellents are substances applied to trees or areas to discourage the visitor. Most work through odor or taste. Repellents work best when other food sources are readily available. A hungry deer or rabbit will eat what is available no matter the taste to avoid starvation. Many different products are available commercially, and home remedies abound. Follow label directions carefully as with all products and realize many will need to be applied more than once, especially after heavy rains. Scientific proof is limited as to efficacy of any repellents.

Castor bean is suggested in the literature as a repellent for moles. There is little data on how effective this is or how many plants are required but is an example of a different type of repellent. Commercially available repellents for moles have been shown to be effective if applied over the entire area and at least twice a year.

Barrier plants can protect other plants. Sharp prickly plants such as barberry, cactus, or holly work well in borders to keep larger animals out. Agartio *Berberis trifoliolata*, a Texas native, deters deer; even a starving deer will not eat this prickly plant. Rabbits dislike garlic, onions, marigolds, and other highly scented plants. Barriers work best planted before the visitors arrive. This prevents them from finding the plants behind the barrier.

Raised beds work against tunnelers where the invasion comes from underground. Prepare the bed as recommended for routine planting, but before filling with soil, line the bottom with ¼ inch mesh hardware screen, nailed tightly to the sides of the frame. Remember when digging for planting or harvesting that the screen is in place to avoid damage to the mesh or digging equipment.

Traps are of two types: live traps that capture for relocation and devices that kill. Traps should be your last option, and before using one check with local authorities regarding laws. In Texas "a landowner on their own land or their authorized agent is not required to have a trapper's license or hunting license if these animals (fur-bearing—raccoon opossum, skunk, nutria, badger, beaver) are taken while causing loss or damage to agricultural crops, livestock, poultry, or personal property. However, such animals or their pelts may not be possessed or sold." Quote from the Texas Parks and Wildlife Outdoor annual hunting and fishing regulations. For additional information contact TPWD.

Several different brands of live traps are available. Trapping and relocating the animal may sound like the most humane method; however, there are several considerations. Just because the animal is wild does not mean it can survive anywhere. Many animals do not survive relocation. Armadillos for example depend on their claws for survival. Trapping often damages the claws to the extent that the animals can no longer forage and will starve to death. All creatures need food, water, and shelter. A new location may have only part of the requirements or may be overpopulated by the species you are setting free. It is illegal to release trapped animals on private property without the permission of the owner. Check with Texas Parks and Wildlife before releasing any captured animals on public land.

Other methods are available commercially but are of questionable value. Ultrasonic devices have not been scientifically proven to work. Animal protection groups have raised ethical questions about how wild animal urine is collected for use as deterrents.

Use the method of control that works best for you, but remember the visitors are the native inhabitants. Man is the real "visitor." Welcome them, accept the benefits, and learn to live with and work around any inconvenience.

Dogs and **cats** can help discourage unwanted visitors; however, neighbors' wanted pets can be bigger nuisances than the native visitors as well as a danger to wildlife. Cats are considered the second-biggest risk to endangered birds! (The first risk is loss of habitat.) Cats, feral and domestic, are responsible for an estimated loss of over one billion wild birds each year in the Unites States. According to an estimate by California ornithologist Rich Stallcup, cats, feral and free-roaming, catch and kill as many as 4 to 5 million birds *every* day. They also kill millions possibly billions of small mammals such as mice, rabbits, squirrels, and chipmunks —all normal prey for native mammal and bird species. By reducing this prey base, the cats negatively impact the population of these natural predators, upsetting nature's normal relationships and balance.

About 66 million pet cats live in the United States with around 40 million allowed outside at least part time. Best estimates indicate 60 to 100 million feral, stray, or otherwise homeless cats roam the nation. A four-year University of Wisconsin study estimated the number of birds killed annually by rural free-roaming cats in the state to be at least 7.8 million and perhaps as many as 217 million. Even well-fed, free roaming domestic or feral cats kill wildlife when presented the opportunity. The animal hunting instinct is very strong. All cats are killers, with very few exceptions killing for the sport not for food.

Cats should be kept inside and controlled not only to curb the hunting instinct, but to prevent spread of disease among the cat population domestic, feral, and native. Feline leukemia, feline distemper, feline immunodeficiency virus, and infectious peritonitis are all suspected of being spread to the endangered Florida panther, bobcat, and lynx by domestic cats. These diseases are easily spread within domestic cat communities and once contracted are difficult to treat.

Most urban and suburban areas have leash laws for dogs and a few include cats. Leash laws are enforced for the dogs and should be for cats. Check your local restrictions. They are in place for a reason. Be a responsible cat owner. Protect your pet from the diseases and protect the wildlife you are trying to attract. Keep your cat inside!

With few exceptions diseases are not transmitted from native wildlife to domestic pets or humans. Skunks and bats are capable of transmitting rabies, but documentation shows the incident to be very low. As a precaution never handle dead animals without heavy gloves. Instruct children to not pick up obviously sick or dying animals and to contact an adult. All communities have wildlife rehabilitators; contact them regarding the care for sick and wounded wildlife. It is illegal to keep wild animals as pets without special permits. Contact Texas Parks and Wildlife or local animal control for details.

Remember man is the true visitor in the environment and the only one capable of protecting others. Observe, respect, accept, and work with the many different forms of nature. Let the visitors help with the pests, and keep domestic pets under control. Know your "enemy" and make them your friend.

CHAPTER 18

SUSTAINABILITY
NATURE KNOWS BEST

Sustainability is the noun form of the verb to sustain, and among its many definitions and uses are to keep up or keep going, as an action or process, and to supply with food, drink, and other necessities of life. Both definitions apply to the current usage with regard to nature. The goal of sustainability is to meet the needs of the present without compromising the resources available to future generations.

Wildscapes, use of native plants, waterwise gardening, elimination of invasive exotics, conscientious pest management, and recycling are all means to accomplish the goals of sustainability. Homeowners are only one part of the picture and as individuals can only accomplish so

much. Businesses and industries both public and private need to be involved. Several programs are in place throughout the United States and in Texas to promote sustainability by example.

In McKinney, Texas, the McKinney Independent School District opened a prototype sustainable school in August 2000. Walker Elementary, the first state-funded sustainable school in the state, is made possible by a grant from the General Services Commission/State Energy Conservation Office. McKinney was one of two school districts picked in 1997 to participate in the pilot program to design a prototype for environmentally responsible schools. State officials hope all schools in the state will eventually be built with lessons learned from the design.

The school features solar energy panels, rainwater collection tanks, a windmill, sundials, a weather station, recycled building materials, and many other components designed to introduce environmental consciousness into the academic program.

The $8.5 million school cost about 15 percent more to build than the traditional school, but the savings on utilities are predicted to make up the difference in about four years. The school has been designed to allow teachers to use the environmental elements of its construction in their lessons—"Eco-Education" —a concept that incorporates the sustainable school into the curriculum, enabling students to understand the design and effects on the environment. They need only walk the halls to see science at work. A clear graduated tube at the school's front door indicates the number of gallons of rainwater collected off the roof and held in cylindrical drums throughout the campus. A windmill at the south end circulates the water in the system, preventing stagnation and bacterial growth. The recycled water is used to maintain the school's landscape, designed for minimal upkeep using native

grasses and heat tolerant Texas natives. Because of the high maintenance required of soccer fields, the school decided against their own and uses nearby public fields.

The classrooms are equipped with light sensors that constantly measure the amount of light entering the room through windows and skylights. Auxiliary fluorescent light gradually brightens to compensate for temporary darkness. A flick of a switch will brighten a room, and shades descend to cover the skylight when the room needs to be darkened for videos or slide presentations.

Studies have shown that not only the environment benefits from sustainable design, but also the children in the classroom. One study of five schools conducted by the Alberta Department of Education in Canada found that students enrolled in schools where daylighting was the principal source of internal light had the following advantages: increased attendance by 3.5 days a year; grew an average of one centimeter (approximately ½ inch) more than their peers enrolled in schools operating under electric light; better scholastic performance resulting from more positive moods induced by natural light; increased concentration levels and significant reductions in library noise; and the biggest surprise, nine times less tooth decay! The study attributes benefits to the natural vitamins found in sunlight. Reduction in tooth decay is attributed to Vitamin D. Natural sunlight is the heart of sustainability as it is the key to all life on our planet.

The McKinney ISD built a traditional school at the same time as the sustainable school and plans to compare all aspects of the two schools. Will nature once again prove it's the best way? Evidently the answer is "yes." McNeil Elementary, a second sustainable school, opened in the McKinney ISD in August 2001.

In Houston the School of Public Health and Central Administration of the University of Texas-Houston Health Science Center have created an Urban Ecology Research Park on the UT-H campus in the Texas Medical Center. The park demonstrates the school's resolve to "behave in accordance with natural laws that influence the connection between the environment and health" and follows the guiding principles: We shall be responsible stewards of our resources; we shall do no harm;

we shall benefit others in the present and future; we shall respect the environment.

The Urban Ecology Research Park and Arboretum is on approximately seven acres located on the southern edge of the densely developed and highly paved Texas Medical Center. The tract was set aside for a park in 1998, and since then the existing plant life has been inventoried and exotics have been eradicated. The low biological diversity of the site has been altered by introduction of native grasses, trees, and other plants.

Poor drainage was modified with the addition of a one-acre wetland including a pond in the upland section of the site. Seven species of wetland native plants were added to the area, which also serves as a water detention site during high rainfall in the Medical Center. The water level is allowed to fluctuate, but when it reaches a set minimum depth, a small pump is activated to maintain the level.

A photovoltaic (solar) panel provides the electricity required for the pump and all other electricity in the park. A small shed in the western corner provides cover for the battery array and controllers for the power system. This area also houses storage sheds and offices for the project.

Vegetable scraps from food service vendors are used for compost to amend soils in the park. In the past all the scraps were sent to the landfill. An organic community garden is planned for one section, using recycled materials for bed construction.

Various studies are planned for the park that are intended to lead to an understanding of how biological communities evolve in an urban environment and to measure the extent to which a seven-acre wildscape contributes to the quality of an urban environment. Discussions are underway to bring students from local schools to learn how to integrate human activities with natural ecosystems. Education is an important part of all sustainability efforts.

Communities across the state recognizing the importance of sustainability are developing plans, guidelines, and indicators. Check out the Sustainability Indicators Project of Hays, Williamson, and Travis Counties at www.centex-indicators.org.

The city of Austin sustainability initiative (SCI) exists to help the greater Austin region achieve economic prosperity, social justice, and ecological health —the highest possible quality of life in the best possible environment. SCI recommends coordinating water resource and air quality and planning activities region wide, in addition to developing sustainable community indicators and green economic development. SCI touches on every area of community life and cuts across traditional political boundaries.

Whether working in your home garden or through a large community sustainability project, consider nature's diversity, interactions among all members of a habitat, and the ways to promote and maintain all aspects. No one part can exist without the whole. Be conscientious stewards for future generations.

CHAPTER 19

LUNCH WITH LUCY
ENJOY YOUR WORK

The time gained by understanding and working with nature is your special time. Use it to relax, heal, relieve stress, and find yourself amidst the busy life generated by today's society. Turn off the radio, TV, phone, pager, and take your lunch outside. Watch. Listen. Breathe. Relax. Close your eyes. Shut out the sound of traffic and air-conditioners and listen. The tapping of a woodpecker, the warble of the purple martin returning to feed her young, the hum of the bees' wings, the chatter of a hummingbird, the raucous call of the blue jay, the rustle caused by the wind through the leaves.

Open your eyes and carefully watch the "living" around you. The dragonfly laying eggs under the water lily pad. The spiny Gulf Coast fritillary caterpillar munching the passionvine leaf. The jewels of light reflected by the fluttering wings of the monarch butterfly. The rich texture of the shades of green leaves punctuated with bright yellow, purple, pink, and red flowers. The patterns created by the movement of sun and shadow.

Take a deep breath (if not too close to a large metropolitan, then maybe only a little breath). Smell the sweet jasmine, the spicy rose, the cinnamon-like fragrance of the dianthus and carnations, the piney scent of the rosemary.

The creatures, the sounds, the smells change not only with the seasons but the time of day. Vary your times. Watch the sunrise and listen to nature wake to take on a new day. Listen to the sounds change from crickets, frogs, and geckos to birds and bees all ready to begin anew. The few minutes spent to listen and watch will enhance the remainder of your day. Watching a female ruby-throat hummingbird at less than an arm's length fly from flower to flower, passing close enough to feel the breeze on my check, is an indescribable way to start a day.

Lucy is the red-eared slider turtle who lives in my large pond. She and I lunch together as often as possible. She basks in her favorite spot in the sun with legs stretched behind her to absorb maximum sun. The dragonflies circle the pond in search of mates and prey. An occasional dragonfly stops on a bamboo stake nearby to commune with me. She turns her head to view me from all angles while I marvel at the delicate wing pattern and brilliant color. My reward for providing the water and plants.

A large garden is not necessary. Everyone can have her own "Lucy." Nature exists all around us even in the pot on the balcony of a high-rise. Provide the proper habitat. The creatures will find you and thank you with a soft "pat."

Sit back, relax, and enjoy nature's rewards for your hard work! You deserve it!

Picture 14. Lucy basking

APPENDIX A

RECOMMENDED READING

1. *America's Neighborhood Bats: Understanding and Learning to Live in Harmony with Them* by Merlin D. Tuttle, University of Texas Press, 1988.

2. *Aquatic and Wetland Plants of the Western Gulf Coast* by Charles D. Stutzenbaker, Texas Parks Press, 1999.

3. *Carrots Love Tomatoes: Secrets of Companion Planting for Successful Gardening* by Louise Riotte, Storey Communications, Inc., Pownal, Vermont, 1975.

4. *Commonsense Vegetable Gardening for the South: The Complete guide to growing old favorites, plentiful herbs, gourmet delectables, and great new varieties for southern soils*, by William D. Adams and Thomas LeRoy, Taylor Publishing, Dallas, Texas, 1995.

5. *Dragonflies Through Binoculars: A Field Guide to Dragonflies of North America* by Sidney W. Dunkle, Oxford University Press, 2000.

6. *Edible and Useful Plants of Texas and the Southwest: A Practical Guide* by Delena Tull, University of Texas Press, Austin, Texas, 1999.

7. *Edible Wild Plants: A North American Field Guide* by Thomas S. Elias and Peter A. Dykeman, Sterling Publishing Co., Inc., New York, 1990.

8. *A Field Guide to Animal Tracks* by Olaus J. Murie, Houghton Mifflin Company, Boston, 1974.

9. *A Field Guide to the Birds of Texas* by Roger Tory Peterson, Houghton Mifflin Company, Boston, 1988.

10. *A Field Guide to Common Texas Insects* by Bastiaan M. Drees, Ph.D. and John A. Jackman, Ph.D., Gulf Publishing, Houston, Texas, 1998.

11. *A Field Guide to Southwestern and Texas Wildflowers* by Theodore F. Niehaus, Houghton Mifflin Company, Boston, 1984.

12. *How to Grow Native Plants of Texas and the Southwest* by Jill Nokes, University of Texas Press, 2001.

13. *The Lone Star Gardener's Book of Lists* by William D. Adams and Lois Trigg Chaplin, Taylor Trade Publishing, Dallas, Texas, 2000.

14. *Native Texas Plants: Landscaping Region by Region* by Sally Wasowski with Andy Wasowski, Gulf Publishing, Houston, Texas, 1991.

15. *Neil Sperry's Complete Guide to Texas Gardening* by Neil Sperry, Taylor Publishing, Dallas, Texas, 1991.

16. *Papa Stahl's Wild Stuff Cookbook* by Carmine A. Stahl, Grass Root Enterprises, Houston, Texas, 1977.

17. *The Organic Gardener's Handbook of Natural Insect and Disease Control, A Complete Problem-Solving Guide to Keeping Your Garden & Yard Healthy Without Chemicals*. Edited by Barbara W. Ellis and Fern Marshall Bradley, Rodale Press, 1992.

18. *Perennial Garden Color: Perennials, Cottage Gardens, Old Roses and Companion Plants* by William C. Welch, Taylor Publishing Company, Dallas, Texas, 1989.

19. *Peterson First Guide: Caterpillars of North America* by Amy Bartlett Wright, Houghton Mifflin Company, Boston, 1993.

20. *National Audubon Society: The Sibley Guide to Birds* by David Allen Sibley, Alfred A. Knopf, New York, 2000.

21. *Southern Herb Growing* by Madalene Hill and Gwen Barclay with Jean Hardy, Shearer Publishing, 1987.

22. *The Southern Living Garden Book: The Complete Encyclopedia of More Than 5,000 Southern Plants.* Edited by Steve Bender, Senior Writer, Southern Living Oxmoor House, Birmingham, Alabama, 1998.

23. *Texas Snakes: Identification, Distribution, and Natural History* by John E. Werler and James Ray Dixon, University of Texas Press, Austin, 2000.

24. *Texas Wildflowers: A Field Guide* by Campbell and Lynn Loughmiller, University of Texas Press, Austin, 1996.

25. *Texas Wildscapes: Gardening for Wildlife* by Noreen Damude and Kelly Bender, University of Texas Press, Austin, 1999.

26. *Wetlands National Audubon Society Nature Guides* by William A. Niering, Alfred A. Knopf, New York, 1998.

ORGANIZATIONS

ASSOCIATIONS AFFILIATED WITH GARDENING AND NATURE

Bat Conservation International. Inc., P.O. Box 162603, Austin, Texas 78716, 1-800-538 BATS, www.batcon.com.

Bureau of Economic Geology, University of Texas at Austin, University Station, Box X, Austin, Texas 78713-7508, 512-471-1534.

Lady Bird Johnson Wildflower Center, 4801 La Crosse Avenue, Austin, Texas 78739, (512) 292-4100, www.wildflower.org.

Master Gardener Program—Contact local county cooperative extension office http://mastergardener.tamu.edu/mg.html.

Native American Seed Mail Order Station, 127 N. 16th St., Junction, Texas 76849, 1-800-728-4043, www.seedsource.com.

Native Plant Society, 117 W. 7th Street, Suite 3, Georgetown, Texas 78626 or P.O. Box 891, Georgetown, Texas 78627, 512-868-8799; fax 512-931-1166, www.npsot.org.

Native Prairies Association of Texas, P.O. Box 210, Georgetown, Texas 78627, www.texasprairie.org.

Nature Conservancy of Texas, P.O. Box 1440, San Antonio, Texas 77098-3114, 210-224-8774, www.tnc.org/texas.

Texas Cooperative Extension—Contact local county cooperative extension office http://aggie-horticulture.tamu.edu/extension/.

Texas Department of Transportation Travel and Information Division, P.O. Box 149249, Austin, Texas 78714-9249.

Texas Master Naturalist Program, 113 Nagle Hall, Texas A&M University, College Station, Texas 77843-2258, http://masternaturalist .tamu.edu. Chapter information available at local county cooperative extension and Texas Parks and Wildlife offices.

Texas National Resource Conservation Commission, Austin headquarters, P.O. Box 13087, Austin, Texas 78711-3087, 512-239-1000 Information line 1-800-447-2827, www.tnrcc.state.tx.us.

Texas Parks and Wildlife, 4200 Smith School Road, Austin, Texas 78744, www.tpwd.state.tx.us/nature.

Wildseed Farms, 425 Wildflower Hills, P.O. Box 3000, Fredericksburg, Texas 78624-3000, 1-800-848-0078, www.wildseedfarms.com.

WILDSCAPE PLAN

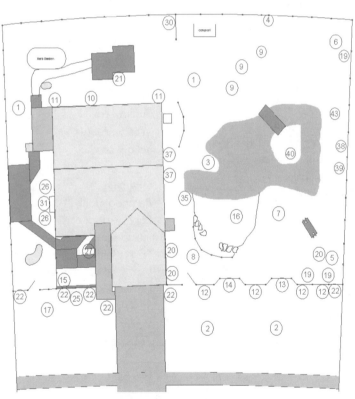

Figure 12. Plot plan of author's wildscape habitat

Trees
American elm-5
American fringe-13
Anacho orchid-14
Bald cypress-3
Black willow-40
Bay tree
Crepe myrtle-15
Desert willow
Eastern red cedar-9
Foster holly-11
Fruitless mulberry-1
Hackberry-4
Live oak (small)-7
Pine-6
Possomhaw
Post oak (small)-8
Roughleaf dogwood
Silver maples-2
Star magnolia-10
Mexican redbud
Two winged silver bell
Texas mountain laurel-16
Windmill palm-17
Wax myrtle-12
Wild plum

Vines
Black-eyed Susan
Carolina jessamine
Clematis pitcheri
Coral honeysuckle
Coral vine
Crossvine
Cypress vine
Evergreen wisteria
Maid Orleans jasmine
Mexican flame vine
Passionvines
Pink jasmine
Potato vine
Snail vine

Annuals
Albmosheus
Castor bean
Claspingleaf coneflower
Bluebonnets
Cleome
Evening primroses
Gaillardia
Gaura
Horsemint
Monarda ssp. Melanpodium
Partridge pea
Plains coreopsis
Red and Pink pentas
Sunflowers
Wild poinsettia
Yellow cosmos

Grasses
Bamboo muhly
Big bluestem
Inland sea oats
Purple leafed fountain
Many self seeding, volunteer grasses, rushes & sedges
St. Augustine (limited)
Vetivir
Zebra miscanthus

Herbs
Basil
Dill
Fennel

Garlic chives
Lemon balm
Lemon verbena
Mexican mint marigold
Mint
Oregano
Parsley
Pineapple sage
Rosemary
Salad burnett
Thyme

Shrubs
Am. beauty climber-30
American beautyberry-19
Azalea-27
Banana shrub-25
Blue point junipers
Buttonbush-35
Cenizo
Compact nandina
Coralbean
Coralberry
Cottoneaster
Duranta-39
Dwarf Barbados cherry lecouthoe
Dwarf palmetto
Dwarf wax myrtle
Esperanza-38
Flame acanthus
Flowering quince
Harlequin glory bower vibernum
Hollywood junipers-22
Japanese yew
Lace cap hydrangea
Lorepetulm-26
Mahonia fortuneii
Mrs. B.R. Cant roses

Mystery gardenia
Old English yellow rose
Pavonia
Pokeweed
Reve d'Or climber-31
Sea green junipers
Spreading juniper
Swamp rose
Sweet olive-20
Texas star hibiscus
Turk's cap-21
Vanity climbing rose
Volunteer citrus
Winter honeysuckle-37

Water and bog plants
Blue waterleaf
Cabomba
Chromatella water lily
Coontail
Dwarf cattail
Dwarf horsetail
Floating heart
Lizard's tail
Native white water lily
Parrot feather
Pickerelweed
Pink water lily
Pitcher plant
Powdery thalia
Purple tropical water lily
Rembrandt water lily
Sagittaria—three varieties
White-topped sedge

Bulbs
Amaryllis
Fortune daffodils

Bulbs cont.
Leucojum
Lycoris
Milk & wine lily
Paperwhites
Pine woods lily
Rain lilies
Spider lily
Swamp lily

Perennials
Arborvitae fern
Boston fern
Brugmansia
Bulbine
Butterfly ginger
Butterflyweed
Candlestick plant-43
Cardinal flower
Christmas fern
Copper canyon daisy Rudbeckia
Datura
Daylilies
Dicleptra
Fall obedient plant
False agave
Goldenrod
Gulf coast penstemon
Halberd leaf hibiscus
Hidden ginger
Holly fern
Indigo spires
Lance leaf coreopsis
Lantana
Louisiana iris
Lyre-leaf sage
Maximillian sunflower
Swamp mallow

Mexican heather
Peacock fern
Plumbago
Prickly pear
Purple coneflower
Red yucca
Royal fern
Ruby creeper
Russelia
Salvia chiapensis
Salvia coccinea
Salvia farencia
Salvia garanetica
Salvia greggii
Salvia lecantha
Salvia penstemonoides
Salvia sinaloensis
Sedums—different varieties
Shell ginger
Shrimp plant
Society garlic
Soft tip yucca
Sotol
Spineless prickly pear
Tropical sage
Wood fern
Yellow columbine

Ground covers
Frogfruit
Katy's reullia
Lysimachia—golden globe
Mexican heather
Peacock ginger
Pigeon berry
Pink buttons
Pink evening primrose
Weigela

Index